GBC

GOVERNMENT BEYOND THE CENTRE
SERIES EDITOR: GERRY STOKER

The world of sub-central government and administration – including local authorities, quasi-governmental bodies and the agencies of public–private partnerships – has seen massive changes in recent years and is at the heart of the current restructuring of government in the United Kingdom and other Western democracies.

The intention of the *Government Beyond the Centre* series is to bring the study of this often-neglected world into the mainstream of social science research, applying the spotlight of critical analysis to what has traditionally been the preserve of institutional public administration approaches.

Its focus is on the agenda of change currently being faced by sub-central government, the economic, political and ideological forces that underlie it, and the structures of power and influence that are emerging. Its objective is to provide up-to-date and informative accounts of the new forms of government, management and administration that are emerging.

The series will be of interest to students and practitioners of politics, public and social administration, and all those interested in the reshaping of the governmental institutions which have a daily and major impact on our lives.

GOVERNMENT BEYOND THE CENTRE

SERIES EDITOR: GERRY STOKER

Published

Richard Batley and Gerry Stoker (eds)
Local Government in Europe

Clive Gray
Government Beyond the Centre

John Gyford
Citizens, Consumers and Councils

Richard Kerley
Managing in Local Government

Desmond King and Gerry Stoker (eds)
Rethinking Local Democracy

Steve Leach, John Stewart and Kieron Walsh
The Changing Organisation and Management of Local Government

Arthur Midwinter
Local Government in Scotland

Yvonne Rydin
The British Planning System

John Stewart and Gerry Stoker (eds)
Local Government in the 1990s

David Wilson and Chris Game (with Steve Leach and Gerry Stoker)
Local Government in the United Kingdom

Series Standing Order

If you would like to receive future titles in this series as they are published, you can make use of our standing order facility. To place a standing order please contact your bookseller or, in case of difficulty, write to us at the address below with your name and address and the name of the series. Please state with which title you wish to begin your standing order. (If you live outside the UK we may not have the rights for your area, in which case we will forward your order to the publisher concerned.)

Standing Order Service, Macmillan Distribution Ltd,
Houndmills, Basingstoke, Hampshire, RG21 6XS, England

Rethinking Local Democracy

Edited by

Desmond King

and

Gerry Stoker

MACMILLAN

Published in association with the
ESRC LOCAL PROGRAMME

E·S·R·C
ECONOMIC
& SOCIAL
RESEARCH
COUNCIL

First published 1996 by
MACMILLAN PRESS LTD
Houndmills, Basingstoke, Hampshire RG21 6XS
and London
Companies and representatives
throughout the world

ISBN 0–333–63852–2 hardcover
ISBN 0–333–63853–0 paperback

A catalogue record for this book is available
from the British Library.

10   9   8   7   6   5   4   3   2   1
05   04   03   02   01   00   99   98   97   96

Copy-edited and typeset by Povey–Edmondson
Okehampton and Rochdale, England

Printed in Hong Kong

Contents

Notes on the Contributors

David Beetham is Professor in the Department of Politics, University of Leeds. His many publications include *The Legitimation of Power* (Macmillan, 1991) and *Max Weber and the Theory of Modern Politics* (1985, 2nd edn).

Allan Cochrane is Dean of the Faculty of Social Science, the Open University. He is author of *Whatever Happened to Local Government?* (1993) and co-editor (wirh James Anderson) of *Politics in Transition* (1989).

Keith Dowding is Lecturer in Public Choice and Public Policy in the Department of Government at the London School of Economics. He is the author of *Rational Choice and Political Power* (1991), and *The Civil Service* (Routledge, 1995) a number of journal articles and is co-editor (with Desmond King) of *Preferences, Institutions and Rational Choice* (1995) He is currently completing a major research project with four colleagues on the governance of London, as part of the Economic and Social Research Council's (ESRC) Local Government Programme.

Elizabeth Frazer is Fellow and Tutor, and University Lecturer, in Politics at New College, Oxford. She is the co-author (with Nicola Lacey) of *The Politics of Community: a Feminist Critique of the Liberal-Communitarian Debate* (1993), and is currently working on normative theories of political relations and public life.

Mike Goldsmith is Professor and Pro-Vice Chancellor at the University of Salford. He is the co-author (with Harold Wolman) of *Urban Politics and Policy: A Comparative Approach* (1992) and editor of *New Research in Central–Local Relations* (1986).

Desmond King is Fellow of St John's College, Oxford. His most recent book is *Separate and Unequal: Black Americans and the US Federal Government* (1995).

Anne Phillips is Professor in the Department of Politics and Modern History, London Guildhall University. Her publications include *Engendering Democracy* (1991) and *The Politics of Presence* (1995).

Gerry Stoker is Professor of Politics, University of Strathclyde. He is Programme Director of the ESRC Local Governance Research Programme 1992–1997. His previous books include *The Politics of Local Government* (1991, 2nd edn), and co-editorship (with John Stewart) of *Local Government in the 1990s* (1995).

Kieron Walsh, who died in May 1995, was Professor of Public Sector Management and Director (designate) of the Institute of Local Government Studies at the University of Birmingham. He wrote on marketing, quality, competition and ethics in the public service, and had recently completed an ESRC local government research project on the new institutional framework. His recent publications include: *Public Services and Market Mechanisms*, (1995) and (with John Stewart and David Prior) *Citizenship Rights, Communities and Participation* (1995).

Hugh Ward is Senior Lecturer in the Department of Government at the University of Essex. His current research is in the fields of rational choice theory and environmental politics. His recent publications include (with D. Samways) 'Environment Policy', in R. Rhodes and D. Marsh (eds) *Implementing Thatcherite Policies: Audit of an Era* (1992); 'Game Theory and the Politics of the Global Commons', *Journal of Conflict Resolution* (1993); 'Purity and Danger: The Politicisation of Drinking Water Quality in the 80s', in M. Mills (ed.) *Prevention, Health and British Politics* (1993).

Harold Wolman is Professor in the Department of Political Science at Wayne State University, Detroit. He is co-author (with Mike Goldsmith) of *Urban Politics and Policy: A Comparative Approach* (1992) and (with Valerie Karn) *Comparing Housing Systems* (1992).

Preface

This book is a product of the Economic and Social Research Council's (ESRC) Local Governance Programme. It emerged following two conferences sponsored by the ESRC and organised by Professor Gerry Stoker. The participants in the first conference at Strathclyde University on 20–21 May 1993 included:

John Benington	Hal Wolman
Desmond King	Davina Cooper
Kieron Walsh	Ann Stewart
John Gyford	Margaret Hodge
Robin Hambleton	Rod Rhodes
Vivien Lowndes	Jim Bulpitt
John Stewart	Dave Marsh
David Beetham	Karen Mossberger
Hugh Ward	Larry Rose
Mike Goldsmith	Gerry Stoker
Patrick Le Gales	

The participants in a second conference held on 26–27 September 1994 at St John's College, Oxford, were:

John Benington	Allan Cochrane
Desmond King	Keith Dowding
Kieron Walsh	Elizabeth Frazer
Vivien Lowndes	Anne Phillips
David Beetham	Hal Wolman
Hugh Ward	Mike Goldsmith
Margaret Hodge	Gerry Stoker

The participants of both conferences contributed to the development of this book. We are grateful to them for their time and insights.

The discussions held at the two conferences were enjoyable and thought-provoking. The development of the book has been a challenge but we are thankful that our contributors proved themselves to be responsible and responsive. Helpful comments from two referees – George Jones and Geraint Parry – helped us to refine the project in its final stages. Jean McDougall and Neil McGarvey eased the process of production.

The book is dedicated to the memory of Kieron Walsh. He was a fine colleague and a good friend. His chapter was complete when he died of a heart attack in May 1995. Some minor editorial corrections have been made with the help of staff at the Institute of Local Government Studies.

GERRY STOKER

In memory of **Kieron**

1 Introduction: Normative Theories of Local Government and Democracy

Gerry Stoker

The transformation of the institutional map of local government in Britain in recent years has been such that local authorities now find themselves working alongside a wide range of other agencies. In the language of the ESRC Local Governance Programme, we are witnessing the transformation of the structure of government beyond Westminster and Whitehall from a system of local government into a system of local governance, involving complex sets of organisations drawn from the public, private and voluntary sectors. The working of this complex system is a important focus for research but there is also a need in the light of this transformation for renewed normative debate about the proper role of local government and the value of local democracy. This book is intended to stimulate and contribute to such debate.

Normative political theory can be defined in broad terms 'to cover all political theorising of a prescriptive or recommendatory kind: that is to say, all theory-making concerned with what ought to be' (Glaser, 1995, p. 21). Normative political thought finds expression in a variety of activities: it can involve the clarification or specification of the meaning of a concept, and it may involve identifying arguments as to why a particular concept – such as democracy – should be valued. Beyond the construction of guiding moral precepts it may move on to more substantive application in which theorists investigate 'the implications of moral precepts for actual political practice' (Glaser, 1995, p. 21). Do existing institutions and practice match normative ideas? How could they be reformed so as to realise the principles in question? Beetham argues in this volume that normative theorising may have to consider further how to balance in practice a number of principles that might be valued. Also it may consider the question of agency: that is, which social

1

groups or political organisations might plausibly act as the bearers of the valued goals?

The various authors in this book engage in all the dimensions of normative theorising outlined above, but the main focus is on its more concrete aspects. Their shared concern is with the nature, purpose and justification of local government and democracy as we approach the twenty-first century.

The context of the debate is the restructuring of local government inspired by Conservative governments since 1979. Three features of the restructuring process are particularly noteworthy (see Stewart and Stoker, 1995). First, the institutional map of local government has been transformed. As noted earlier, the term 'local governance' has been used in an attempt to capture the increasingly differentiated range of agencies and organisations that have responsibilities for strategic decision-making and service delivering within localities. There is little doubt that the emerging structure of local governance marks out a lessening of local government within that structure. As we shall see, the traditional advocates of local government have since Victorian times emphasised the value of multi-purpose local government as against *ad hoc* administration. The reforms of recent years are seen as a direct threat to that tradition, as powers and responsibilities have been taken away from local authorities. In the past the range of responsibilities and legitimacy held by local authorities made them relatively dominant within the overall system, even though there were other agencies involved in providing local services. The multiplicity of agencies, along with the weakening of the relative position of local authorities, represents a fragmentation within the overall system.

A second feature of the restructuring has been an extension of central control. Many of the new agencies of local governance are subject to direct influence from central government through the appointment of their controlling boards or by way of their funding coming directly or indirectly from the centre. Local authorities have been brought under extensive and closer supervision of their spending. The débâcle of the poll tax has left local authorities heavily reliant on non-local sources of revenue. In 1993–4 local taxation accounted for only about 20 per cent of total local authority income. The heavy reliance on non-local revenue creates a substantial opportunity for central government to dictate the level of local spending in aggregate terms. In addition, it is able to influence the spending decisions of individual authorities through defining what needs to be spent by way of an annual standard spending assessment (SSA) and by holding capping powers over local budgets to ensure that they do not rise above government-approved levels. In short, the traditional concept of a local government system guaranteed a degree of autonomy through locally-controlled powers of taxation would appear to be almost fatally undermined by the restructuring since the early 1980s.

A third element in the context is the rise of a managerialist vision of central–local relations and the organisation of public services. Public services are to be operated by a nationally driven set of priorities and standards and managed through a complex network of 'contracts'. Central government sets the broad guidelines of what is needed and what can be afforded. It then devolves responsibility by way of contract-style relations to a range of other agencies, including local authorities, to meet those needs. These agencies, in turn, operate internally and externally through contracts. Customers too will have contracts, giving them strengthened rights to redress for unsatisfactory service – plus, increasingly, the right to go elsewhere.

This model, as Mather (1989, p. 234) notes, leaves 'the elected status of local government somewhat behind', with the onus 'on the elected politician to show that they are necessary to this service provision'. A similar message emerges from Government Minister William Waldegrave's defence of management reforms. Output in terms of better quality service delivery is the challenge: 'The key point in this argument is not whether those who run our public service are elected, but whether they are producer-responsive or consumer-responsive' (Waldegrave, 1993, p. 13).

The changes since the 1980s raise fundamental questions about British local government and democracy. Some see the fragmentation leading to a weakening of democratic local government as local authorities lose power and include. The managerialist model with its consumerist vision raises doubts about the value of local political activity as an exercise in collective choice. The constraining financial system seems to confirm local authorities' relegation to the status of one among a variety of instruments for providing nationally regulated service delivery. Others, however, see new opportunities for public participation through the variety and diversity of local political institutions, as well as a new role for local authorities in supporting a range of service delivery and decision-making platforms.

The changing institutional features of the British system and the distinctive character of central–local relations provide a unique backcloth to our debate. Yet other elements of the context for the debate are shared in broad terms by all Western democracies. One issue is uncertainty about the future of the Keynesian welfare state. Another is how best to manage economic change and development. A third is concerned with how to meet popular disenchantment with politics and enhance public involvement in decision-making. These issues, which have implications for local government and democracy, can in turn be placed in context of what Held (1992) calls the 'emerging cosmopolitan order'. What are the implications for local democracy in the face of both globalised forces of change and transnational interdependent decision-making? In the context of globalisation, the idea of a community governing itself becomes deeply problematic.

This book provides the material for a reformulated normative debate. The need for such a debate reflects the particular doubts thrown up by recent trends in the British system and by a broader pattern of change which contributes to an aura of uncertainty about the value of local government and democracy. The starting point for the book is the need to move beyond the traditional literature on justifications for local government. This is not deny that there are many useful and worthwhile arguments within this literature; it is merely to suggest that the opportunity to search in an imaginative and open-minded way should not be missed. There is considerable scope for introducing ideas and arguments from neglected perspectives, and indeed from other countries.

The remainder of this introductory chapter examines the core propositions of the traditional literature, and then moves on to discuss the problems and limitations of that literature. It then reviews themes and issues within the reformulated debate presented in this book. The case for local government and democracy that unfolds shares some common ground with the established literature but moves beyond it in a number of significant ways. A final section of the chapter guides the reader through the contents of chapters in the remainder of the book.

Theories of local government: an evolving orthodoxy

Much British thinking about local government is rooted in the nineteenth century. It was in that century that local government in Britain came of age, and broad arguments about its value and worth were promoted which, in the course of the twentieth century, have become what can be termed the 'traditional orthodoxy'. Orthodox propositions can be found in academic writings but also in official reports. Indeed, there is a close interaction between academics and practitioners in the evolution of the orthodox position. It is appropriate to refer to an evolving orthodoxy because although core arguments are shared the emphasis and character of orthodoxy has shifted over time as circumstances have changed.

In analysing the development of the traditional literature it is useful to distinguish three phases: the early advocates; the debates of the post-war reformers; and the localists of the 1980s. Each of these phases will be examined briefly in turn.

The early advocates

John Stuart Mill is quite rightly seen as the seminal writer among the early advocates of local government in Britain. In his *Considerations on Representative Government*, first published in 1861, he presented a series of arguments in favour of local government that provide the main elements of the orthodox position. Mill's work goes beyond the perspective of the early Utilitarians with their emphasis on administrative efficiency and central supervision. He shared with Jeremy Bentham a belief in a systematic hierarchy of administrative bodies, but placed more faith in the capacity of local institutions (for a critical discussion of this literature see Magnusson, 1986).

Mill's position rested on two main arguments. First, that local political institutions would be an essential element in a system of democratic government, because they widen the opportunity to participate and provide the capacity to educate the citizen in the practice of politics and government. Second, that substantial scope for local administration made practical sense because local interest, knowledge and capacity to oversee made the prospect of achieving efficient and effective service provision much more likely: 'In the details of management, therefore, the local bodies will generally have the advantage' (Mill, 1911, p. 2357).

The Fabians and Guild Socialists also deserve attention as theorists with an interest in local government (Sancton, 1976). Hill (1974, p. 30) identifies a number of arguments for local self-government propagated by the Fabians and in particular by Sidney and Beatrice Webb in the early years of the twentieth century:

> The Webbs and Fabians believed working people must combine together (and with other sympathisers) to work for representation and social reform. This would not be handed to them by the existing ruling classes. The best way of achieving these aims was to pursue the programme of municipal socialism: local self-government, ruled by the majority (not just by property owners) and the provision of a wide range of services, municipally (i.e. publicly owned for the improvement of local life).

Sancton (1976) argues that the Fabians' vision took inspiration from Mill and the even earlier Benthamite theory. Of the Webbs, he comments that they may have been socialists of 'an extremely bureaucratic nature, but it would be wholly inaccurate to call them centralising socialists' (p. 163).

The Guild Socialists drew their inspiration from other sources. Given their emphasis on functional democracy, they were less strong advocates of territorial democracy, but G. D. H. Cole in particular saw scope for local and regional self-government as a base for participation and as a focus for co-ordination and service provision (see Sanction (1976) for a fuller discussion).

A further strand of thought identified by Hill (1974) is the perspective of Toulmin Smith and the mid-Victorian romantics. For them, local self-government is a cherished tradition in opposition to a centralising drive to more efficient and democratic government. The historic involvement of local élites in running local affairs was a means of safeguarding their interest and fostering responsibility. Localness was itself to be valued as a bulwark against centralism.

The nineteenth- and early-twentieth-century theorists established three core arguments for local government which have dominated the literature. First, local government provided an opportunity for political participation. Second, it helped to ensure efficient service delivery. Third, it expressed a tradition of opposition to an overly centralised government. The vision of local government they offered was of a relatively autonomous, multi-purpose institution providing a range of services, with a tax-raising capacity and controlled through the election of representatives to oversee the work of full-time officials. Their vision stretched from a commitment to a local democracy to support for a particular form of local government. It has provided a dominant influence on the normative debate about local government and democracy in Britain.

The debates of the post-war reformers

The second phase in the evolution of theories of local government can be identified with the attempt of post-war reformers to grapple with the operation of local government in the context of an expanded and extended welfare state. The scale and scope of local government service delivery was more substantial than that envisaged by early advocates of local government. The issue became how to reconcile local government with the requirements of the welfare state.

In Royal Commissions, and through other investigations, the details of reform options were debated. Underlying these debates there remained a strong commitment to the virtues of local self-government. Local government was an essential element in the expanded welfare state; it could achieve even more if it was modernised and given greater local autonomy.

Not all theorists were convinced that local government still had a place in a modern welfare democracy. A debate in *Public Administration* in the 1950s found Langrod (1953) taking the view that the local arena was more likely to reinforce narrow sectional interests and undermine the virtues of democracy in the nation-state as whole, which could better reflect majority rule, equality and uniformity. The Mill-inspired defence of local government was presented by Panter-Brick (1954). Local government was still essential to allow individuals to voice their needs and to learn the art of practical politics.

Academic theorising about the value of local government fed directly into policy debates. W. J. M. Mackenzie was a member of the Herbert Commission on London's local government. In his review of the justifications for local government he argued that it was to be valued because of the traditional loyalty it attracts, its efficiency in the delivery of services, and its capacity to provide scope for public involvement (Mackenzie, 1961). The Commission itself produced a similar credo in its affirmation of the traditional values of local government (Herbert Report, 1960, paras 219–242). As Self (1962, pp. 159–60) comments, 'hardly a word would have failed to win the approval of John Stuart Mill'.

Self (1962) further notes that the Herbert Commission's unwillingness to rethink fundamentally the role of local government led them to neglect some of the complexities of metropolitan government in a modern world. In effect, they proposed more of the same but on a larger scale. It was 'a great gesture of faith in the potential elasticity and vitality of local representative institutions' (Self, 1962, p. 162).

Another noteworthy contribution to the debate in the context of a reorganisation is provided by Sharpe (1970), a former Director of Intelligence to the Royal Commission on Local Government in England which reported in 1969. A slightly reworked form of the paper was published as a research paper by the Layfield Committee in 1976.

L. J. Sharpe takes the discussion of the values of local government in a number of new directions. His aim is to provide a review of past theories but ultimately 'evolve a consistent theoretical justification for local government that claims to bear some resemblance to actual practice' (1970, p. 159). With this criteria in mind, Sharpe is less convinced by arguments about local government as a bulwark against possible central tyranny. He has more time for another element of the traditional arguments, namely the opportunity for participation afforded by local government. He notes the limits to participation in practice but concludes: 'participation in its different forms emerges as an undoubted value, if not in the full glory of some of its promoters at least as an important justification for local government in a democracy' (p. 165).

It is in relation to efficiency that Sharpe develops a series of interesting and new arguments. He notes how John Stuart Mill had offered a cast iron case for local government as an efficient provider of services such as refuse collection which are essentially local in character. But with the rise of the welfare state and the expansion of services provided by local government, a substantial rethinking and development of the functional case for local government is required.

Sharpe promotes the efficiency value of local authorities as the strongest argument in favour of modern local government. He stretches the claim of efficiency to cover a range of roles offered by local government. He argues: 'as a co-ordinator of services in the field; as a reconciler of community opinion; as a consumer pressure group; as an agent for responding to rising demand; and finally as a counterweight to incipient syndicalism local government seems to have come into its own' (1970, p. 174). It is worth looking at each of these arguments in a little more detail.

The argument over co-ordination is premised on a recognition that the British system of central administration lacks the local generalist superior role common in other countries (for example, the prefect). Yet some co-ordinating role is essential: 'There must be some compendious, horizontal co-ordinating agency which can gather together the separate vertical services coming down from the centre and adjust their content and character to the particular needs of each community' (Sharpe, 1970, p. 167). Local government in Britain contributes to efficient service delivery by providing this co-ordinating function.

Sharpe also stresses the role of local government as a reconciler of community opinion. Providing services requires judgement at two levels: what is deemed desirable within the locality; and the problem of deciding between relative priorities. Given the inevitable differences of opinion within the community, local government becomes the mechanism through which priorities are agreed upon, and the conflict between demand and resource-raising is reconciled.

A further quality of local government promoted by Sharpe is a consumer pressure group. Local authorities provide a check on the domination of the political system by producer groups and speak for and promote interests that are unorganised such as 'the retired, the young, married women' (1970, p. 170). Local authorities, notes Sharpe, are local monopolists and are not subject to the discipline of consumer sovereignty, but are responsive to consumer concerns expressed through the ballot box. Elections may be influenced by national or all sorts of other factors but 'what matters is that an elected body is produced that acts as *if* it is a representative of its constituents' interest' (p. 172, original emphasis).

Sharpe, in a subsequent passage, notes the inevitability of rising demand for public services and the need to have a capacity to expand spending to meet demand in a smooth and orderly manner. Unlike those agencies more directly under the influence of the centre which find their investment plans shackled by the vagaries of the national government's stop/go management of the economy, local authorities can offer a more controlled and planned vehicle for service expansion: 'Rising demand is likely to be a permanent feature of a large slice of the personal health, welfare and education services. The ability to respond to it thus becomes an important, possibly even vital, consideration in assessing the relative merits of alternative administrative arrangements' (Sharpe, 1970, p. 173).

The final argument unveiled by Sharpe in support of the efficiency value of local government relates to its capacity to keep professional groups in check. He recognises that the specialisation and techno-logical sophistication of government policy has given professional groups a considerable degree of discretion and power: so much so that a public service can come to be run in the interests of the professionals rather than society at large. Some form of external control is necessary to challenge professional power, and local government offers the best option: 'It does so by creating an additional focus of loyalty for professional group members – the local authority itself – on a scale that makes political control feasible and subjects the group to the moderating influence of a face-to-face relationship with other comparable and competing professional groups' (1970, p. 174).

Sharpe's arguments represent an attempt to construct a strong justification for local government in the context of a powerful and expanded welfare state. Local government has had to embrace a much expanded range of functions as the welfare state has devel-oped. It is the efficiency it brings to this expanded role that justifies its existence. Its multi-purpose character means that it can co-ordinate provision and balance competing priorities. Its representa-tive institutions provide a mechanism for responding to demand, and a check on the power of organised interests. The basic form of local government remains appropriate even in the new conditions of an expanded welfare state. What is required is for it to be moder-nised, enlarged and reorganised to increase its technical and func-tional capacity.

Local government is justified more by its ability to deliver rather than involve, according to orthodoxy developed in the post-war reform debate. D. M. Hill, writing in the early 1970s, comments: 'Perhaps the majority of people would now agree with L. J. Sharpe that local government is justified as the effective provider of services rather than the means of liberty, participation or democracy' (Hill,

1974, pp. 235–6). Hill herself is only partially convinced. She warns that local government runs a risk if it neglects the involvement of the public in a meaningful way:

> To be the effective provider of services local authorities must be more than efficient. They must still be judged by that justice, fairness, equality and openness by which democratic society as a whole is judge. (Hill, 1974, p. 236).

A decade or so later, L. J. Sharpe himself was moved to agree that 'the sociogeographic and service efficiency arguments in the British reform process were exaggerated' (Sharpe, 1988, p. 114). By that time, however, the debate about local government had moved on.

In defence of local government: the localists

The changed environment of the 1980s is outlined by Jones and Stewart (1985, p. 3) in the following terms:

> Since 1979 – as in previous governments – ministers have sought to increase their control over local authorities but the pace of centralisation has increased. The message of central government was that it needed to control disobedient local authorities. Its measures and proposals were designed to increase centralisation and to weaken local government. By July 1982 one minister (Leon Brittan) was openly questioning the case for local autonomy over priorities and in the administration of services. The very existence of local government appears under serious threat.

The supporters of local government led by Jones and Stewart mustered a range of arguments in defence of the local autonomy and local government. The localists developed orthodox arguments in a range of ways.

The threat to local autonomy had been identified in the working of the Layfield Committee on local government fiance, in which both Jones and Stewart were involved. The Layfield Report (1976) was quoted enthusiastically by the two authors in their *The Case for Local Government*, because it identifies, for them, the most important issue about local government, namely:

whether all important governmental decisions affecting people's lives and livelihood should be taken in one place on the basis of national policies; or whether many of the decisions could not as well, or better, be taken in different places, by people of diverse experience, associations, background and political persuasion. (The Layfield Report, quoted in Jones and Stewart, 1985, p. 5)

Jones and Stewart make it plain that they value a governmental system where there is considerable scope for local autonomy and decision-making.

In their review of the arguments for local government, Jones and Stewart stress many of the familiar positions of the traditional orthodoxy. Local government ensures that resources can be better matched to the diversity of needs. It is local and therefore closer to the citizen. This visibility makes it open to public pressure. However, Jones and Stewart (1985, p. 5) emphasise the argument that local government is an expression of the diffusion of power:

> Local government is no passing luxury. It should be a guardian of fundamental values. It presents, first and foremost, a spread of political power. Power is diffused among many different organisations. Local authorities, however, are the only institution other than the House of Commons within the country that can claim the authority that comes from election. Local authorities can represent the dispersion of legitimate political power in our society.

They conclude that 'concentration of power is a danger to a free society' (1985, p. 9). Local government is to be valued above all because it limits the concentration of power.

The theme that local government makes a fundamental contribution in diffusing power in society was followed through by several other authors in the 1980s. Young (1986b), in a contribution that reflects the work he did for the Widdicombe Committee, criticises Sharpe's (1970) work because it sees the case for local government mainly in terms of the service delivery role, Young argues that 'any valid theory of local government must be a political theory' (p. 18). Drawing on the broad tradition of theorising about the value of local government, he places particular emphasis on two political dimensions. The first is described as the 'argument about pluralism'.

Local government is to be valued because it undermines centralised, concentrated power. The second argument is about political education and the value of political participation at the local level. Young recognises the service efficiency arguments for local government, but gives them a particular political twist. First, it is the multi-purpose character of local authority service delivery that is to be valued because it enables the making of political choices between priorities. The responsiveness of local government is also displayed in its ability to innovate in response to changing needs and demands. The thrust of many of Young's arguments are reflected in the section on the value of local government in the report of the Widdicombe Committee (1986, pp. 47–52).

Chandler (1989) develops the theme that local government is best justified by arguments about the value of local autonomy. He comments:

> The principal justification for local government is therefore that it is the political arrangement for ensuring that conflicts concerning a territorially delineated community are resolved solely by those affected by these conflicts. (p. 606)

Drawing on and adapting J. S. Mill's arguments about individual liberty, J. Chandler's position is that people should, through local government, be able to make decisions that are primarily of concern to their local community. Intervention by outside parties and interests is appropriate only in limited circumstances.

The 1980s saw arguments for local government shifting ground, although the debate remained within the territory of the traditional orthodoxy. In contrast to the post-war debate, the localists of the 1980s made less of local government's contribution to efficient service delivery and placed more emphasis on the political value of local government as a bulwark against an over-centralised state. The strong link between academic theorising and official investigations into local government characteristic of the evolving orthodoxy is also present.

The localists want to see the basic multi-purpose, representative character of local government sustained (see, in particular, G. Jones' contribution to Jones and Ranson, 1989). However, they recognise the need for some reforms. Jones and Stewart (1985), for example, recommend the introduction of proportional representation for local elections, and that the proportion of the cost of local services met by local taxes should be increased to ensure local accountability. They retain a fundamental faith in the existing structures of local self-government:

> There are inefficiencies in local government, local authorities that are unresponsive to local pressures, and local bureaucracies that pursue their own interest. But even where such accusations are made, and justifiably so, they are made because of the very visibility of local government . . . The system is open and provides thereby correctives to revealed defects. (p. 8)

The defects of local government institutions are as nothing compared to the alternative of centralism. Local government constitutes a 'visible local bureaucracy' controlled by 'councillors close to their officials and involved in the affairs of their localities' (p. 9).

The problems of the orthodox debate

The orthodox debate has some considerable residual value, but it provides a very shaky foundation for local government as we move towards the twenty-first century. It is struggling to provide a solid support and clear vision for local government in the context of the fragmentation, centralisation and manageralism associated with Britain's emerging system of local governance. It is possible to recast some of the arguments, but the limitations of the established literature indicate there is considerable scope for a radical rethink. This argument is established below by the way of a review of the difficulties associated in sustaining the orthodox claims for local government as an expression of pluralism, a platform for participation and as a mechanism for efficient service delivery.

Local government and pluralism

The first set of claims involves promoting local government as a counter-weight to autocratic central power and as a bulwark of pluralism. Local government spreads and limits political power and so promotes individual liberty. How convincing are such arguments?

The main problem is that such arguments belie the fact that local government *is* government and, as such, might have as damaging an effect on individual liberty as could central government. It is difficult to see why local government is less likely to engage in arbitrary, questionable or unnecessary restrictions on individuals than are other forms of democratic government (see Sharpe, 1970). Indeed, central government often claims for itself the moral high ground in protecting the rights of individuals against the possible depredations of local authorities. Recent cases would include the issues of council house sales, local taxation capping, and parents' rights over schooling. Local government as a special protector of negative.liberty emerges as a rather dubious argument.

There is perhaps more substance to the claim that by diffusing power local government helps to promote pluralism. Yet this is not a claim that is unique to local authorities, and other institutions would appear to have a case for claiming that role. Political parties, pressure groups, trade unions, the media and social movements could all be seen as stronger defenders of pluralism than local authorities. Because local authorities are part of a national system of government and administration, notwithstanding their local election, their claims to promote pluralism might be considered as being modest against these societal forces and actors.

A final issue to consider is whether the 'local government as a protector of our liberties' argument can be dusted off in the context of the politics of the 1990s and be given a new lease of life. Two possibilities present themselves. The increased intensity of central government intervention and its use of non-elected local agents to manage strategic and service delivery responsibilities has led to creation of what has been described as a new magistracy – a lay, non-elected elite (Jones and Stewart, 1992). Perhaps even more problematic is how layers of professional officials have escaped traditional political scrutiny by being transferred to such agencies. Could local authorities offer themselves as the voice of the community, to check and bring to account central government and its unelected agents? A second possibility is that local authorities could provide a meaningful forum through which local interests might organise to express their concerns to the European Union (EU). The counterweight argument might still have some life left in it if recast in these terms.

Local government and participation

The second arm of the case for local government is as a platform for participation in politics. Notwithstanding the paternalistic overtones of some versions of the argument, it is difficult to deny that the accessibility of local government is greater and the opportunities for an active political role are more varied than they are at central government level. However, doubts can be raised about the breadth and quality of participation that is offered.

The first set of difficulties revolves around the limited range and diversity of those figures central to local government participation: the elected representatives. According to a survey undertaken in 1993, only 25 per cent of councillors were women, 77 per cent were over 45 years old, and a third were retired (Young and Rao, 1994). Moreover, there are relatively few of them. The ratio of councillors to citizens is 1:1800 in England and Wales, against an average ratio among Western nations of somewhere between 1:250 and 1:450 (Norton, 1994).

The limited range of very active participants and their socially unrepresentative nature, of course, could be considered irrelevant. For some, the web of participation spreads through the operation of political accountability. Councillors are held accountable to the public through their election, their surgeries and daily contact with their constituents. However, doubts about the 'actual practice' of electoral accountability in local government can be raised. Stoker (1991, pp. 49–55) reviews four main critical themes:

- the weak connection between decisions on local spending and decisions on local taxation levels;
- the low turnout in local elections compared to parliamentary elections, and the turnouts achieved in other European Western democracies;
- the influence of national factors on local voting behaviour; and
- the absence of effective conditions of political competition in many localities, so that many local authorities are one-party states.

Defenders of local government could argue that many of the criticisms noted above apply to the operation of electoral democracy at the national level. Moreover, although the value of electoral accountability may be obscured, it does not mean that the discipline of the ballot box has been lost altogether. Nevertheless the operation of local electoral accountability leaves much to be desired.

However, local government provides a forum for participation which extends beyond the mechanisms of electoral democracy. An active world of local interest groups exists and since the 1970s there has been considerable evidence of local authorities opening out to encourage a strengthening and widening of the base of local interest group activity (Stoker, 1991, ch. 5). Again, some qualifications need to be made. Interest groups remain as supplicants to the local authority, and the extent to which they become an effective channel for expressing local interests depends on the reaction of the authority. In short, the terms of the participation are generally defined by the authority, and not by its public. Some authorities are more open than others, some have a more active base to deal with, and the nature of participating groups varies.

Further qualifications can be made. The resource advantages of groups with a professional or middle-class membership are still often considerable. Business interests with substantial investment and employment capacity are perhaps more likely to enjoy a sympathetic hearing from a local authority. However, none of these qualifications would apply with greater force at the local level than at any other level of government (unlike, perhaps the situation in the United States).

One further area of uncertainty that surrounds the status of participation in the 1990s is the uneasy relationship between representative and more participatory forms of public involvement. These latter forms of participation can involve the control and definition of the relationship being taken beyond the veto of the authority. School governing boards, housing management co-operatives and other user influenced organisations provide a new channel for participation outside the immediate ambit of the elected local authority. Does involving people on the basis of their direct material interest in an issue provide a more meaningful basis for participation than traditional representative forms? Or does local representative democracy have some right to claim an overseeing role over these more direct forms of democracy?

Local government and efficiency

Allocative efficiency, it is claimed, is a core value provided by local government. Elected local authorities have the capacity to produce goods and services which best match the preferences of their local communities. Sharpe (1970) felt that local government was on its safest ground in terms of such efficiency claims. What a difference two decades can make!

Public choice arguments have led to the counter-charge to these claims in the 1980s and 1990s. (The following passages draw on Stoker (1991) pp. 238–42.) For public choice theorists, the optimal mechanism for allocating goods and making decisions is the market. Public bureaucracies and representative democracy are both seen as being seriously flawed in comparison. In particular, public sector expenditure is seen as being inherently prone to excessive growth. This in-built tendency to over-supply reflects weaknesses in representative democracy. Vote-seeking politicians look to establish constituencies to support existing and increased levels of spending. Vocal and highly organised interest groups are formed which constantly push more and better provision to meet their special interests. The losers are the disorganised and silent majority who finance this expenditure. More generally, public choice theorists regard existing democratic arrangements as very poor predictors of citizens' preferences and demands. Elections every few years force people to decide on a whole range of choices and options provided by the market mechanism.

The tendency to over-supply is reinforced by key features of public bureaucracies. All organisations, it is argued, tend in the long run towards the abandonment of collective goals and in their place is the pursuit of self-interested goals by those holding official positions. In particular, a characteristic goal of bureaucrats is budget maximisation through the expansion of their departmental programmes. Politicians 'in charge' of the bureaucracies are often sympathetic to the process of budget expansion. In part, this reflects the inadequacies of the representative system outlined earlier. it also reflects the ability of bureaucrats to 'capture' politicians, given that they control much access to information about the need for services and the costs involved in providing existing services. In the case of local government, public-choice-inspired theorists have been highly critical. Self-interested professionals and trade unionists are dominant, with managerial and political controls weak and ineffective. Consumer preferences are rarely taken into account, resulting in the over-supply of inadequate services.

The public-choice theorists offer a number of remedies aimed at tackling these problems:

- performance contracting rather than direct labour through open-ended employment contracts;
- fragmented, multiple-provider service structures to ensure competition and citizen choice; and
- the introduction of user charges for services rather than the funding of these through general taxation.

These quasi-market mechanisms will better ensure that public goods and services match the preferences of local communities than will provision through the traditional producer-dominated monopoly provision of local authorities. Moreover, there may be additional x-efficiency gains, with reductions in the level of inputs required to produce a given level of output.

The reform prescriptions of the public-choice theorists have found expression in much of the Conservatives' restructuring programme (see Chapter 3). If the central thrust of their argument is accepted, then responsiveness in service delivery relates not to the elected status of an organisation but to the degree it is subject to the forces of competition and consumer choice. Elected local authorities are left with no special claims in relation to the value of allocative efficiency. Rather, they have to battle it out in practice, contract by contract, with competing service providers.

If a case for local government in the 1990s is to be rebuilt, the critical thrust of the public-choice challenge needs to be met. The public choice view goes to the heart of the orthodox claims about local government's special qualities as a service provider. In particular, Sharpe's (1970) arguments about responding to demand are challenged flatly; as is the claim that local government is a consumer champion against producer and professional interests. Sharpe, however, also commented on the role of local government as 'a coordinator of services in the field' and as 'a reconciler of community opinion'. It is perhaps through these broader governmental roles that claims about local government's contribution to allocative efficiency could be reassembled, an argument developed by Walsh in this volume (see Chapter 4).

The orthodox arguments for local government are limited and in some respects flawed. Yet despite these problems it is clear that variations of the arguments could be advanced to still provide a viable set of arguments about local government and democracy. The robustness of the core propositions are in many ways a tribute to the qualities of J. S. Mill's original analysis.[1] Yet, equally, the review provided here suggests that it might be appropriate to move beyond the orthodox territory, and widen out the focus of the normative debate about local government and democracy.

Beyond orthodoxy: emerging themes and enduring tensions

What is different about the way the normative debate around local government and democracy is developed in this book? First, the procedure we adopt is different.

From John Stuart Mill onwards the traditional orthodoxy has developed through abstracting general principles from the practice of local government. Such a mode of arguing has coloured the character of the theorising and reflects in part its closeness in many instances to official reports and investigations. It is little wonder in these circumstances that theorists tried to relate their arguments for local government and democracy as closely as possible to the actual or reformable practice of local politics.

This book takes a different perspective. It begins with some major currents in political and social theory and asks what is the place of local government and democracy within these schemes of thought. Thus, for example, David Beetham considers what is the contribution of democratic theory to clarifying the relationship between local government and democracy, and Anne Phillips asks whether there is a feminist case for local democracy. Green, communitarian and other strands of social and political thought are similarly quizzed within the book. This procedure creates a more open and wide-ranging set of perspectives. It liberates the discussion and enables the authors to move beyond the traditional orthodoxy and to widen the debate.

A further element in the process of mould-breaking in this book is provided by the introduction of comparative material into the normative debate. Harold Wolman and Mike Goldsmith explore the evolving traditions of, respectively, the United States of America and Western Europe in comparison to the British experience. The implications of the wide-ranging debate for practice are not neglected. Many chapters move from evaluating normative values to examining the institutional practice of local government and democracy. Kieron Walsh's chapter is a particularly strong example. Allan Cochrane in his chapter draws on and extends the discussion of the relationship between theory and practice.

What else is different about this book compared to the traditional orthodoxy? The second general feature of the book is the way it goes beyond the prevalent, 'economist' conceptions of local government which underlie much of the orthodox literature. As Magnusson (1986) suggests, much of the orthodox literature has struggled to escape its utilitarian foundations and as a result there is a 'tendency to understand local government in economic terms and to make economic welfare the main criterion for assessing political arrangements' (p. 2). From a utilitarian perspective, 'the State's legitimacy depends on its ability to enhance the welfare of its subjects – and welfare is normally conceived in terms of consumer satisfaction' (p. 16). The traditional advocates of multiple-purpose local representative government and their public choice critics share a common underlying understanding of the role of government. Their argument is over which system is likely to lead to greater consumer satisfaction. Their vision of the purposes of politics and government is limited by their shared conception that government is their to satisfy the consumption requirements and needs of its citizens. What is missing from the debate, according to Magnusson, is a broader conception of local government as a political unit. Several contributions in this book confront this issue directly and offer an explicitly wider vision of the polity which goes beyond a narrow 'economism'.

One key theme, which follows from the commitment to avoiding 'economism', is an emphasis on the distinctiveness of the political realm as a focus for collective decision-making. This argument finds expression in Keith Dowding's critique of public choice theorists. Their use of economic and economic-like tools to study politics 'involves certain tools which *are only applicable* to market situations; they use a hammer to drive in a screw'. In particular their work is tainted by Pareto-efficiency assumptions which tend to lead to a preference for market allocations as opposed to decision-making through a political form. The basic Pareto-optimising principle espoused by economists is that if some gain and none lose there is an improvement in welfare. The problem is that democracy will, according to this ethical postulate, always produce Pareto-inefficient outcomes unless votes are unanimous. What is more, public choice theorists have twisted the criterion even further to suggest that if some people lose from a change, then that change should not be made. The conservative nature of this position becomes even more obvious once it is further realised that the Pareto-efficiency postulate assumes an initial distribution of resources and a fixed technology. To rule out by definition the issue of property rights means that public choice theorists ignore one of the most important dimensions of politics.

Politics involves more than the working out of a calculus of gainers and losers. As Beetham comments, politics is about collectively binding rules and policies, and about the resolution of disagreement about what those policies should be. Situating democracy in the sphere of the political indicates that it is not simply a means of maximising individual choice or freedom. Politics presupposes that we are social creatures, living interdependent lives, and therefore requiring common rules and procedures. Politics involves making decisions on behalf of other people and not ourselves alone. It is a process of collective decision-making to which democratic theory rather than simplistic Pareto-style ethical postulates should provide a guiding light.

A second theme running through the book is a concern with the value of a local democratic polity rather than a particular preference for local representative government. Beetham makes a distinction between the concept of representative government and a commitment to representative democracy. The former may be more or less democratic, but the latter assumes government conducted according to democratic principles. The latter does not make a fetish out of the particular and special qualities of representatives: rather it suggests that representative democracy 'cannot be realised or sustained without an active citizen body'. Other contributions in this book similarly break from the traditional orthodoxy in that their arguments are for the value of locality as a political space and democratic arena rather than for a particular institutional form of representative local government.

A third and related theme is the importance of local politics in revealing and reconciling preferences. Phillips, for example, emphasises the importance of deliberative capacity within a political system. Politics which takes preferences as given is unsuited to the needs of women, and, by extension, to any group defined out of the dominant consensus. A more participatory, involving and reflective politics is required in order to encourage the articulation and refinement of previously unspoken needs. There is a broad case for deliberative capacity, which is shared by several of the contributors to this book. Elizabeth Frazer, while criticising the formulations of the communitarians, shares their concern with how to create a polity that displays the 'civic' virtues of trust, co-operation and reciprocity. What is required is the sharing of experiences and a process of collective deliberation. This capacity is particularly important given the increased uncertainty and complexity of many of the issues confronting the local arena.

Political institutions must be designed to enable citizens to relate to each other as deliberators or reason-givers and not as bargainers engaged in exchange. Local political institutions, with their accessibility and closeness to communities, would seem well-equipped in principle for this task.

A final feature of the presentations in this book is a commitment to a form of local government that emphasises its capacity for framework-setting rather than its role in direct service production. Walsh offers the most detailed examination of the form and structure of local government and concludes that what is required is a complex process of institutional design. If efficiency in the sense of responsiveness to citizens is to be the goal, what is required is a diverse and flexible system which mixes markets and networks with traditional bureaucracy. Hugh Ward, writing from a Green perspective, endorses a view of local authority as a broker, an organiser of coalitions, and as a consensus builder. Day-to-day politics, in his view, should involve a complex range of non-territorial associations in which people participate and which correspond to the diversity and variety of their circumstances and interests. Local authorities should play a key role in bringing the fragments together. Frazer develops a similar line of argument. Local government is attractive as a conductor, facilitating and leading a complex range and variety of organisations in civil society. The active civil society needs to be sustained and nurtured, and local authorities would have a key role in establishing a framework for interest expression and co-operative problem-solving.

These four shared themes in the book are joined by a recognition from authors of a number of enduring tensions in the debate about local government and democracy. First, several of the authors are keen to avoid what might be termed 'the trap of localism': that is, a tendency to view the local and local autonomy through romantic eyes. Smaller communities do not necessarily behave in a more democratic way. They can be stifling or disabling in reinforcing relationships of subordination and narrow parochialism.

A further enduring tension is the recognition that opportunities for participation at the local level can be undermined by a lack of system capacity at that level. Localities are buffeted by a range of global forces and must place themselves within a complex architecture of government. Moreover, individuals may in a mass-communication and highly mobile society find the local political sphere more difficult to identify with and work through. The viability and importance of a local political space can still be claimed but it cannot be assumed.

Finally, there is an enduring tension between the scope for local political choice and a concern for achieving social justice. It is this tension that is a particular focus of attention in Desmond King's concluding chapter in the book. It is, however, a concern of a number of authors throughout the volume. Can local choice be reconciled with a concern for equality of treatment for all citizens?

The structure of the book

The previous section identified a number of core themes in the book but it does not fully capture the richness of the arguments presented. It may be helpful to provide the reader with further guidance as to the contents of individual chapters.

Beetham in Chapter 2 considers what contribution democratic theory can make to clarifying the relationship between democracy and local government. He outlines a reformulation of the main arguments for representative democracy. Authorisation of decision-makers, accountability to citizens, responsiveness to public opinion and the representativeness of elected representatives comprise different aspects of the democratic principle of popular control, he argues. Local government has the potential to fulfil these principles in practice to a greater extent than a system of local administration organised by an elected government at the centre. There is, therefore, according to Beetham, a strong democratic case for elected local government. However, if the democratic potential of elected local government is to be fulfilled, a number of reforms will be necessary to improve the practice of the existing system. A concluding section of the chapter identifies a number of difficulties in connecting democratisation at the levels of government and civil society. In the context of an emerging local governance, Beetham argues that the political party might have a crucial role in forging the links between the two spheres.

As already noted, public choice arguments have led the challenge to the orthodox justifications of local government and democracy. Dowding in Chapter 3 shows how a range of writers from the public choice tradition have been suspicious of representative democracy and large public bureaucracies. He notes how these suspicions and an associated reform programme advocated by public choice theorists are reflected in a limited and partial way in the Conservatives' restructuring of the system of local governance since 1979. The final section of his chapter opens out a critique of traditional public choice theory. The fundamental problem, as noted earlier, is the ideologically tainted use of Pareto-efficiency arguments. Freed from such a bias, the rational choice perspective has much to offer, argues Dowding. He notes in conclusion a number of potential areas for further investigation.

In Chapter 4, Walsh examines the arguments about the efficiency of local government. As he notes, the dominant argument since the mid-1980s has been that public services will only be efficient if they are subject to market forces. Yet, as Walsh demonstrates, this is a simplistic argument and neglects the complexity of the meaning of efficiency. He identifies three concepts of efficiency – technical, allocative and x-efficiency. Each type of efficiency indicates some scope for local administration, but the arguments around allocative efficiency provide the strongest arguments for democratic local government. Efficiency arguments about the structure and form of local democracy suggest a highly differentiated system of local governance. However, this pattern needs to balance against a broad concern for the ability of citizens to understand the system. Walsh concludes that if efficiency arguments are to be followed, what is required is a wider democratic mix of institutions and instruments at the local level.

In Chapter 5 Frazer explores the debate about communitarianism and examines its implications for the normative underpinnings of local government. Communitarians believe that local government should be strengthened. Yet, on closer examination, communitarian arguments are clouded by inadequate conceptions of community and locality. Similarly practitioners' regular references to community obscure the normative argument for local government. Frazer argues that a prescriptive case for local government needs only to emphasise the value of care for localities and the needs of people living and working in and using localities. The civic virtues prized by communitarians can be promoted at the local level without necessarily following the communitarian perspective.

Phillips in Chapter 6 asks if there is a feminist case for local democracy. In some respects the openness of local politics makes it an attractive arena for feminists. On the other hand, the coercive implications of community and the limited capacity for change at the local level argue against radical decentralised power. Phillips reviews the arguments on both sides of the fence and concludes that the best argument for local democracy is that, at the local level, those seeking to challenge existing agendas will get their first break. Feminist politics is about transformation and a vibrant local democracy can play a crucial component in any politics of innovation.

Ward in Chapter 7 examines the political thought of the Green movement and argues that it has profound implications for rethinking the role of local government and, indeed, the conception of local political processes. He divides the arguments of the Greens into four categories: those which relate decentralisation to the development of a Green consciousness; those that claim the self-interested pressures that threaten the environment are best managed at the local level; those that suggest that sustainable communities require small-scale organisation; and finally, those that argue that grassroots democracy is a necessary condition for sustainability. Ward is not convinced by all the arguments of the Greens, but suggests that a number of aspects of Green thinking present a strong case for the decentralisation of power and enhanced grassroots democracy.

In Chapter 8, Wolman shifts the focus of the book to an examination of normative debates about local government and democracy in a comparative perspective. Wolman reviews the dominant theories of local democracy in the USA and shows how they are flavoured by the broader American emphasis on individualism and localism. Goldsmith, in Chapter 9, examines the ways in which local democracy has been interpreted within other European countries. He draws a broad distinction between a Northern group of countries that emphasise the formal constitutional status of elected local government and a Southern group that emphasise a tradition of territorial representation.

The book concludes with two chapters that provide a range of reflections of the contents of the volume. Cochrane presents the more optimistic assessment in Chapter 10. He notes the uncertainties and difficulties surrounding the promise of democratising the local polity. Yet he notes that it is possible to point to emerging thinking and practice within local politics that may come together to help transform traditional understandings and build a more positive way forward.

King in Chapter 11, presents a more pessimistic picture. He develops a commentary about an underlying concern about the volume: how can local autonomy be made compatible with the maintenance of nationally valued rights of citizenship.

The case for local autonomy, democracy and government is not self-evident. If this book moves the debate beyond the propositions of the traditional orthodoxy it will have achieved its purpose. The emerging system of local governance demands some radical rethinking in normative theorising. This book makes a starting contribution to that process of rethinking.

Note

1. This argument draws on some notes sent to me by John Stewart.

2 Theorising Democracy and Local Government

David Beetham

'There is now no universally accepted notion as to the proper nature of local democracy,' wrote John Gyford in his contribution to the Widdicombe Report, 'and many of those who use the term are simply talking past one another' (Gyford, 1986, p. 106). In the decade or so since he wrote that, the terminological confusion he remarked upon has intensified. The purpose of this chapter is to consider what contribution democratic theory can make to clarifying the relationship between democracy and local government.[1] My starting point will be with the meaning of democracy itself, and an understanding of what kinds of principle and practice it entails. With this foundation secured, I shall then address three questions: (i) What case is there, from a democratic point of view, for an elected system of local, in addition to national, government? (ii) What changes might make it more democratic, and how desirable and practicable would they be? and (iii) How might democracy be realised at the local level, other than through the formal structures of government?

Before I embark on this agenda, it will be worth offering some introductory comments on the nature of normative theorising and its uses, which will help to structure the argument of the chapter. Normative theorising is a complex and many-sided activity that includes a number of distinct elements. There is, first, an analytical or conceptual component, addressing the question: What is the meaning of a given concept (democracy, freedom, justice and so on), and what are the criteria by which we can tell whether, or how far, it has been attained in practice? Second there is a justificatory component answering the questions: Why should we value it? And why is it important to us? Third is a critical component, answering the questions: How far are the criteria or principles entailed by the concept realised in a given situation or set of institutions? and How far does practice measure up to a justifiable normative standard or ideal? Fourth is a practical aspect, addressing two rather different questions: What institutional arrangements are, or might be, most effective in realising the principles in question? and At what point does realising these principles bring us into conflict with other principles that we value? Finally there is the question of agency: Which social or political groups might plausibly act as the bearers, protagonists or beneficiaries of the values in question?

Giving a full answer to these different questions – conceptual, justificatory, critical, practical and agential – is a large undertaking, beyond the scope of a single chapter. However, they provide a useful map of the route to be followed, and will help to clarify exactly what commentators on local democracy are disagreeing about, when they do so.

First, then, the meaning of democracy. Democracy belongs to the sphere of the *political*, which is the sphere of collectively binding rules and policies, and of the resolution of disagreement about what those policies should be. Situating democracy in this sphere of the political excludes immediately one misconception about democracy, recurrent in the British culture, that it means the maximisation of individual choice or individual freedom. Democracy certainly entails a variety of individual rights – of free speech, association, the suffrage and so on – but their point of reference is the process of collective decision-making, which is necessarily prior to – because it provides the preconditions and boundaries for – individual choice and action. Democratic politics, like any politics, presupposes that we are primarily social creatures, living lives that are interdependent, and therefore requiring common rules and policies.

From the above definition of 'the political' it follows, secondly, that democracy is not confined to the arena of government alone, but can be realised wherever there are common rules and policies to be made, and disagreement about these rules to be resolved, whatever the collectivity or association happens to be, from the family outwards. What makes collective decision-making at the level of government especially important is that its association (the state) embraces everyone within a given territory, that membership and tax contributions are compulsory, that disagreement about its rules and policies is correspondingly intense, and that the institutions for deciding and enforcing these rules and policies are highly developed. Although our concern here primarily will be with democracy at the level of government, in view of its significance, it is important to recognise not only that there are many other fields for the practice of democracy than that of government, but also that the decisions of many institutions other than government can have a considerable impact on people's lives, both nationally and locally. How such decisions are taken, therefore, and to whom they are accountable, is a legitimate matter of both public concern and democratic consideration.

If, then, democracy belongs to the sphere of the political, of decision-making for an association or collectivity, then a system of collective decision-making can be defined as 'democratic' to the extent that it is subject to control by all members of the relevant association considered as equals. Popular control and political equality are the key democratic principles.[2] They are most fully realised in small groups or associations where everyone has effectively an equal right to speak and to vote on policy in person. In larger associations, and especially at the level of a whole society, practical considerations of time and space necessitate that collective decisions be taken by designated agents or representatives acting on behalf of the rest. Here democracy is realised in the first instance, not as direct popular control over decision-making, but as control over the decision-makers who act in their stead. How effective that control is, and how equally distributed it is between individual citizens, and between different groups of citizens, according to their numbers, are key criteria for how democratic is a system of representative government.

At this point it is useful to distinguish between the concept of representative government, which may or may not be particularly democratic, and representative *democracy*, which is a representative government conducted according to democratic principles. Of the former – representative government – it may or may not be true, as is frequently alleged, that 'it assumes that citizens are passive, that they are incompetent to participate in decisions about complex issues' (Stewart *et al.*, 1994, p. iii). Representative democracy, on the other hand, as I shall show, cannot be either realised or sustained without an active citizen body.

Popular control and political equality constitute simple but powerful principles which can be used both to assess how democratic a system of collective decision-making is, and as ideals to be realised in practical institutional form. The history of popular struggles to make government more democratic has developed a set of intermediate, or lower order concepts, entailed by the two main ones, and a set of characteristic institutions for their realisation, which stand in continual need of renewal if government is not to regress from a democratic point of view. These mediating concepts or ideas are those of popular authorisation and accountability of public officials, and the responsiveness and representativeness of decision-making bodies. A key instrument for realising each is that of competitive election; but the electoral process also needs to be supplemented by a variety of other institutional arrangements and practices if popular control and political equality are to be secured effectively.

Let me consider briefly each of these mediating concepts in turn.

The basic idea of a representative democracy is that of the popular *authorisation* of the key governmental decision-makers through election by universal equal suffrage. Such authorisation embodies the idea of popular sovereignty: the people constitute the only rightful source of political authority. Consistent with this idea is the requirement that the relationship between electors and elected, and the respective powers of each, should be established in a written constitution that has been directly approved by popular vote; and that any subsequent changes should require popular approval through a referendum. Whatever disagreements there may be otherwise about the role of referenda in a representative democracy, it is difficult to contest the conclusion that, if the rightful source of political authority lies in the people, then they should have the final say directly on the constitutional terms on which that authority is surrendered to others.

From the popular authorisation of public officials follows their *accountability* to the people for the policies and actions undertaken while in office. Here the other side of the electoral process to that of authorisation is central: the credible threat of being turned out of office in the event of 'failure' or abuse of trust. To be effective, such a threat requires not only that the public have access to independent information about government activities, but also that the electoral process itself is not tilted to the advantage of the incumbents. Effective public accountability also requires a set of supplementary procedures and institutions in addition to elections: the accountability of non-elected officials to elected ones; an independent judiciary to ensure legal accountability and uphold the freedoms of speech, association, and so on, on which electoral accountability depends; independent accounting officers to ensure financial accountability; independent media with a commitment to investigative journalism, and so on.

The criterion of *responsive* government goes beyond accountability or answerability, to embrace the requirement that governments take note systematically of the full range of public opinion in the formulation and implementation of law and policy. Elitist critics of democracy have always been scornful of the idea of government responsiveness. They argue that the so-called 'will of the people' is more the product of the political process than its initiator, and that governments should resist being always blown off course by short-term unpopularity.[3] However, to recognise a creative role for politicians in reconciling conflicts of opinion and interest, and in securing continuity and consistency of policy, does not entail belittling public opinion. Responsiveness requires that there be a legally recognised right of consultation and access to government on the part of all sections of opinion with an interest in a given policy or piece of legislation. The electoral process, although here too the ultimate guarantor of responsive government, is also too crude an instrument on its own to assess public opinion on any issue, and needs to be supplemented by a variety of other institutions and procedures.

While the above concepts comprise different aspects of the democratic principle of popular control, the final concept of *representativeness* is closely linked to the other democratic principle of political equality or equality of citizenship. For an elected assembly to be properly representative of political opinion requires that individuals' votes should be of equal value, wherever they happen to live and whichever party they happen to vote for. For it to be socially representative requires that there is effective equality of opportunity to stand for public office, regardless of the social group to which a person belongs. For public opinion to be representative requires that access to the media and to government should not be weighted in favour of wealth or connection, and against the socially disadvantaged. None of the above guarantees that the outcomes of policy will satisfy everyone, but rather that the procedures are fair, and that all sections of society and opinion are guaranteed an equal chance to have their views considered according to their numbers.

Representative democracy, then, requires that government is popularly authorised, accountable, responsive and representative, through a process of competitive election, and a variety of other institutions and procedures. For these criteria to be met, however, it requires more than a particular set of institutions and their associated popular rights. It also requires that citizens are active in the exercise of their rights, and in ensuring their access to, and control over, the government of the day. Here lies the validity of the much discussed concept of 'participation': without an alert and active citizen body, governments will not be representative, responsive or accountable; nor will they enjoy the full legitimacy that comes from popular authorisation.

On its own, however, the term 'participation' is far too vague a concept to serve as an equivalent for 'democracy', in the absence of any specification of participation in what, by whom, or to what effect. The most 'participatory' political regimes of the twentieth century were the communist systems, so-called people's democracies; yet that participation delivered little popular control over the personnel or policies of government. Extending participation in the Western democracies, on the other hand, can simply mean more power for already advantaged groups. Participation is also often advocated, *de haut en bas*, as a means for the political education of those considered to be in need of it.[4] How far an extension of participation is to be judged 'democratic' depends on its contribution to securing greater popular control over collective decision-making, and greater equality in its exercise; participation is thus subordinate to, and to be judged in terms of, these two prior democratic principles. Moreover, as the above argument also makes clear, popular participation (in voting, in standing for election, in associating with others to influence opinion, lobby office holders and so on) is a necessary condition for, not an alternative to, representative democracy.

If clarifying what democracy means in the context of a representative system requires a lengthy exposition, the justification for democratic principles can be stated more briefly.[5] Democracy shares with Western liberalism a core value – that of self-determination, or controlling our own lives; a core assumption – every adult is in principle capable of taking responsibility for themselves; and a core epistemological premise – that there is no independently ascertainable good for people other than what they themselves, equipped with appropriate knowledge, freely determine. The important difference is that these three features are to be understood in a collective or political – rather than an individual – context. This means not only that everyone's interest is entitled to equal consideration in the formulation of public policy, but also that everyone is entitled to a say in it, and to the information necessary to make an informed judgement about it. If these values provide the justification for the characteristic institutions and freedoms of representative democracy, they also await to be more fully realised within it.

The above discussion about the meaning and justification of democracy should help to clarify what is relevant to answering the three questions about local government which were posed at the outset of the chapter. They will now be considered in turn.

The democratic case for local government

How strong is the case, on *democratic* grounds, for a system of locally-elected government, or representative government at the local, in addition to the national, level?[6] More precisely, can a government only be accountable, responsive and representative at the local level if there is a popularly authorised tier of local government, rather than a system of local administration organised by an elected government at the centre?

This question confronts us with a serious methodological difficulty at the outset. Are we talking about general principles abstracted from specific UK circumstances, as J. S. Mill does in his chapter on local government in *Representative Government* (1861, ch. xv)? Or are we considering institutional arrangements as they operate in practice in the UK? Or again, is it such institutional arrangements as they might realistically be modified to work more democratically? Consider the following situation. It is becoming abundantly evident that we suffer from a deep malaise of representative institutions at all levels in the UK, in respect of accountability, responsiveness and representativeness alike. Critics of a centralised model can point to the democratic deficiencies of a national parliament which is dominated by the executive, electorally unrepresentative, and unresponsive to all but a limited range of sectional interests. From this perspective, the idea that a system of local administration run from the centre could ever be democratic in the context of an unreformed parliament, is simply ludicrous. On the other side, critics of UK local government as it operates in practice can point to parallel, if not identical, deficiencies from a democratic point of view. On either side the case can be rigged by contrasting an unreformed system on the one hand, whether local or national, with assumed perfection on the other. The only way to overcome this problem of comparing like with like is to explore the *intrinsic potential* for democratisation of given institutional forms, or institutional models, abstracted from their particular circumstantial defects. Although what counts as intrinsic and what extrinsic or accidental is necessarily contestable, the distinction can be defended, as with any ideal-typical method, by appropriate argument and evidence, including cross-national comparison. Thus, for example, the issue becomes, not whether the existing Westminster Parliament could hold a system of local administration effectively to account, but whether any national parliament, however constituted, could cope realistically with the workload of supervising simultaneously local as well as national and supranational levels of administration. And so on with the other criteria of democracy. I shall take each of them in turn.

Accountability

The most clearly defined alternative to a system of local government accountable to a local electorate is a system of administration accountable *upwards* to an elected minister (and through the minister to Parliament), and *downwards* to its customers through an ombudsman, citizens' charter or other mechanism of legally enforceable redress in the event of minimum standards or procedures not being observed. This model applies widely in the UK, both to local offices of national departments, and to 'quangos' of all kinds; Desmond King calls it the 'informal local government system' (1993, pp. 205–15; see also Davis and Stewart, 1993). Let us suppose, for the sake of argument, that this model were to lose its most obvious defect in practice, from the point of view of accountability, and that all agencies in receipt of public funds were required to meet the same conditions of openness as currently apply to local government.[7] Although it might be argued that this is not an accidental defect – since it is intrinsic to a philosophy which assumes that the norms of private sector management can be transferred without remainder to the public services – nevertheless there is no reason to regard secrecy as being intrinsic to such a model of administrative accountability. Indeed, the case for it would be strengthened considerably if the openness necessary to any effective public accountability were legally required.

There remain, however, three defects which can be regarded as intrinsic rather than accidental to such a model of accountability for a local administrative system. First, it must be doubted whether a national parliament can have either the capacity or the interest to subject local administration to the same degree of scrutiny as people in the locality have. This limitation of both capacity and interest was the primary reason why J. S. Mill advocated a system of locally-elected government, which would also enable the national parliament to do a more effective job of scrutinising strictly national affairs. 'It is but a small portion of the public business of a country which can be well done, or safely attempted, by the central authorities,' he wrote, '. . . Not only are separate executive officers required for purely local duties, but the popular control over those officers can only be advantageously exerted through a separate organ' (1861, pp. 346–7; see Jones and Stewart, 1983, p. 10; also Weir and Hall, 1994, pp. 41–4).

Second, a system of separate local agencies or quangos, accountable only to their several ministries, overlooks the way in which different services are interdependent at the local level, and require co-ordination to be properly effective. Separation simply encourages the dumping of problem cases from one agency onto another, and the externalisation of their costs in the interests of a narrowly defined administrative efficiency. If, on the other hand, institutional arrangements for local co-ordination are established, it is difficult to see how they can be held effectively accountable within a centralised model, which assumes answerability to individual ministries. To whom should a co-ordinating body for local services be accountable if not to a local electorate?[8]

Third, there is a crucial limitation to the model of individual redress as the only form of downward accountability. Not only do the consumers of a service have no say in what the standards of service delivery should be, or whether these might be varied or improved upon locally. Treating citizens simply as consumers also removes them from any influence over political decisions about priorities in the use and distribution of resources, which are treated simply as a managerial prerogative at the level of local agency or quango.[9] Indeed, accountability itself in the centralised model tends to be reduced to the narrow concept of 'accountingability', that is, public protection against the misuse of funds, rather than the justification to a local public of decisions about their use and prioritisation.

In the light of these intrinsic deficiencies of accountability in a centralised model – in respect of supervisory competence, of inter-service co-ordination and of political answerability – the argument in favour of a separate tier of local government, directly accountable to a local electorate, must be considered to be strong. At this point, critics of contemporary local government in Britain will point to the inadequacies of electoral accountability in a situation where only a minority of the electorate bothers to vote; where voting is on national rather than local issues; and where single-party fiefdoms can remain immune to any realistic electoral reckoning. These are serious defects. Yet to make the case against local government stick, critics would have to show that these defects were intrinsic to local electoral processes as such, and were not amenable to reform.[10] They would also need to show that the lack of accountability was not due to the very process of centralising government power, which had so narrowed the scope for local political choice that people did not think it meaningful to vote. Such a process would make the centralising model itself a cause of, rather than simply a response to, deficient electoral accountability at the local level.

Responsiveness

When we turn to the second criterion of democratic government, that of responsiveness, we shall find good reason to conclude that a nationally organised system of local administration cannot be as responsive to local interests and local opinion as can elected local government. What it can ensure is that there are common standards of service across the territory of the state, without arbitrary dis-crepancies between citizens simply because of where they happen to live. However, this requirement of equal citizenship – itself an important democratic requirement – can be met sufficiently through national legislation on minimum standards of service provision, and through a resource distribution mechanism between richer and poorer local authorities, without surrendering the responsiveness to local opinion that is the hallmark of an elected system.[11]

The case for elected authorities here rests on a number of considerations. One is the sheer diversity of situation and needs between different localities. The problems of rural areas are not the same as those of towns, nor towns the same as those of suburbs or inner cities. Even where the problems are similar, the most appropriate solutions may not be the same. These can be devised most effectively by those who have the advantage of local information and experience, and who also have to live with the consequences of their decisions. Diverse solutions also produce a fertile ground for innovation and experimentation, and for different models of good practice. A uniform and centralised system of administration, is unlikely either to develop or to tolerate such diversity.[12]

A second consideration is that those responsible for running a service typically are found to be much more accessible if it is organised by a locally elected authority rather than a national one. This is partly a question of numbers. Local councillors, who represent a few hundred or thousand electors, are much more accessible than Members of Parliament, who represent many tens of thousands. In a tradition where elected representatives are regarded as an important avenue for complaint and assistance, both because of the weight they carry with non-elected officials, and because they also share responsibility for the policies being pursued, their accessibility to their constituents is an important consideration. So too is the much easier access that groups of organised opinion have to policy makers when these are located in the town or county hall rather than in Whitehall or Westminster (Parry *et al.*, 1992; Young, 1986a).

Finally, an elected authority has a greater incentive to develop and extend the practice of local consultation, and to experiment with new forms of it, than a non-elected one. We may agree with critics of the electoral mechanism itself, that it constitutes a very crude instrument of choice compared, say, with the choice available in the consumer market place (Seldon, 1990, ch. 5). But such a contrast is based on two fallacies. One is that individual choice can ever be an adequate substitute for the collective choices of public policy; indeed, surrendering to individual choice (in transport, education, health care and so on) simply becomes a form of collective choice by default for a particular pattern and distribution of service provision. A second fallacy of the market contrast is the assumption that elections constitute the only collective mechanism for responsiveness to citizens' preferences. Just as there exist all kinds of devices for consumer survey and market testing in the provision of private goods, so these can have their counterpart in the public sphere to complement the electoral process. What elections provide is the incentive for policy makers and service providers to develop more responsive modes of consultation (and a legitimate ground for citizens to demand them) that are lacking in a non-elected administration.

Representativeness

A number of considerations combine to favour a locally elected system of government on grounds of representativeness. First is the importance of having all the main strands of public opinion, and all the significant political forces of a country, represented in government at some level.[13] This consideration becomes all the more urgent, the more one party is able to monopolise power at the centre. Majority rule (let alone minority rule) is only defensible on some consideration of reciprocity: the expectation on the part of the losers that they will have their turn in power. While a share in power at the local level may be no substitute for this, it at least works to mitigate the force of exclusion at the national level, and prevents alienation from the political process on the part of significant sections of public opinion, and of whole localities. The experience of having all the public agencies in an area run by the appointees of a ruling party with very little popular support there only adds insult to injury, and reinforces a conception of politics as the exclusive property of one party or section of opinion and its representatives.

A second consideration in favour of elected local government is that it enables not only more people, but also a wider range of people, to hold public office than if elections are limited to the national level alone.[14] When J. S. Mill compared the character of local representatives with national ones, his main point of contrast was the 'much lower grade of intelligence and knowledge' of the former (Mill, 1861, pp. 356). This is probably still the view from Whitehall. From a democratic perspective, however, other points of contrast are more significant. The fact that local elected office is indeed local and also part-time makes it more accessible to women and to people of varied occupations and occupational status. The fact that it is based on much smaller constituencies gives members of ethnic minorities a greater chance of being elected than to a national parliament. Whether it is political or social inclusiveness, therefore, that we are concerned about, local government can be defended as enhancing the overall representativeness of elected institutions, though there remains much room for further improvement (see below).

Taken together, the democratic case for elected local government, on grounds of accountability, responsiveness and representativeness alike, must be judged to be a strong one, when compared with the alternative of a local system of administration that is accountable upwards to a nationally elected parliament, and downwards to individual 'consumers' through an ombudsman, citizens' charter or the like. The limits to the possible democratisation of the latter model are quickly reached. They are constituted, on the one hand, by the practical limits to a pyramidal structure of upwards accountability, where the base of the pyramid comprises a multitude of decisions taken in hundreds of different localities; and, on the other, by the conceptual limits to a model of downward accountability based upon individual redress alone. These limits to accountability are intrinsic rather than accidental, and have in turn corresponding implications for responsiveness and representativeness. How the much greater democratic potential of an elected system might be realised in practice will be explored in the following section.

The democratisation of local government

If the conclusion of the previous section is sound, namely that the model of elected local government has much greater intrinsic potential for realising democratic values than a centrally-organised system of local administration, then it follows that anyone concerned with democracy is committed to exploring how that potential might be realised more effectively. In the context of the UK, this means exploring how the acknowledged defects of existing local government practice might be remedied. Although the individual ideas that follow make no claim to originality, their relevance for democratisation can best be brought into focus with the help of the criteria already elucidated.

Two preliminary comments are in order about the political context of such a discussion. First, as suggested earlier, any debate about the future of local government in the UK must recognise the deep malaise of representative institutions at all levels, national as well as local. Any proposals for local government, therefore, which imply that it is uniquely problematic, or which treat unreformed central institutions as a 'given', will necessarily be one-sided and incomplete. Second, although the specific malaise of local government is a long-standing phenomenon – witness the plethora of reports, commissions, reorganisations, disbandments of previous reorganisations and so on since the 1970s – the acuteness of the present malaise can be traced to the way in which the democratic deficiencies of a centralising model have progressively been exposed to view. This exposure only makes more urgent the task of exploring how the long-standing defects of the local electoral model, in respect of its accountability, responsiveness and representativeness, might be addressed.

Accountability

Insufficient accountability to a local electorate is the most obvious weakness of the local government system as it currently operates in the UK. This has a number of dimensions. Low electoral turnout indicates little interest in the outcome. The tendency to use the vote to pass judgement on the national government means that the exercise bears only a slight relationship to the policy or performance of elected councillors. The chance of one party retaining power indefinitely reduces the incentive to be responsive and removes the sanction on outright misgovernment. Low accountability, in turn, encourages the seepage of power and authority to the centre, which further reduces electoral choice and local accountability (see Miller, 1988, ch. 17, for a review of the electoral evidence; also Miller, 1986; Jones, 1992).

This vicious circle can only be broken by reform from two directions simultaneously. One is to increase the autonomy of local government, so that it is less a purely administrative arm of the centre, and can offer more imaginative policy choices to the electorate. Removing the *ultra vires* limitation, so that a local authority could undertake whatever measures it saw fit in the interests of its inhabitants, has been canvassed widely, most recently by Donnison (1994, p. 30). Indeed, such a general competence within the law would seem to follow from the principle of electoral authorisation, and is widely supported by local electors themselves (Miller, 1988, p. 239). Equally important is to achieve a more defensible division of labour between centre and locality in respect of those policies and services in which they both have a legitimate interest. If the task of the centre is to define minimum standards and minimum conditions of eligibility for the main public services, the task of the locality should be to deliver these by whatever means, and by whatever mix of public/private provision, it sees fit. Nothing has contributed more to the erosion of local autonomy than the historical tendency of both major parties to elevate state and market respectively from means into ends, when it should be a matter for local judgement and experimentation how nationally determined standards should be met. Overall financial limits for local authority spending and borrowing should be a matter of mutual agreement between central government and representatives of local authorities, possibly with a finance committee of an elected upper house acting as final arbiter.

Increasing the autonomy of local authorities will not on its own, however, ensure their accountability, without a reform of electoral arrangements. A shift to a proportional representation system would break the stranglehold of one-party regimes, and prevent the Leninist deformation of democracy, whether from left or right, whereby a determined minority can capture a party for its exclusive programme, and construct a ruling majority out of minority electoral support. Elections could be held for the whole council at the point in the national electoral cycle that would have least impact locally (say twelve months into a four-year fixed-term national parliament). To focus local interest and media attention, ruling parties could be required to publish and debate a yearly programme of government alongside an annual budget, and at other times in the event of a change in a ruling coalition.[15]

Strengthening local government accountability in these and other ways would not exclude arrangements for individual redress where minimum standards of provision were not maintained. It could also be complemented by introducing a measure of local elected representation in respect of those services and agencies which remained under central control. The key principle in each case is that, wherever policy decisions are taken affecting the use and distribution of public resources, there should be a transparent and effective form of accountability to a relevant public. No system of political accountability is perfect. But it is only those with an interest in monopolising executive control at the centre who can be satisfied with arrangements as imperfect as those we currently have.

Responsiveness

Whereas improving the electoral accountability of local government would require substantial changes to its legal status, its electoral arrangements and the relationship between centre and locality, considerable experimentation has already taken place to enhance the responsiveness of local service provision (Gyford, 1991). Many authorities have undertaken a radical decentralisation in the delivery of their services, to improve their accessibility to clients. Others have sought to empower previously marginalised groups, and encourage their contribution to policy-making or the administration of services. Yet others have undertaken market testing or opinion surveys to improve the sensitivity of the policy process. North American and European experience in the use of local referenda is being studied, as well as in a variety of other consultative devices: deliberative polls, consensus groups, citizens' panels or juries, and roving consultative commissions.[16]

All these devices involve an acknowledgement that the electoral process *on its own* cannot ensure responsive government. The choices that people make at election time are 'broad brush' choices between representatives and their policy programmes or tendencies, at a particular moment in time; they do not entail agreement with everything that the representatives may do in the future, even on the part of those who voted for them. Nor does election itself guarantee that the elected know what their constituents may think about particular issues. Systematic and regular consultation is therefore a necessary democratic complement to the electoral process.

Two questions recur, however, in respect of many of the consultative devices mentioned above. One is how representative they are. Empowering previously marginalised groups, for example, may give voice to self-appointed spokespersons whose claim to be representative of their constituency might be doubtful – a problem that applies, of course, to all pressure groups. Even carefully selected citizens' panels or juries can hardly claim to be a true cross-section of the relevant electorate, unless they are so large as to be unwieldy for their deliberative purpose. Opinion surveys, on the other hand, comprise at best snap responses rather than considered judgements on a given issue. The fact that these devices are less than perfect is not an argument for abandoning them. But it does emphasise the significance of a second question: what should be their status in relation to the decisional competence of elected councillors, whose representative credentials are more secure, and who are also publicly accountable for their decisions? The only device which can 'trump' the legitimacy of the elected representative is the referendum, which is one reason why it should be used sparingly outside issues of constitutional reform. Councillors cannot be required to bind themselves to the findings of any other consultative process. They can, however, be required to have a strategy for undertaking them, both generally and in the context of specific services. And a national foundation for experiment and advice on consultative processes, and for the dissemination of good practice, would provide significant consolidation to the existing impetus for more responsive local government.

Representativeness

The case for elected local government has already been argued on grounds of representativeness, in terms of including a wide range of political opinion and social identity alike in government. Both forms of representativeness can be improved further within a local system. A move to elections by some form of proportional representation has already been defended on grounds of improved accountability; its advantage over first-past-the-post (FPTP) in terms of its superior representativeness of political opinion is even stronger. The democratic principle of political equality requires that votes should have equal value, regardless not only of where people live, but also for which party they vote. The present regional distortion under FPTP whereby Conservative votes in southern England and Labour votes in Scotland carry a political weight out of all proportion to their share of the population, is wholly at variance with this principle, as is also the underrepresentation of Liberal Democrat votes in all regions. Similar inequities can be found at the level of local government (Hill, 1994, p. 120).

The above assumes that a key purpose of elections is to register and represent *political opinion*, on issues of both policy and leadership, and that parties are necessary to focus electoral choice in respect of both. Advocates of a *socially* representative assembly sometimes defend it on the grounds that from social representativeness will follow representativeness of political opinion, but this is erroneous. Social groups defined by sex, age, race and so on cannot be assumed to have a common opinion on most issues, nor elected members to be representative of such opinion simply because they share the relevant characteristics (Phillips, 1991, pp. 70–3). The case for a more socially representative elected body has to be argued on different grounds: on its symbolic force for those who share a given social identity; on the value of having a wide range of social experience among those responsible for public policy; and above all, on the democratic criterion that everyone should have equal opportunity to stand for public office, whatever the social group to which they belong.

Whereas improving the political representativeness of an elected assembly can be addressed simply through a reform of the electoral system, making it more socially representative is less straightforward. How far legal measures are appropriate is a controversial matter, beyond the normal anti-discrimination clause of equal rights legislation. Selecting which groups should be eligible for special treatment is itself controversial, and a matter of changing values. At the beginning of the twentieth century it was the lack of working class MPs that gave rise to the Labour Party. Today it is the underrepresentation of women and ethnic minorities that causes concern. Tomorrow it might be age or occupational status. Responding to these concerns is in the first instance the responsibility of political parties through their own selection procedures for candidates. The role of legislation is perhaps best that of ensuring that the conditions of work for elected representatives are such as to facilitate and not discourage participation from any social group.

Strategies for the democratisation of local government, then, involve working to improve its accountability, responsiveness and representativeness. Some of these improvements cannot be envisaged without corresponding changes at the national level. At the same time, they do not exhaust all that is relevant to a consideration of 'local democracy'. This brings us to the last of the three questions raised at the beginning of the chapter.

Democracy beyond local government

It is currently fashionable to advocate a concept of politics that is quite separate from the sphere of government, and which is practised precisely in those social spaces that government does not occupy: from the development of new forms of life-style and personal identity on the one side, to participation in a variety of lateral networks and social associations on the other (Mulgan, 1994a). As a corrective to an exclusive preoccupation with the formal structures of government, and an overestimation of their potency, this tendency has its value. Indeed, the conception of democracy advanced at the beginning of this chapter allows for just such an extension of the 'political'. There is a danger here, however, of constructing a new orthodoxy that is equally one-sided in its preoccupation, and which overlooks the way in which the spaces for informal politics, and the powers that people are able to develop or deploy within them, are both fashioned and circumscribed by governmental policy. Exclusive preoccupation with informal modes of politics may well be a symptom of a wider powerlessness that itself needs confronting directly, rather than merely acquiescing in.

Concepts of quite varied theoretical provenance have contributed to this more informal notion of the political. The concept of 'governance' underlines the way in which publicly-financed services and other government functions are undertaken by non-governmental organisations, or by groups within civil society. The idea of 'civil society' itself, as a network of autonomous, self-organising associations, is advanced as a necessary condition for limiting the power of the state, and ensuring any societal control over it. From a different direction the concept of 'community' charts the limits of any self-chosen individual identity or interest, and recalls us to a sense of mutual responsibility within and for a shared social space. In their different ways these ideas extend our conception of the political, and the potential field of democratic practice.[17] They also connect with more traditional concerns of democratic theory, such as how the powerful social and economic institutions of civil society may be rendered accountable, both to their own members and to the public at large, or how a vigorous associational life can serve as a basis for democratisation of government itself.

The advantage of the tradition of democratic theorising over the more recent tendencies is precisely that it links the projects of democratisation in the informal and formal spheres of politics, by demonstrating their interconnection. In so doing, however, it also confronts a key contemporary problem about our conception of political space, which is most acute in any consideration of what is meant by the 'local'. The formal political sphere is defined as a bounded territory, which may or may not (in the UK usually *not*) correspond to any coherent geographical entity with which people can identify. The informal political sphere, on the other hand, is now a potentially boundless space, whose associations may comprise anything from a local group of neighbours to an international group of communicators on the Internet. This disjunction between the spatial ranges of government and civil society respectively poses a serious difficulty for a project of democratisation that seeks to link the two. It also renders problematic the apparently simple concept of 'local democracy'.

A second difficulty in connecting democratisation at the levels of civil society and government relates to the final aspect of normative theorising not so far addressed, that of political agency. Who today are the bearers of democratic values, who might conceivably act as the agents of democratisation? It is no longer possible, if indeed it ever was, to point with confidence to a single social class or stratum whose situation and interests align them unreservedly with democratic struggle. On the other hand, there are many people in all kinds of social situation who recognise that their pressing problems cannot be solved by individual action alone, but only through collective self-organisation or by a form of government that is more responsive to their needs. The idea that constitutional reform is only of potential interest to the so-called 'chattering classes', when ordinary people pay such a high cost for a system of government that is unaccountable, unresponsive and unrepresentative, is one of the self-fulfilling myths of our time.[18] Yet the connections have to be *demonstrated*, between the processes and the outcomes of government, and between the content of policy and the structures of influence that determine it. The agency for political change, in other words, is not socially given, but has to be politically constructed from a broad coalition of potential interests.

The vehicle for such a construction can only be that much maligned institution, whose demise has so often been heralded – the political party – which belongs to both civil society and the state, and hence is uniquely placed to link democratic initiatives in the two. Whether any political party measures up to the requirements of such a task will determine the future of democratisation at both national and local levels in the United Kingdom.

Notes

1. For a historical survey of democratic theory and local government, see Hill (1974); for a succinct recent treatment, see Phillips (1994).
2. For a fuller treatment of this definitional issue see Beetham (1994).
3. This view received its 'classic' exposition in the work of Schumpeter (1952, chs. 20–22). It is significant that the value of responsiveness is given a substantial place in most defences of local government (see for example, Gyford, 1991a; Jones and Stewart, 1983; Stewart, 1989; Widdicombe Report, 1986).
4. Most famously by Mill (1861, chs viii and xv), but many have since followed him. For a critique of its paternalist thrust in the context of local government, see Sharpe (1970, p. 162).
5. For a fuller justification, see Beetham and Boyle (1995).
6. It should be evident that this chapter confines itself narrowly to the democratic case for local government, as distinct from the case that is made on other grounds in different chapters of this book. Much of the existing literature on the 'case for local government' does not in fact distinguish sharply between democratic and other grounds (for example Jones and Stewart, 1983, ch. 1; Sharpe, 1970; etc.). Miller, on the other hand (1988, p. 229), argues that it is only democratic criteria that can justify using the term local *government*, rather than *administration*.
7. Their sorry record in respect of openness is exposed in Weir and Hall (1994, pp. 27–30 and appendix 5).
8. The alternative of a new centralised Ministry of the Interior could only worsen accountability still further (Sharpe, 1970, p. 162).
9. The contrast between citizens and consumers is now a standard feature of the critical literature on the neo-liberal conception of accountability. See for example, Clarke and Stewart (1992, pp. 19–21), Donnison (1994, p. 23), Gyford (1991a, ch. 7), Hill (1994, ch. 8).
10. A comparison of turn-out rates in UK local elections with those in other established democracies shows that the UK comes at the bottom of the league (Game, 1991, p. 17).
11. Hoggett and Hambleton (1987, p. 4) argue that democracy and responsiveness are quite separate; however, their supporting examples are drawn largely from the private sector, which is not a relevant comparator here.
12. The argument for innovation and diversity has been put particularly forcefully in Stewart (1991). For the degree to which councillors are rooted in their localities, see Mabileau *et al.* (1989, pp. 158–62).

13. The argument for pluralism as *inclusiveness* is different from the more familiar, and contested, argument for pluralism as *liberty* protecting (see, for example, Jones and Stewart, 1983; Sharpe, 1970; Widdicombe Report, 1986).
14. Although studies of local participation tend to emphasise the discrepancy between the electors and the elected, the discrepancy between the elected at local and national levels is equally striking (compare Hill, 1994, ch. 3, with Chapter 6 by Anne Phillips, in this volume).
15. A discussion of possible changes to improve accountability is to be found in Hill (1994, pp. 119–23).
16. A range of such practices is described in Barber (1984, ch. 10), Fishkin (1991, ch. 8), Mulgan, (1994b), Phillips (1994), Stewart *et al.* (1994).
17. See the chapters by Frazer (Chapter 5), Phillips (Chapter 6) and Ward (Chapter 7) in this volume.
18. For a dramatic example of this cost, see Butler *et al.* (1994).

3 Public Choice and Local Governance

Keith Dowding

Public choice

Writers in the public choice tradition have tended to be suspicious of representative democracy for a number of reasons.[1]

Arrow's general impossibility theorem (Arrow, 1951; Riker, 1982)

Arrow's theorem demonstrates that any system of voting may produce 'arbitrary' or 'unfair' winners. This means that we cannot be assured that the result of any election represents the outcome preferred by most people over all other possibilities, and thus there is no such thing as the (uncontroversially acceptable) social choice of any community. This result challenges the faith placed upon democratic procedures for making social decisions.

Rational actor models of party competition (Downs, 1957)

According to Downs, plurality systems such as those in British local elections lead politicians and parties to seek the median voter on each policy dimension, building up coalitions of support to win elections. In doing so, parties are led to produce inconsistent sets of policies. They try to conceal from the electorate their own inconsistencies while advertising those of their opponents. Voters do not have a great incentive to spend much time or effort trying to ascertain the true policies of the parties, but rather vote on the basis of party or 'brand' loyalty. Again this reasoning devalues democracy as a rational process of discovering the overall preferences of the community.

Rent-seeking arguments (Buchanan *et al.* 1980; Olson, 1984; Rowley *et al.* 1988; Tullock, 1990)

These accounts suggest that inefficiencies in society are generated by organised groups demanding from government rents for their own existence. Thus farmers receive subsidies for growing certain types of crops or using certain types of chemicals; local governments encourage firms to locate in their region with tax breaks or help for infrastructure (King, 1990); the poor receive housing allowance, allowing landlords to charge more for rents than under a free market. Such rent-seeking activity increases year by year; for example, the Greater London Council gave grants to voluntary bodies totalling £82 million in 1984–5, up from £427,000 in 1965–6 (Wilson and Game, 1994, p. 283).[2] Local authorities in Britain contributed over £590 million to voluntary organisations in grants and aid in 1990–1 (Wilson and Game, 1994, p. 288). Such rent-seeking activities may often appear to be socially desirable if considered 'one-case-at-a-time', but overall are socially undesirable, pushing up tax rates, stultifying the market and thereby making everyone worse off.

Budget-maximising and bureaucratic slack-seeking arguments (Tullock, 1965; Niskanen, 1971, 1973)

This body of literature suggests that the structures of large public bureaucracies create incentives to bureaucrats to press for larger budgets, produce more goods for society than society would choose to pay for, and provide few incentives for bureaucrats to look for productive or allocative efficiencies.

Underlying all these arguments is the problem of discovering the 'true' demand function of society for 'collective' (Samuelson, 1954, 1955, 1958) or 'worthy' (Savas, 1987) goods. A collective good is one that exhibits jointness of supply and non-excludability entailing that rational individuals will try to avoid paying for its production and supply on the grounds that they will receive its benefits anyway. A 'worthy' good is one from which it is perfectly possible to exclude consumers but for which society has (by whatever imperfect decision procedure) decided to provide. Arrow suggests that there is no such demand function; Downs suggests that parties are not interested in discovering the true demand function; Tullock *et al.* suggest that pressure groups will press for demand functions that are socially inefficient, and Niskanen argues that bureaucrats will want to supply at a point beyond the 'true' demand function. While it can be seen that these arguments are not all completely consistent (Arrow's theorem and budget-maximising arguments, for example[3]) together they lead to an impressive attack upon the institutions of representative democracy, particularly if the underlying normative principle of Pareto-efficiency is adhered to.

Pareto-efficiency has been described as a 'very weak ethical postulate' (Buchanan and Tullock, 1962, p. 172; see also, for example, Boadway and Bruce, 1984), though given the way it is *used* in the models listed above (particularly the rent-seeking and budget maximising arguments) it is inconsistent with other ethical principles such as equity and utility maximisation and it is difficult to see how it can be weaker than they are (see Dowding, 1995, esp. chs 3–5).[4] Thus underlying the public choice approach is a strong normative principle, which is what leads it to its right-wing or 'new right' flavour (King, 1987). But the methods of economics do not necessarily require these 'new right' normative principles (Hindmoor and Dowding, 1994).

The four sets of arguments have led public choice writers to believe that a leviathan state has developed and constitutional principles of local governance are required to cut the leviathan down to size (Buchanan, 1975; Brennan and Buchanan, 1980). Five sets of institutional arrangements may be identified as part of that programme to cut the leviathan down.

Direct as opposed to representative democracy

Some writers in the public choice tradition have argued for direct rather than representative democracy at the local level (Santerre, 1986). Through direct debate, citizens may come to persuade others to their own views and surmount the heterogeneity of preferences that leads to the Arrow paradox. Direct democracy is thought to subdue both rent-seeking and budget-maximising by giving greater control to tax-payers, mitigating the demands of rent-seeking groups which lobby local bureaucrats and politicians. In Britain, the idea of direct rather than representative democracy at the local level has not received much attention.

Small-scale jurisdictions

Introducing (or reintroducing) small-scale jurisdictions breaking up large-scale metropolitan government is the solution to which most public choice attention has been directed. Arrow's result is less likely to occur in very small electorates, particularly if the preferences and interests of the community are largely homogeneous. Rent-seeking is also thought to be more difficult the smaller the community. Concomitantly, the smaller the bureaucracy, the harder it is for successful budget-maximising by public servants. However, most of the public-choice literature recommending small jurisdictions derives from Tiebout's (1956) model of small-scale jurisdictions in metropolitan areas competing for 'consumer-voters' by the package of tax and services they offer. This market-analogue is thought to encourage productive efficiency as governments are forced to produce goods at competitive prices; encourage allocative efficiency as local governments will be forced to provide the goods that (potential) residents desire; and reduce tax burdens as governments attempt to encourage rich residents to locate in the area in order to receive the higher marginal tax payments.

Let the market provide

According to standard economic theory, the market both reveals preferences (allocative efficiency), and through competition produces productive efficiency, and therefore automatically provides Pareto-efficiency. Public-choice writers thus argue that wherever possible the market should be allowed to provide goods and services. A government should intervene only when strictly necessary and even then local governments should contract out most of their business to the private market. While public-choice writers do accept that government action is sometimes justified, they adhere to Tullock's (1994) dictum: 'where there are no externalities the market is good and the government mediocre, where there are externalities the market is bad and the government is still mediocre'. To some extent both left and right may agree with this dictum, the difference lying at the point at which externalities are thought to bite, and the degree to which the government needs to intervene. I shall return to this point later in the chapter.

Single-purpose agencies

Many public-choice writers favour single-purpose agencies within given geographical boundaries, or even within boundaries that are determined by technical or economic factors, creating flexible solutions to supply problems (Ostrom *et al.*, 1961; Bennett, 1989). For example, the fire service may be organised in small jurisdictions for quicker response times, while the water supply and sewerage agency are determined by the naturally-occurring water catchment areas. Two solutions are possible: one is that each agency will have its own democratically elected board; or, more recently, public choice writers assume that these agencies will be private-sector companies awarded contracts by the local governments for providing their services (as above, in small-scale jurisdictions) (Bish and Ostrom, 1973; Parks and Oakerson, 1993). This system has the advantage of fewer elections, easier accountability, yet at the same time small-scale local government can take advantage of economies of large-scale by using the services of large, perhaps multinational companies, providing local services (Ostrom *et al.*, 1961).

Consumption equals disbursement

Underlying these principles is the idea that one should pay for what one receives, that is, there should be a clear relationship between the taxpayer and the services in order to overcome 'fiscal illusion', which leads to leviathan behaviour. When one pays directly for what one consumes there is no problem with misrepresentation of demand ensuring 'allocative efficiency'. Of course, consumption equals disbursement in the private market, so once again this institutional principle uses the market-analogue.

That consumption should equal disbursement led some public choice writers to favour the poll tax (Bennett *et al.*, 1991) and to oppose open-ended central grants (Foster and Jackman, 1982). It also leads others to recommend that all redistributive polices, large-scale collective or 'worthy' goods should be paid for through national taxation, organised nationally and only involve local government structures as agents for the national state. Federalism thus is a key component of public choice (Tullock, 1969; Oates, 1977; King, 1984; Ostrom, 1987; Bish, 1987; Bender and Mookherjee, 1987).

This brief review of some of the conclusions of public choice analysis will be used as a template to analyse Conservative administrations' attitude to local government reform since 1979 in the next section. We see that the Conservatives' adoption of public choice is partial, limited and indeed inconsistent with aspects of the public choice approach. Later in the chapter I shall make some brief comments upon what may be learned from public choice, taking especial care to draw out normative underpinnings and thus partition possible right-wing from possible left-wing conclusions from the same logical and empirical evidence.

The Conservative transmutation of local governance

During the 1980s and 1990s the Conservatives have brought about a transmutation of the system of governing at the local level. This radical transformation of the structures of local governance may been seen to have three theoretical driving forces:

(i)   The attempt to reduce public expenditure.
(ii) The attempt to increase accountability.
(iii) The attempt to increase efficiency.[5]

These can be seen to be related to the public choice account elucidated above in a number of ways.

Reducing public expenditure

The most obvious way to reduce the size of the state is to reduce public expenditure. In 1979, local government expenditure constituted a quarter of all government expenditure. Thus, reducing local government expenditure comprised an important part of their overall economic strategy.[6] The acts changing the nature of local government finance were: the 1982 Local Government Finances No. 2 Act, abrogating the right to levy supplementary rates; the 1984 Rates Act, giving the Secretary of State the right to cap or limit the rates set by local councils; the 1988 Local Government Act, abolishing the rates, introducing the uniform business rate and the poll tax. These were all attempts to reduce local expenditure by making it harder for councils to levy taxes.[7] The first two took power away from local government and gave power to the centre, demonstrating a lack of trust by central government for local government to show willingness and the ability to reduce public expenditure. The poll tax was supposed to tie consumption to disbursement and make local expenditure less popular, although the 1992 Local Government Act (and Margaret Thatcher's downfall) showed that central rather than local government received most blame for the hated tax (Butler *et al.*, 1994). Despite proclamations that the aim was to give local government back to the local community, the result of these finance bills and other changes to the nature of the Rate Support Grant (becoming the Block Grant) in the 1980 Local Government Planning and Land Act gave much greater discretion to the Secretary of State over the payment of central grants, thus allowing central government to determine local needs, something which has proved a great boom to the two 'Tory flagship' London boroughs, Wandsworth and Westminster. The poll tax also led to central government taxation taking up a greater proportion of total local government spending in a desperate attempt to control poll tax increases.

The overall effect of the financial legislation and legislation proclaiming to free local government from central control was to centralise powers (Duncan and Goodwin, 1988, esp. chs 3 and 4). This first aim of freeing citizens from the leviathan had the opposite effect. The power that wished to free others from control, ended up controlling more in order to ensure that the freedom is not abused. That is one problem for 'new right' interpretations of local democracy. If their axiomatic belief that people want to pay less tax and receive fewer services is false, then it is democracy that suffers when less tax and fewer services are foisted upon 'consumer-voters'.

Increasing accountability

The Conservatives have wanted to increase accountability of local governments. This has been attempted in numerous ways. The Poll Tax was supposed to increase accountability as a tax paid by all, thus overcoming the problem that some could demand more services as they would never feel the burden of paying for them (Butler *et al.*, 1994). Abolishing the metropolitan counties was also justified on the grounds of increasing accountability as 'consumer-voters' would be less confused about services if they were provided only by single-tier authorities rather than by the remote bureaucrats in city hall. This idea of single-tier authorities was also supposed to underlie the Local Government Commission's work (Adam Smith Institute, 1989a, 1989b), though this has not quite worked out as planned. Shifting power away from local governments and over to those using the facilities was also designed to create greater accountability. The 1988 Housing Act created new Housing Action Trusts (HATs) in areas of derelict council housing, and empowered residents to replace council tenancy with landlords of their own choice. The 1988 Education Reform Act abolished the Inner London Education Authority, empowers parents to remove their schools from local authority control, and ended local authority control of polytechnics and colleges of further education. How far these increase accountability is open to question. In part it depends upon the nature of the democratic processes that exist within schools, HATs and other such Extra Government Organisations (EGOs) and their ability to have financial control. For opted-out schools for example, one can easily see that power has moved to the Department for Education as much as it has to parents (Whitty, 1990), and now under the 1993 Education Act to a newly created EGO, 'Funding Agency for Schools', which shares planning with local education authorities. The whole flowering of EGOs is taking powers away from elected councils and giving them to appointed boards. The number of these EGOs and the fact that they control nearly a third of all public expenditure (Weir and Hall, 1994) has nothing to do with public-choice theory. Run by the 'new magistracy' (Stewart, 1992), the organisations are predicted by the budget-maximising models of Niskanen (1971, 1973) and other models which demonstrate principal–agent problems (see, for example, Milgrom and Roberts, 1992) to be allocatively, productively and Pareto-inefficient, subject to core budgetary growth and suffer major malversation problems. The story of the Welsh Development Agency (Beckett, 1994), in place since 1976, could soon be repeated throughout the nation and across policy sectors.

Increasing Pareto-efficiency

The major objective of the Conservatives was to increase efficiency. The market is seen as Pareto-efficient. Since a perfectly competitive market automatically reveals demand for private goods at any given price (allocative efficiency), and competition forces firms to search continually for productive efficiencies, it automatically provides Pareto-efficiency. Traditionally, it has been recognised that the government steps in where the market fails. But the refrain of public choice is that the government fails as often as the market. Where government is necessary, they argue that it should try to behave like the market as much as possible. Forcing local governments to put services out to competitive tendering (1988 Local Government Act) was one attempt to bring in greater marketisation. The 1985 Transport Act limited councils' abilities to regulate and subsidise public transport, thus forcing a new market upon reluctant councils, while the Housing Act of 1980, and the Housing and Building Control Act of 1984, encouraged council house sales, thus creating a broader housing market.

The professed aim of creating 'enabling councils', which do not themselves provide services by direct labour organisations but rather enable services to be provided by creating the political structure through which demands can be made and the market facilitated to respond (Ridley, 1988), can also be seen as a part of this element of the public choice approach.

Another element of marketisation is provided by the Tiebout (1956) model. The abolition of the metropolitan counties can be seen as one attempt to produce greater competition between councils in metropolitan areas. British academics usually demonstrate a great scepticism about the possibilities of competition between boroughs, based upon household mobility (for example, Sharpe and Newton, 1984), though Dowding *et al.* (1994a) and John *et al.* (1994) demonstrate that there does seem to be evidence that households were attracted to low-poll-tax boroughs in inner London. Similarly, the government announced a preference for smaller, single-tier councils throughout Britain. The early reports of the Local Government Commission demonstrate that it is not carrying out this brief. The Local Government Commission (LGC) have professed that they are not being led by any theoretical considerations, following a report they commissioned from the Policy Studies Institute which, through lack of time, resources and intellectual capacity, felt unable to recommend any underlying principles for the LGC to follow (see Leach, 1995 for a history). The result appears to be a mishmash based upon the loudest voices to be heard from the groups which have pressed the LGC during its deliberations. Power play demonstrated by the bargaining model of power (Dowding, 1991) is what is actually driving the proposals for local government reform from the LGC.

There have been some dimly understood precepts of public choice theory which bear some similarity to the motivations which, following the principle of humanity we can detect in the Conservative justification for its programme of local government transmutation. As political scientists interested in historical explanation of policy generation we should not want to make too much of these observations. Within a normative critique of their local government transmutation we cannot make too much of them.[8]

Some normative notes

The problem for public choice theory is the problem it has in understanding market failure.[9] To some extent this is a bizarre criticism. The first volume of *Public Choice*, the house journal of the American Public Choice Society, was entitled *Papers in Non-Market Decisionmaking*, and the whole purpose of public choice is to study politics and the institutions of governing. The problem is that in their 'use of economic and economiclike tools developed for special application in a field that political scientists traditionally taught' (Tullock, 1990, p. 195) involves certain tools which *are only applicable* to market situations; they use a hammer to drive in a screw. In order to model a perfectly competitive market we need to draw the demand and supply curves. In this model we can be assured (by our assumptions) that given initial resources and current technology, what is supplied *is* what is demanded at a given price. But once we move outside the assumptions of the perfect market and into the world, what is demanded and what is supplied are not the same thing. The early history of local government in Britain is the history of local communities petitioning central government for the right to raise taxes and regulate local communities precisely because the market failed to provide all their wants. At first, local denizens wanted the right to end certain street market activities such as slaughtering animals, scalding and dismembering carcasses in the street (for example, Prest, 1990, p. 66), and later to provide services such as sewerage and lighting, partially but not completely provided by private enterprise (Waller, 1983). Markets may have some of the features of 'spontaneous order' (Hayek, 1982; Sugden, 1986) but where the spontaneity of the market has failed to produce the goods, communities have sought political powers to provide them for themselves. Demands to provide goods through coercive means (local taxation and local by-laws) are political demands every bit as legitimate as demands revealed through market processes, though public choice insists on analysing them through the same procedures as demands in the perfect market. But there is an important difference; the market for private goods involves a host of decisions to buy or not buy which together constitute society's demand curve for the private good. The political forum involves one decision to provide or not provide a good made up of many decisions in some voting procedure. That one decision is the only demand curve that makes sense (Dowding, 1995, ch. 3). The difference is vital, for the former can be said, given initial resources and technology, to reveal Pareto-efficiency; the latter, unless the vote is unanimous, will always be Pareto-inefficient. While the Pareto-principle, that 'very weak ethical postulate' remains at the heart of its analysis, public choice will always wish to replace government with the market. Democracy does, by definition, produce Pareto-inefficient outcomes. If one is not prepared to trade efficiency for democracy one cannot be a democrat – though that is not to say that all issues need be up for democratic grabs.[10] Hence public choice's anti-democratic stance. However, if Pareto-efficiency is ignored or replaced more explicitly with other normative commitments, then rational choice does allow careful deductive reasoning leading to a variety of possible conclusions.

This is particularly acute since Pareto-efficiency revealed by demand and supply curves is Pareto-efficiency only given current technology and the initial distribution of resources. Initial distribution of resources depends upon political conditions which determine the nature and distribution of property rights (Bromley, 1989; Eggertsson, 1990; North, 1990; Williamson, 1986): perhaps the most important issue within the scope of political science concerns the distribution of property rights. As Pink Floyd pithily sang in the early 1970s, 'With, without; And who'll deny it's what the fighting's all about'; well, public-choice writers apparently. Public choice is so deeply conservative precisely because it denies, by its very methods dependent upon searching for Pareto-efficient solutions, that redistribution is an issue with which political discussion should concern itself (Dowding and Hindmoor, 1994). Public-choice writers sometimes claim that redistribution is not an issue that should concern their 'positive' science, but the way in which Pareto-efficiency is used by them to judge rent-seeking, social choice functions and non-market provision entails that this is an issue through which they elidingly glide. We may approach essentially this same issue from another direction. Above I quoted Gordon Tullock, who suggested that markets are good where there are no externalities. It could be rejoined that all markets have externalities, so perhaps all markets are bad. This retort is too simplistic, despite the easy demonstration that markets require government intervention, if only to preserve property rights. The essential market production problem to which Tullock was referring concerns the collective–private good distinction. This is deeply problematic. One way of defending government production is to say that it provides collective goods, which the market fails to do. The problem is that the distinction between the private and the collective is not clear-cut, depending upon a set of at least five logically intermingled but distinct characteristics; moreover, these characteristics of goods are relative to both technological and demand conditions (themselves dependent upon initial distribution of resources) existent in any community. The modalities of 'collective' and 'private' are not ones of logical necessity, but of natural possibility (Dowding and Dunleavy, 1994). Crudely, this means that sometimes the market will provide, say, sewerage systems, and sometimes it will not. In fact, Dowding and Dunleavy argue (harking back to Ostrom *et al.*, 1961) that government versus private production is not the key political issue. Public versus private disbursement is the political concern, and that necessarily is a distributional issue.

Tiebout's model, the most famous (and seemingly, as far as some are aware, the only) public-choice model of local governance, is an attempt to provide a market-analogue solution to the provision of local collective goods. For those goods which, for free-rider reasons, it is difficult for the market to provide, but for which it is desirable that essentially the user pays, the market-analogue may work. Dowding *et al.* (1994a) find that households in London claim to take into account tax-service factors when deciding to relocate, and John *et al.* (1994) further demonstrate that the moves are consistent with such rationality and, over a five year period, are sufficiently great to generate a market-analogue. But it should be noted that by far the strongest Tiebout motivation for relocation was low (poll) tax, not better services; and the services desired tend to be private goods publicly disbursed (such as swimming pools and libraries) rather than 'worthy' goods such as social services. Evidence (reviewed in Dowding *et al.*, 1994b) from the US suggests strongly that welfare recipients will engage in long-range migration to achieve better welfare services. Such competition here is more likely to bid down welfare than bid it up; welfare recipients are not the type of 'consumer-voters' most local politicians and their tax-paying constituents will want to encourage (Dye, 1990; Dunleavy, 1993). Indeed, as Buchanan (1971) has noted (see Hoyt, 1993), such 'club' competition will encourage regressive taxation as communities try to entice the rich to relocate.

The left-wing appraisal of the Tiebout analysis should recognise the truths the model contains. If communities do compete, then redistributional welfare services and 'worthy' goods will suffer. Therefore such communities should not be allowed to compete and redistributional issues must be decided and disbursed at the higher level.[11] (There is nothing in the work of Tiebout that contradicts this normative claim (Tiebout, 1956, 1957, 1961; Ostrom *et al.*, 1961).) This says nothing about the production issue. Contracting-out production and privatising (if it produces competition) do bring productive efficiencies. Nor should the fact that the easiest way to bring about productive efficiencies is to reduce wages and lower standards of working conditions mean that contracting-out is flawed as a concept: it may simply be flawed in the form in which it was introduced (Ascher, 1987).

The rational-choice approach deductively produces a number of problems for the organisation of local government. Together with normative assumptions it can also suggest numerous solutions to those problems. Once we have separated the deductive framework from the ideologically tainted use of Pareto-efficiency with it anti-redistributional bias, we can utilise rational choice to frame the normative framework we wish to adopt. I end with some brief notes about the tasks that we may set ourselves in this direction.

The Tiebout effects need to be placed explicitly within a normative context of what we (by whatever social choice mechanism deemed appropriate) want from government. Only once it is decided what we want from the government can we begin to discuss at what level the government should disburse the good. There is a trade-off to be made between providing welfare (or 'worthy' goods), and allowing local tax-service discretion. If 'worthy' goods are to be disbursed locally, then tax-migration may well result, as has been demonstrated in the USA (see Dowding *et al.*, 1994b) and, arguably, in Britain (see John *et al.*, 1994). The redistributionalist will want to see public disbursement of worthy goods at the highest levels of government, although this does not entail that local government cannot play some role as the service-provider.

Further analysis of the strategic possibilities open to rational communities to combine in areas of 'antagonistic cooperation' is required.[12] Overall welfare loss will almost certainly follow competition between communities over business location if this involves tax incentives or special infrastructural incentives. Game-theoretic analysis of the types of strategic manoeuvreing may suggest which institutional procedures are normatively preferable. Again, how much discretionary power of local governments is appropriate may depend on the degree of antagonism and convergence of interest that occurs across policy domain.

We must expect principal–agent problems at all levels of government. Careful scrutiny must be goven to what sort of principal–agent problems are emerging between public bodies, central government departments, local authorities and EGOs. And we must be aware of the dangers of the 'accountability conspiracy' (Dowding, 1995, ch. 5) that can emerge in complex principal–agent structures. In the absence of democratic accountability, what other forms of accountability can be developed? Are these preferable to democratic accountability, given any truths contained in the public-choice critiques of representative democracy?

Rent-seeking can make everyone worse off (Riker and Brams, 1973) but can also make everyone better off (Schwartz, 1975). Theory does not help us to decide whether rent-seeking should be encouraged or discouraged; rather, it should make us wary and consider institutional devices to validate decisions. Is there a role for regular referendums on local decisions, as happens, for example, in some US states such as California, and in Swiss cantons? How far do these mitigate rent-seeking and the Arrow general impossibility theorem? (See Frey, 1992; and Nurmi (n.d.), for some discussion of this.)

How great a problem is budget-maximising and bureau-shaping (Dunleavy, 1991) in local government (Cope, 1994; Biggs and Dunleavy, 1995) and within local government EGOs and agencies? Strategies such as contracting-out, privatising, auditing, even creating line-hierarchies need to be re-examined, along with more radical alternatives such as direct democracy can be reconsidered given these new tools of analysis.

While urban analysis will always concentrate on local communities defined by the interests of those who occupy a given geographical space, full recognition of the effects of the power and interests of groups in a much wider sphere is required. In other words, a definition of the local to focus attention, but explicit recognition of the traditional problem for urban analysis – that the processes explained fail to have any clear 'local' or 'urban' referent. Events on the world stage affect local communities as much or more than decisions within the local council chamber.

We need explicitly to recognise and study the separation of institutional issues from political processes. This requires the analysis of rules and institutions demarcated from, but underlying, analysis of political processes within those rules. The levels of analysis methods suggested by Kiser and Ostrom (1982), Ostrom (1991) and Buchanan's (1991) 'constitutional economics' point the way to understanding that the relations between the constitution, institutional form, conventions of behaviour and the preferences of the actors all affect the type of policy outcomes. In choosing a new form for local government all levels and the interrelationships between them need to be understood and analysed carefully. Institutions and preferences together determine policy outcomes, but institutions also create preferences even as we choose the institutions we want, given our preferences (Dowding and King, 1995). This circle cannot be squared, but at least we can try come to terms with it.

In conclusion, we can see that the time of local governance studies being a sub-branch of political science consisting of quiet research of local community decision-making outside of the big questions of social justice and political economy are long gone. Rethinking the normative basis of local government is required, if only because the radical transmutation of local government in Britain has opened up all those questions which perhaps urban scholars had once thought that political philosophers had largely settled.

Notes

1. Any account of a 'tradition' will misspecify the detailed views of any, if not all, members of that tradition. In this chapter I try to elucidate general principles that may be detected in the public choice tradition, but do not make the claim that all writers adhere to each of them.
2. The 1984–5 figure is inflated somewhat by the ending of the GLC's 'Fares Fair' policy, which left resources to be spent and the desire not to have reserves left when the GLC was abolished.
3. Consistency may be attained if, for example, Tullock's (1992) attack upon Arrow's result as having little empirical generalisation is correct.
4. What Pareto (1906, Appendix, para 89, pp. 451–2) actually wrote and the way the concept tends to be used by public-choice writers (and other welfare economists) is rather different. Brian Barry (1991, pp. 50–1) expresses neatly the ideological move: 'The definition [of Pareto-efficiency] requires that if some gain and some lose in a change from one situation to another nothing can be said about its desirability. But the principle is instead sometimes taken to entail that if some people will lose from a change that change should *not* be made . . . It of course includes in itself the optimizing principle already discussed – that if some gain and none lose there is an improvement and *vice versa* – but it then goes on to say that if some lose, whether or not others gain, there is *no* improvement.'
5. Other more politically motivated driving forces could be identified, of course, but here I consider only the theoretical reasons which may be given for Conservative reforms using the most charitable version of the Principle of Humanity (Grandy, 1973). The political motivations may indeed be culpable for failures for practice to match theory.
6. This was also a part of the previous Labour strategy from at least 1976.
7. The Treasury's long-held opposition to local income tax is based almost entirely on the belief that this relatively popular tax will enable local authorities to spend more with growing economic prosperity without having to raise taxes.
8. The term 'rational choice' has broader connotations than 'public choice' both in terms of the scope of explanation and in ideological labelling, see Dowding and Hindmoor, 1994.
9. As Brian Barry (1989, p. 7) has remarked, replacing the simple-minded view that setting up a public organisation to do what you want cannot be replaced by the equally simple-minded view that all one requires is a market. He writes, 'anyone who gets past the first chapter of an economics textbook will soon realise how restrictive are the conditions under which there is any reason for expecting people pursuing a profit to bring about a socially desirable outcome'.
10. I slide deliberately between using the terms 'Pareto-efficiency' and 'efficiency', since this is precisely the ideological trick employed by the new right. See Dowding (1995, ch. 4) for a discussion of different types

of efficiency and logical problems of comparing in Pareto-terms market and non-market provision.

11. The same holds for national communities as well, as the European Commission realises in its bid to end the British opt-out over welfare issues, and as those who unquestioningly support GATT (General Agreement in Tariffs and Trade) may begin to realise as the decades pass.

12. This useful phrase is from Marin (1990).

4 Public Services, Efficiency and Local Democracy

Kieron Walsh

An influential argument used to justify local government is the claim that it is more efficient than a centralised system (see, for example, Sharpe, 1970). This justification for traditional patterns of local government in Britain has been challenged by central government since 1979, and by the rise of 'new right' thinking with its emphasis on market solutions to problems of public service management. Put simply, the argument has been that public services will only be efficient if they are subject to market pressures, which can be achieved by making citizens into consumers with choice, able to take their business from one provider to another. It is not then necessary for government to be local, because the centre can set standards for a disaggregated system of market-based administration, and efficiency will be ensured by the normal market processes of exit and choice, as well as inspection and regulation.

The British government's argument goes further than simply maintaining the efficiency value of the market. Efficiency, markets and democracy go together; as Waldegrave (1993, p. 13) argues:

> there is no guarantee – indeed there may not even be a sporting chance – that by periodically expressing his or her democratic decision at the ballot box, the citizen (by the use of that sovereign power) will necessarily obtain on a continuous basis efficient, properly accountable, responsive public services. You don't have to go far back in history to see that.

There are obvious difficulties with this argument, notably how 'publicly approved standards' are determined, but the challenge does require us to reconsider the extent to which democratic local government can be justified on the basis of its claim to efficiency.

The persuasiveness of the argument upon which the government's reform of local government is based depends upon the extent to which markets operate efficiently to meet individuals' choices. The problem of public bureaucracies is that they have been driven by producer interests. Choice in public service markets will act as an incentive mechanism for ensuring that producers do not dominate. There are obvious problems with the concept of choice (Dowding, 1992, Shackle, 1979), and little knowledge of how it operates in practice, but it is clear that market mechanisms may have more to contribute than has been recognised in the traditional pattern of organisation and management of the public service. There is evidence, for example, that the introduction of market mechanisms, such as compulsory competitive tendering in local government, have improved the quality and responsiveness of services (Walsh and Davis, 1993). It can also be argued that rationing decisions have been made more explicit by market mechanisms – for example, in health and community care. The argument has long been made that the market is more efficient than government; it is now being maintained that it is more democratic.

The dimensions of efficiency

There are three concepts of efficiency: technical efficiency, allocative efficiency and x-efficiency. Technical efficiency is an engineering or production concept, involving the maximisation of outputs with given inputs, and the use of the best available technology. It takes as given what we want to produce, and concentrates on achieving the best method of production. Allocative efficiency assesses whether the correct balance of outputs is produced; that is, whether outputs reflect preferences and needs, whether an appropriate combination of inputs is used in their production, and whether the pattern of distribution is acceptable. Allocative efficiency is commonly analysed in terms of Pareto optimality; that is, the assumption that there is an improvement in efficiency if one person's welfare is improved, and nobody is made worse off. The third concept, x-efficiency, is a measure of the extent to which avoidable waste in an economic system is minimised, given the set of technologies in use. Increasing x-efficiency makes welfare gains possible without any countervailing loss. All three dimensions of efficiency raise important issues about processes of social evaluation; a 'green' theory, for example, might evaluate production and distribution systems differently from more traditional approaches (see Ward, Chapter 7 in this volume).

None of these concepts of efficiency is simple, and they also interact with each other. Technical efficiency can only be considered in terms of some set of preferred outcomes: that is, some valuation of outputs. As the terms in which valuation is made change, for example with changing tastes, so what is technically efficient will change, since relative output values will alter. Equally, technological possibilities will determine patterns of allocative efficiency to some degree, as the relative costs of production change, and rates of substitution are altered. The concept of x-efficiency is related to technical issues. One reason given for x-inefficiency is that 'the production function is not completely specified or known' (Leibenstein, 1966, p. 412). Stigler (1976) contests Leibenstein's concept of x-efficiency on the grounds that a complete specification of organisations' inputs and outputs, taking account, for example, of leisure taken by workers during working hours, will show that production takes place on the production frontier. The issue of x-efficiency is therefore partly a matter of allocation. Any analysis of the overall efficiency implications of local government and local democracy will have to take account of the way that the different concepts of efficiency interact. One of the key arguments for democracy in public services is that the level and nature of efficiency, whether allocative, technical or x-efficiency, is a matter of judgement, both in terms of a value base and the overall assessment of total effectiveness, given the interaction of its various dimensions.

Further complications arise when we introduce change and time. Technological possibilities change as learning takes place, even if the mechanisms by which organisations learn may be debated (Pettigrew and Whipp, 1991, ch. 1). Economic systems need to generate an appropriate level of technical advance if they are not to be left behind in the world economy, as the British case has famously shown. I shall argue that similar problems apply within local government. Allocative efficiency will also be affected by change. Population changes may change the basis on which welfare judgements are made. Items that are scarce will be more valued, and the optimal pattern of output will change as technological possibilities modify levels of scarcity. Valuations will also change over time because of experience, and the pattern of outputs in any society is likely continually to be revalued. As Hirschman (1982) has argued, our patterns of involvement shift, for example, as our preferences about preferences lead to revision of our valuations of goods and services.

It is more difficult to measure efficiency, however defined, in the public sector than in the market-based manufacturing centre. Not only are there significant difficulties of moral hazard and adverse selection, but the very basis of evaluation, not simply the ordering of preferences, may be disputed by people holding opposed political views. The service character of much of the public sector means that it is difficult to separate producer and product, and to develop objective measures of efficiency. The consumer may also be involved directly in the production of the service. The problems of measuring quality, apparent in the case of any good, are more difficult to deal with in the public services (Walsh, 1991). It is commonly argued that there is some trade-off between equity and efficiency in the public service (Okun, 1975), though, as Le Grand (1991, p. 29) argues, since efficiency is a means to an end, it is:

> not an objective in the sense that equity is an objective; rather it is a secondary objective that only acquires meaning with reference to primary objectives such as equity.

On this argument we cannot make judgements about technical efficiency until we are satisfied about the initial distribution of income, power and opportunity.

The conceptually embedded character of efficiency makes it difficult to analyse in the public sector, because of its concern with the production and distribution of primary goods. There will also be issues particular to the public service in the general consideration of externalities, and the particular example of public goods, where collective and individual judgements of each dimension of efficiency may differ. The public sector is subject to prisoners' dilemma-type problems, in that the interaction of individual decisions, made on a rational basis, may produce collective results that are not optimal for those individuals. No single system of governmental organisation is likely to yield unambiguously the most effective pattern of output, produced in the most efficient way.

Decentralisation and efficiency

The traditional arguments for government provision of services do not imply that there should be local government; indeed, if anything, quite the opposite. There may be an argument for the production of local public goods, but, since there are few pure public goods, the case is not strong. The arguments from externalities and for government provision of merit goods do not provide strong justification for decentralised government. Growing complexity is likely to mean that the size of governmental unit that is necessary to internalise spill-over effects is increasing. Nor do arguments from increasing returns to scale and monopoly, and from the existence of asymmetries of information, justify decentralisation. The efficiency based arguments for decentralised government, if they exist, are likely to follow from the internal dynamics of government, rather than arguments for its necessity, which are generally based on theories of market failure. Local government, if it is designed effectively, overcomes some of the efficiency problems in the operation of public bureaucracies identified by public choice and government failure theorists (Wolf, 1988). The argument for decentralised government is secondary to that for government in itself. I shall take for granted the argument that there is a case for government provision of services, though it is clear that that case is being revised, given the challenge of the 'new right'.

Technical efficiency

The existence of many producing organisations may lead to greater technical efficiency, through learning from diversity, and therefore justify the decentralisation of production. Redundancy in governmental systems may be inefficient in the short term, but efficient in the long term (Bendor, 1985). On the other hand, there is the Schumpeterian argument that large corporations will become the centres of technical advance, supplanting the individual entrepreneur. Certain technologies will involve large-scale investment, and economies of scale; in other cases, there will be diseconomies of scale. As technology changes, then the level of scale and centralisation that leads to greater technical efficiency will also change. Two conclusions follow: first, that the optimal scale of organisation for different services will differ; second, that the optimal scale of organisation for the production of services will change over time.

Services that involve high levels of capital investment – for example, public utilities – are more likely to exhibit economies of scale. Factors that make decentralised approaches to the control and delivery of services more appropriate include the degree to which it involves direct contact between user and provider, and the degree of variation required to respond to local circumstances. Decentralised control and delivery is less easily justified the more specialised skills are scarce and expensive to buy. A standard argument for large public organisations is that they are necessary to recruit highly-skilled and qualified staff and to provide career structures for them.

Decentralisation is more important if the technology necessary for the production of a service is not well understood, and the more that methods of production vary. The more a service is repetitive, unvarying and well understood, the less local control will be needed. Public services frequently involve poorly understood production processes, weakening the case for centralisation. Generally, decentralised control and delivery is more appropriate the less there are economies and the more there are diseconomies of scale, the more it involves human services, and the less well understood and the more variable the nature of the service. This would suggest that local control of gas, electricity and water services is less appropriate than is the case for policing, social care or health provision.

Allocative efficiency

Oates, in his classic study, *Fiscal Federalism* (1972), develops the decentralisation theorem:

> in the absence of cost-savings from the centralized provision of a good and of interjurisdictional external effects, the level of welfare will always be at least as high (and typically higher) if Pareto-efficient levels of consumption of the good are provided in each jurisdiction than if *any* single, uniform level of consumption is maintained across all jurisdictions.

Allocative efficiency requires decentralisation because of the variation of preferences. There are many qualifications to this theory, for example the level of externalities, but it provides the most persuasive argument for some degree of decentralisation in government, and for local democracy. An important issue will be the extent to which locality is a causal factor in the variation of preferences, and recent work on the importance of place (Gyford, 1991b) would suggest that this is so. The greater the variation of preferences from one locality to another, the greater will be the efficiency loss from national uniformity in service provision. If preferences vary in a way that relates to locality there is an argument for decentralisation. Preferences may vary with factors other than locality – for example, race or gender – and cases can be made for taking these into account in designing governmental systems, both locally and nationally (Guinier, 1993).

The allocative-efficiency-based argument for decentralisation is limited by the existence of externalities which it may only be possible to internalise in relatively large jurisdictions. Oates points to two other problems with decentralisation. First, there is the cost of decision-making, which increases as the number of decision-making agencies increases. Second, there is the problem of congestion that follows from movement into a locality, with people moving to attain an advantage that the movement itself may destroy. One might add the costs of decision aggregation and the costs of the centre responding to a more dispersed system. Decision aggregation will be more costly the more local governments there are.

X-efficiency

It is possible to argue that decentralised government will be less wasteful than a centralised system. Certainly it is the highly centralised systems, as in Eastern Europe and the Soviet Union, that have made the grandest mistakes, but the case against centralisation on grounds of waste can be made more generally. The argument of public choice theorists such as Niskanen (1971) are partly based upon the assumption that politicians will be unable to monitor bureaucrats effectively. It seems plausible to argue that monitoring will be more effective in decentralised systems where politicians and administrators are closer to each other. Size leads to problems of loss of control, and larger organisations are more complex. Size may also be linked to absenteeism and other organisational causes of *x*-

inefficiency (Ingham, 1970), though the relationships are not simple (Clegg and Dunkerley, 1980).

Centralised systems may also be costly because of the incentive that is created to exercise upward influence. Milgrom and Roberts (1990) argue that:

> any centralisation of authority, whether in the public or private sector, creates the potential for intervention and so gives rise to costly influence activities and to excessive intervention by the central authority. (p. 87)

Central control may lead to costly and inefficient avoidance activities of the kind that were apparent during the period of creative accountancy in local government in the second half of the 1980s in Britain. High levels of central control of finance (such as now operate) lead to wasteful attempts to influence the centre, as the Audit Commission (1993) argues.

Dynamic efficiency

Decentralised administration can be argued to be significant for the dynamic character of technical, allocative and x-efficiency efficiency in government because it makes possible variation, experimentation and learning. As North (1990, p. 81) argues the consideration of technical efficiency from a dynamic perspective leads directly to issues of centralisation and decentralisation:

> Adaptive efficiency . . . provides the incentives to encourage the development of decentralised decision-making that will allow societies to maximise the efforts required to explore alternative ways of solving problems.

The pursuit of static and dynamic efficiency may take one in different directions, depending on the period over which efficiency is assessed. Various studies have shown the way that innovations are made first in a small number of leading public organisations, from which they then spread (Zucker, 1988). Wainwright (1994) argues for decentralised governmental systems on the grounds that much knowledge is tacit and local in character. Decentralisation may create incentives to each form of efficiency through competition; as Tiebout (1956) argues, the possibility of movement from one locality to another may provide a spur to greater efficiency. Competition between localities – for example, for grants from central government – or schemes such as City Challenge, or to attract industry, may act as incentives to innovation.

Discussion

Those human services where capital investment is relatively low are most likely to benefit from decentralisation. Centralised systems will tend towards an imposed uniformity unresponsive to variations of local circumstance and need. The greater the variation in preference, and the less prevalent the externalities, the more appropriate is decentralisation. These arguments do not establish the case for local democracy as opposed to local administration; nor do they tell us what form any system of local governance should take. They simply suggest that decentralised systems will have advantages over centralised systems in some circumstances. They also suggest that there will not be infinite advantage from decentralisation because of the countervailing costs. Even if there is a case, say, for the decentralisation of a particular service because of the need to respond to local variation in preferences, and to avoid the dominance of central preferences, the decision costs of an excessively fragmented system may be difficult to justify. The variation of size impacts by service suggests that the debate will not only be over the level of decentralisation, but also the distribution of functions at the local level.

Local democracy and efficiency

It is easier to make the case for local administration, and variation in the character of local services, on efficiency grounds, than it is to make the case for local democracy. The technical efficiency arguments for decentralisation, or smaller size, do not necessarily imply that local services need to be controlled democratically. Arguments, for example, about economies of scale have little to contribute, in themselves, to the normative arguments for or against local democracy, though they may influence the practical possibilities. Direct democracy may only be possible in small jurisdictions, meaning that economies of scale might have to be sacrificed. Democracy can create incentives to technical efficiency through the threat of loss of office. Though there may be little evidence that local voting patterns do depend upon technical service efficiency, politicians may behave as though that is the case. Technical efficiency considerations generally are, if anything, likely to provide a case *against* democracy, and arguments that there are trade-offs between equity and efficiency are in fact arguments about technical rather than allocative efficiency.

Democracy may be seen as one means of overcoming problems of x-inefficiency, in that the likelihood of loss of office provides an incentive to reduce waste. The elected politician at the local level can more easily be identified as being responsible for failure, and can more effectively monitor the behaviour of officials, than can a more distant national politician. It could be argued that it is not so much the fact of election that is important as that individuals will be held to be accountable for failure, and this could be done by local appointees. The impact of such a system is likely to depend upon the accountability of appointed individuals. It might be maintained that what is needed is performance statements and units for monitoring performance against standards, such as audit bodies and inspectorates, rather than political accountability. The limitations of performance management have been widely discussed (Carter *et al.*, 1992), and the issue about auditors and inspectors is how they are held to account for their actions, and how those actions are evaluated. Excessively detailed performance measures may limit adaptiveness (Stewart and Walsh, 1994). The public sector needs political accountability for x-efficiency reasons, because the mechanisms that provide incentives to private managers, such as share price and the threat of take-over, are not present. Holding to account through central politicians would not be adequate because of the implied overload of decisions.

Allocative efficiency is much more significant than technical or x-efficiency for decisions affecting the democratic character of local institutions. If there is to be variation in services to reflect local differences in preferences and needs, then the geographical distribution of preferences and needs has to be known or expressed, and the system of government has to be designed to allow variation of provision. Any system of local administration, if it is to be allocatively efficient, requires a means of ensuring preferences and needs are known and responded to. The means of determining needs and preferences might involve voting in a variety of forms, but also other mechanisms, such as surveys, citizen panels and juries and so on, that might not be seen as being inherently democratic. Markets could play a role. It is not necessary to accept the superiority of the market in all circumstances to argue that it can have a role in supplementing democratic procedures. Market and quasi-market choices may be the most appropriate means by which people can reveal, and perhaps discover, their preferences. It seems feasible to combine democratic and market mechanisms, especially when it is possible to vary the level of service provision rapidly. Voting for the overall control of a local authority might create incentives to technical efficiency, while saying little about individual preferences about services (especially when they are subject to change). Markets might support, rather than replace, democracy, just as participative forms of democracy might make representative forms more effective.

Burnheim (1985) has argued that voting can do little to deal with the complexities and paradoxes of expressing and reconciling contrasting values, although he underestimates its importance in creating a legitimate mechanism for doing so. Local voting, with the variation of spatial provision that it makes possible, is more likely to contribute to allocative efficiency than can solely national elections, but no more than that. Whatever output level is chosen, voters' preferences will always be distributed round it:

> within any single community there will be a distribution of voters' preferences around the actual output level, implying the continued existence of allocative inefficiency, although now on a smaller scale, since the local electorate might have greater control over output decisions which should then reflect local conditions and local needs. (Jackson, 1982, p. 206)

Analogous problems arise with markets; for example, with monopoly. Voting may be argued to be important for reasons other than revealing detailed preferences; for example, legitimating decisions, or because elections serve to highlight and perhaps create preferences on key issues, but it does not contribute greatly to the detailed pursuit of allocative efficiency. Elected politicians may argue that they have been granted the legitimate authority to make decisions, but the idea that they know the mind of the electorate is not plausible, though it may be more likely at the local than the national level.

The pursuit of allocative efficiency would suggest that there should be more extensive and detailed voting (for example, through referenda on specific issues or annual elections), but such systems are likely to run into both theoretical and practical problems; for example, in reconciling decisions. Moreover, it is possible to argue that people do not necessarily know their preferences, and that the point of democracy is not simply to reveal, but, through deliberation, also to generate preferences. Voting is not a particularly effective route to social and political deliberation. Representative democracy has advantages in reconciling differences but is of limited value in revealing preferences. Participative democratic approaches may work better in revealing preferences, though there are obvious dangers of disproportionate levels of participation, and the emergence of oligarchy. If democracy is to contribute to allocative efficiency then the democratic system will need to be designed with care, and to be multidimensional.

The difficulty of operating local democracy as a route to allocative efficiency may be overcome partly by the development of such approaches as citizens' juries or standing panels to supplement more traditional methods. Experience with such approaches – for example, in determining patterns of health care in Oregon – illustrates the problems in reconciling preferences, whatever combination of approaches is used. The pursuit of allocative efficiency would suggest the use of multiple and overlapping methods of involvement and of determining what people need and want, while recognising the need for deliberation, debate and judgement in political decision-making. Changes in technology make possible different approaches to democratic deliberation about what should be provided. New approaches, such as Fishkin's (1991) 'deliberative opinion poll' are being developed. Most important, perhaps, market mechanisms might be used to supplement voting systems: for example, through the use of vouchers, making possible the development of different mechanisms for the revelation and aggregation of preferences.

It is the value-laden nature of the determination of allocative efficiency, and, ultimately, other forms of efficiency that provide the best basis for arguing for local democracy rather than local administration. Decisions about efficiency in all its forms are always bound up with values. The market will only be a satisfactory means of reaching an acceptable, value-based system of production and distribution if we are satisfied with the initial conditions. Such an assessment involves democracy at some level. The values on which we base our assessments of systems of production and distribution may well be incommensurable. If the criteria for judgement could always be set unambiguously before the decision then there would be few problems in assessing allocative efficiency, but this is rarely the case. As Gray (1989, p. 251) argues:

> Reasoning, on this view, is not from principles to cases, but from case to case. Far from principles determining our judgments in particular instances, they are abridgments or summaries of our judgments in these particular instances.

There is no 'agreed territorial welfare function against which output can be assessed' (Keating and Midwinter, 1994, p. 177).

If allocative efficiency requires deliberation based on judgement, because of differences in values, then some form of democracy is appropriate. The dynamic nature of value-based judgement would suggest that the system of democracy will need to be interactive, to make possible preference revelation, discovery and aggregation, and this is difficult in a centralised system.

The issue is not simply one of whether there is democracy or not, but the form that democracy takes if allocative efficiency is to be achieved. Market mechanisms may provide means of enabling us to express choices; they are less appropriate in determining levels of need or desert. It may be, as public economists tend to argue (Musgrave, 1959), that redistributive decisions should be made at central government level. It is less clear that the centre will be able effectively to determine appropriate levels of welfare spending in local areas or to decide the detailed nature of services required. The argument for democracy in the pursuit of allocating efficiency in government is likely, therefore, to be for a differentiated system of government using a variety of methods for democratic involvement. One could argue that if democracy is needed then it can be provided at the central level, but all that we know about central planning systems (Nove, 1983) suggests that a highly centralised system generates large allocative, technical and x-inefficiencies. The separation of powers is an argument that can be made not only on political, but also on efficiency grounds.

Dimensions of local democracy

The nature of democracy at the local level may vary along a number of dimensions. The most important of these, from the point of view of efficiency, would appear to be: size; the degree of aggregation of functions; and the mode of operation of the local system. I shall consider each of these dimensions in turn, and then argue that the various efficiency considerations point to a highly differentiated pattern of local government and local democracy, which may not be desirable for other reasons: for example, the ability to understand the way that the system operates. In designing systems of local administration and democracy there will need to be decisions on how different dimensions are balanced.

Size

The size of local unit has implications for each of the dimensions of efficiency. The debates over the appropriate size of local government for the provision of different services have tended to concentrate on technical efficiency, and have yielded few definitive results; Bennett (1980, p. 126) concludes that:

> whilst there may be an optimum size for any service or any one community, there is no general optimum size for all services in all communities, since the economies of administration, distribution, economic activity, and personal contacts differ widely for different functions and different areas dependent on the different environments, divergent patterns of historical development and settlement and differences in the range of local preferences for services.

More recently, Travers *et al.* (1993) drew an equally sceptical conclusion from their review of the evidence:

> there is evidence to suggest that within some parts of provision there are results which show larger authorities to have lower costs

and/or be more effective. In other services and areas of provision, smaller authorities appear to perform better. (p. 56)

These arguments imply that there needs to be a differentiated pattern of government at the local level, to take account of these different size characteristics, everything else being equal. The advantages of size are not independent of other features of local organisation. Local authorities in most other countries are far smaller than in Britain and operate through various forms of inter-authority contracting, involvement of voluntary and private organisations and other mechanisms. It is a commonplace of contemporary organisation theory (Clegg, 1993) that organisational networks are becoming more important as a response to increasingly diverse and rapidly changing markets. Even if this case is overstated, it is possible to argue that the advantages of small and large size can be combined in a diversified system. The review of local government structure in the 1990s has prompted many local authorities to devise imaginative schemes to combine the advantages of large size and decentralisation. Market mechanisms will enable local authorities to gain economies of scale without becoming excessively large. Size, even though it has relevance, cannot be a determining factor without taking into account other factors that will influence whether beneficial scale effects can be gained – for example, the aggregation of function and the mode of operation of the system.

In terms of allocative efficiency there are arguments for being both large and small at the same time, to cope with variation in preferences but also to incorporate externalities. There are also arguments for being both large and small if local authorities provide more than one service. Even within services, distinct elements may be better provided by organisations of different sizes; for example primary schooling compared with further education. The need to be large and small at the same time suggests local authorities that operate systems of decentralisation, at least for some services, and local government systems that have more than one tier. Differentiation is necessary to ensure that the various aspects of democracy can be incorporated. Small authorities are good for the expression of preferences and for making responsive decisions. They are less appropriate for decision aggregation. The variety of size that seems necessary for technical and allocative efficiency in different services implies that the form of democracy will have to adjust to the requirements of scale. Small local authorities, or decentralised units within larger authorities, might be able to operate levels of participative and direct democracy that would not be possible in large organisations. Such approaches have been developed in recent years both in Britain and elsewhere.

Aggregation of functions

The issue of the separation or aggregation of functions has been a traditional topic of debate in considering the efficiency of local government. Single purpose authorities will be technically more efficient because of clarity of focus. In the United States it has sometimes been maintained that high levels of disaggregation of function are costly and technically inefficient because of overlap and duplication. By contrast, Burnheim (1985) argues that:

> it is much less risky to hand over control of public goods to a variety of very limited agencies than to one omni-competent agency. The risk of irresponsible action is dispersed. Total disaster is less likely . . . the watch one can keep over an omni-competent agency cannot be very effective. (p. 15)

Isolation of services from each other may insulate them from failure.

This argument tends to assume that agencies can, in fact, be kept separate. Some issues arise because of the overlap between functions, and the possibility of one agency shifting costs on to another. It is commonly claimed, for example, that hospitals have discharged people with mental health problems to shift costs and responsibilities on to the local authority. Burnheim's (1988) argument is less telling if we consider an omni-responsible organisation, but one that is not necessarily self-sufficient in provision, perhaps purchasing from other agencies or on the market. The disadvantage of single-purpose agencies is the shift of allocative decisions, or the distribution of resources between services, to the centre. This problem can be avoided to the extent that local single-purpose bodies are taxing agencies, and local people can choose different levels of spending for each agency. The need for grant systems tends to make this more difficult. The argument for single-purpose bodies is strengthened in so far as financially they are autonomous from the centre, but there are then problems of equalisation.

The arguments for multi- or single-purpose local service agencies is fairly evenly balanced from a technical point of view. There are arguments for integration to achieve scope economies because of surplus asset capacity or the public good character of assets (Willig, 1979). Moore (1992) has developed a theory of the firm as a collection of assets, with the pattern of ownership and control determined by technology and transaction costs. On similar lines, the degree to which multi-purpose local authorities are appropriate will depend, from a technical efficiency point of view, on complementarity of action and technological issues. Moore (1992, p. 499) argues that assets which 'are strictly complementary should be owned together'. Complementarity arguments could be made for bringing together services, such as housing and social services, or the emergency services, police, fire and the ambulance service, which are highly interdependent, and where the actions of one influences outcomes in the other. Equally, complementarity arguments would lead us to question the present pattern of educational organisation, or the relationship between health and social services, which involve high levels of disaggregation of strongly overlapping services. The technical efficiency argument for multi-purpose authorities would be for limited integration of like and complementary services. It seems unlikely that economies of scope or complementarity arguments would justify highly diversified organisations.

The more plausible argument for the multi-purpose authority follows from the pursuit of allocative efficiency. The extent to which the market can allocate finance between services is limited in the public service, both for technical and political reasons. If local services are provided by market mechanisms and single-purpose, or limited-purpose bodies, then initial allocative decisions have to be made at the centre unless issues of equalisation are ignored completely. The more such decisions are made at the centre, the more inefficient they are likely to be because of ignorance of local preferences, needs and circumstances. Central influence would seem most appropriate where uniform standards can be agreed fairly easily. The problems are apparent in some cases of specific grants and the funding of grant-maintained schools. There is evidence, for example, that local authorities have found difficulty in spending the special transition grant on community care because of lack of freedom over how it was spent. Spending has been skewed towards residential care, where most local authorities, given the choice, would have developed other elements of community care. A multi-purpose local authority, closer to the point of delivery, will make more appropriate decisions. This would be an argument, though, for small authorities, with some central control to cope with externalities.

It is now commonly argued that government networks can be more efficient in the production and delivery of services than can multi-purpose organisations. In the United States, the Advisory Commission on Intergovernmental Relations (1987, p. 1) concludes that:

> a multiplicity of general purpose and special purpose governments is not an obstacle to good governance. On the contrary, a diversity of local government can promote key values of democratic government – namely efficiency, equity, responsiveness, accountability and self-governance. A multiplicity of differentiated governments does not necessarily imply fragmentation; instead such government, interactively linked through a variety of arrangements, can constitute a coherent local political economy.

There is evidence for the efficient operation of networks in the private sector, especially in Asian countries (Gerlach, 1988). Networks might be effective in the public service, though initial evidence from an ESRC study suggests that the effectiveness of networks depends upon the local authority to provide support and integration.[1] Studies of local government have also pointed to the difficulty of co-operation between different organisations. It is far from clear that networks can operate effectively to deliver public services. The less effective are networks, the more important it will be to bring together services in multi-purpose organisations. Networks are only likely to be effective within an appropriate institutional framework. The number of linkages between organisations will increase exponentially as the number of organisations grows arithmetically, creating logistical problems. Just as this suggests that a multiplicity of small organisations might create technical efficiency problems, so it suggests that too many single-purpose organisations might be inefficient, both technically and allocatively. A degree of multi-purpose responsibility, if not provision, seems appropriate. If there is to be allocative efficiency, then local single-purpose agencies would need autonomy from the centre and the ability to raise finance.

Mode of operation

The 'enabling' local authority, purchasing services from a range of other organisations, is an alternative to the integrated, self-sufficient local authority. Local authorities would be more technically and *x*-efficient if they operated through a combination of externalisation, contracting, competition and direct provision. Users with choice would produce pressures for allocative efficiency. This model is being pursued by authorities such as Brent, Rutland and Berkshire, who claim cost savings and improved services. The use of 'enabling', market-based, mechanisms creates the possibility of reaping the benefits both of large and small size, and combining market and government. The small authority can contract with large companies or larger local authorities, thereby gaining the advantages of economies of scale as is common in France. Monopoly problems can be overcome as long as the market is contestable – that is, if competition is possible for the market, even if not within it (Vining and Weimer, 1990).

The evidence on the technical and *x*-efficiency effects of alternative systems of service delivery tends to show that there are savings to be made from contracting out in simple, repetitive services, such as refuse collection (Domberger *et al.*, 1986), but that equivalent technical and *x*-efficiency gains are less likely in the case of contracting for complex, human services (Gutch, 1992; Smith and Lipsky, 1993). There is limited evidence on the costs of operating market-based systems, and preparing for competition, but what there is show that such costs are significant. The transaction costs of contract and specification writing, tendering, performance monitoring and contract management are high.

A broader view of the enabling debate suggests a range of possible models. In France, there is the provision of monopoly goods such as water by large private providers working with small local authorities. In the United States there is the prevalence of contracting between local authorities as well as contracting out in the private sector. In Europe and Australia there is extensive use of voluntary agencies. Joint ventures and co-production are increasingly common – for example, in Canada. The technical efficiency of the local authority is likely to be dependent upon the nature of the institutional framework within which it operates, particularly the extent to which principal–agent relationships are designed to minimise transaction costs, and to create an appropriate allocation of property rights. The operation of a more differentiated system also requires changes in the way that democratic mechanisms operate. The purchaser/provider split and markets, for example, pose challenges to the traditional pattern of representative democracy in local government. Elected members are required, for example, to separate the consideration of service delivery from service specification, which poses difficulties for traditional committee-based decision systems. Purchaser/provider splits also affect the openness of the system – for example, because of claims about commercial confidentiality.

The development of market-based mechanisms may have advantages in making possible a more specific expression of preferences. The 'mixed economy' of social care may create some opportunity for expression of choice, though the evidence is limited. The evidence on the impact of market mechanisms on the ability of users to choose is not yet clear. Market mechanisms have led to new approaches to involving the user – for example, in monitoring services subject to compulsory competitive tendering and in the design of service specification – but only to a very limited degree. Some means of setting the conditions for the market is required, and the market itself cannot create these conditions. The evidence so far is that the enabling authority may have some advantages in technical and x-efficiency terms, but has done little to increase allocative efficiency.

Conclusion

An efficient democratic system is likely to be differentiated, with a mixture of participative and representative approaches operating at a number of levels. Allocative efficiency is enhanced by participation in clarifying the differentiation of views and preferences. Decision aggregation requires some level of representative democracy. Allocatively efficient decisions are also likely to require the operation of democracy at various levels and in different forms. It might be argued, for example, that direct, participative democracy is appropriate at the neighbourhood level, but that it is difficult to operate such a system at the level of the city or locality. Where appointed bodies were considered appropriate for example, because the need for technical knowledge – allocative issues might suggest an element of election, or some other means for the democratic expression of preference and holding to account. Markets could also play a role.

The democratic 'mix' is restricted in Britain. There is a dominance of indirect, elected representation and, increasingly, appointment by central government. The arguments that have been presented, at least from an efficiency perspective, suggest that the forms of democracy need to change to achieve a fit between the patterns of organisation, and what is needed to be more efficient. Voting systems might need to be changed to create better technical efficiency incentives. It can easily be argued, for example, that local elections will not operate as pressures for technical, allocative or x-efficiency where there is little chance of control changing hands between political parties.

Corruption, or simply ignoring the public, is more likely where there are, effectively, single-party systems. Recent experience of appointed bodies suggests that they may also give rise to corruption, or ignore public wishes. Efficiency arguments for local government point in a number of directions. There are arguments both for large size and for small size. There are arguments for multi-purpose and single-purpose authorities. Recent developments – for example, in the debate over the nature of the enabling authority – have begun to show the way that technical efficiency gains can be made by using more varied approaches. Small authorities may gain economies of scale by contracting. The overall efficiency of local government depends upon a complex process of institutional design. The number of factors to be taken into account is potentially large, and the interaction of the various dimensions of efficiency makes it difficult to achieve a system that is best for each dimension.

If, as I have argued, the dominant factor in designing a local government system is the achievement of allocative efficiency, then there is a need for local democracy. It is unlikely that the present system (with its limited involvement, high levels of appointment, and strong centralisation) meets efficiency criteria. The main arguments for freedom of local from central government are those of loss of control, the costs of bureaucracy, and the dominance of uniform, central preference. There are arguments for centrally-defined standards, but too much standardisation is likely to limit adaptation to local and changing circumstances. Most countries allow local authorities much greater freedom than is the case in Britain, and do not spell out standards in such detail, or use them to determine grants. The limits of central knowledge in setting standards and allocating finance must also be recognised.

It is difficult to refute the argument that local government and local democracy is inefficient, partly because it is made in such general terms, and, more importantly, because the way that the concept of efficiency is used constantly shifts. My argument is that democracy is necessary to allocative efficiency in particular, and that centralised democracy is unlikely to be adequate.

Note

1.   The New Management – Citizenship and Institutional Change in Local Governance – ESRC Grant Number L311253017.

5 The Value of Locality[1]

Elizabeth Frazer

Introduction

Since the early 1980s political theory has been dominated by the debate about 'communitarianism' (Avineri and de-Shalit 1992). In the academic context, communitarianism engages critically with recent Anglo-US liberalism, especially its emphasis on individualism. More recently, communitarian ideas and values have taken a central place in mainstream UK politics.[2] References to communitarianism and invocations of the value of community reflect a widespread fear, to the left, right and centre of the political spectrum, that market individualism threatens to atomise society.

Communitarianism in political thought is pertinent to a reconsideration of the normative underpinnings of local government in two ways. First, communitarian theorists believe that local government should be strengthened. Second, theorists and practitioners concerned to defend or strengthen local government institutions appeal frequently to the needs or interests of local communities, and to the duty of government to be accountable to the community.

In this chapter I subject these two claims to critical scrutiny. First, I examine the grounds for the communitarian belief in strengthened local government, and put these in the context of the communitarian debates in general. In so doing, I develop some sceptical arguments about the conceptions of community and locality which are explicit and, for the most part, implicit in this work. Second, I question the meaning of local government theorists' and practitioners' references to 'community'. I argue that a prescriptive argument for local government needs only to emphasise the value of care for localities, and the needs of people living and working in and using localities. To invoke community muddies the normative argument with specious sociological reasoning, and will lead to policy mistakes.

Communitarianism and community

In recent political theory communitarians have launched a series of telling attacks on 'liberal individualism'. First, against the liberal picture of individuals as disconnected egoistically rational choosers, communitarians offer a picture of people who are connected with others in a given social world of patterned relationships, traditions and institutions. They favour a social constructionist theory of both the self and social reality. Second, communitarians emphasise the importance of intersubjective, collective and public goods. Third, against the liberal ideal that principles of justice or judgements of value are universally applicable, communitarians insist that justice and value can only be adjudged by reference to the contexts of particular communities and their associated traditions, cultures and social institutions. It is important to note, and relevant to the current argument about local government, that although the target in recent debates has overwhelmingly been liberal individualism and associated empiricist methods in the social sciences, simultaneously communitarianism constitutes an attack on certain varieties of Marxism, which emphasise the normative status and role of the state, and on associated structuralist methods in social science.

Both the liberal emphasis on the individual, and the Marxist emphasis on the state, are challenged fundamentally by recent crises of the welfare state which have not been resolved by resort to purely market mechanisms; by the fragmentation of the Soviet Union and the claims of ethnic groups; by ethnic divisions and competing claims in liberal democratic states such as Canada; and by the challenges facing people attempting to build or rebuild civil society. It is in the context of such significant social changes that community is invoked as an ideal form of social organisation and set of relationships. Attendance to the needs, wishes and values of actually existing communities is urged as a guide to social policy, against the pressures of individualism, market relations and bureaucratic state policy, or the values of a nation state.

However, at this point a problem that is central to the concerns of this chapter becomes clear. Within communitarianism there is a fallacious inference from an appeal to the proper recognition of the relational basis of social identity and human society, to the prescription of community as the ideal form of social organisation. The emphasis on a range of intersubjective relationships, such as reciprocity, solidarity, neighbourliness, shared ethnic or other cultural identities, and sociability, all conduce against the straightforward individualism and faith in market mechanisms for solving social dilemmas that have been intellectually and politically influential in recent decades. Similarly, they conduce against a simple faith in action and mechanisms at the level of the state for the solution to these same problems. This means that the individual, on the one hand, and the state, or nation, or 'people', on the other, are less salient than a variety of social organisations and institutions such as kinship groups, neighbourhoods, voluntary associations for voluntary work, voluntary associations for fellowship or shared purposes, communities, parties, corporations, and other economic enterprises. But community is a rather specific form of association, and by no means the most significant one in modern societies.

Within communitarian writing we find a peculiar combination of acknowledgement and denial of this. A recurrent theme is that community has been lost. This is consistent with the sociological thesis about the historical transition from traditional to modern societies, from community to society, from status to contract as the dominant normative basis of social relations, from particularism to universalism in knowledge claims and social relations and so on. The details of this sociological and historical thesis are, of course, argued about; and some sociologists and historians who are inclined to emphasise continuities rather than discontinuities, incremental change rather than dramatic restructuring, dispute the thesis itself. Nevertheless, it is true that the early sociologists were preoccupied with the ills of modernity – alienation, anomie, the brutality of capitalist relations, the iron cage of bureaucratic rationality. At least part of their project was to seek resolutions to these new conflicts and contradictions. But it is by no means a valid inference to associate these ills with the loss of community itself, nor, further, to presume that the solution to the ills of modernity is the reinstatement of community.

Recent communitarian thinkers tend to argue that the story of discontinuity misrepresents the human condition in certain crucial ways. The picture of the liberal autonomous rational choosing individual de-emphasises certain characteristics of human social existence which are distorted or repressed (but not done away with) in modernity. These must be properly acknowledged in theory and in practice if certain ills of modernity are to be cured. So, in the communitarian writings we find an emphasis on the facts that language, and therefore communication, rely on prior shared meanings (Taylor 1985a, 1985b, 1985c). We find arguments that our social identities (and, in a stronger version our subjectivity) are generated by social relations (Sandel, 1982, p. 179; Selznick, 1987, pp. 450– 3). We find the powerful argument that even liberal individualism relies on a culture and a tradition to sustain it as a normative way of life (MacIntyre, 1981, pp. 326– 48).[3]

It is a big leap from this emphasis on the interconnectedness of human individuals to a full-blown prescriptive theory of community. But the leap, or rather, a slide, is certainly made, for the communitarian theorists do not hesitate to use the term community, with, however, a variety of references. Michael Walzer, for example, argues that 'community itself is largely an ideological presence in modern society . . . it is intermittently fashionable only because it no longer exists in anything like full strength' (Walzer, 1990, p. 7). But it does still exist, and has a central place in Walzer's normative scheme: he mentions the fragility of communities in the modern world, and asks how we can sustain them (Walzer 1990, pp. 16, 20). Michael Sandel thinks of communities as one kind of institution of which we might have membership (like families, or nations, or peoples) (Sandel, 1984, p. 90). Alasdair MacIntyre, by contrast, makes 'community' a term which encompasses a range of subcategories: he mentions 'communities such as those of the family, the neighbourhood, the city and the tribe' (MacIntyre, 1981, p. 221). Charles Taylor, in a more abstract argument which nevertheless puts community at the centre of social theory, argues that 'common meanings are the basis of community . . . only with common meanings does this common reference world contain significant common actions, celebrations and feelings. These are objects in the world that everybody shares. This is what makes community (Taylor, 1985a, p. 39). Philip Selznick, commenting on the vagueness and elusiveness of the concept, argues that, in current contexts, community 'is not a special purpose organisation. It is a comprehensive framework for social life . . . in a genuine community there must be a minimum of integration, including shared symbolic experience, (but) we also expect to find relatively self-regulating activities, groups and institutions' (Selznick, 1987, p. 449).

The meaning of 'community', like so many concepts in social analysis, is imprecise. In community studies within sociology there has been disagreement about whether community entailed any or all of: a bounded geographical area; a dense network of non-contractual relations including those of kinship, friendship, and cultural membership; a particular quality of identification on the part of members with place, or culture, or way of life, or tradition; shared symbols, values, meanings, language, norms; shared interests, such as occupational interests, as in 'a fishing community' or a 'mining community'; or political or cultural interests, as in the 'gay community' or 'the feminist community' (Bell and Newby, 1971; Stacey, 1969). It is not necessary for all these to be present together; equally no one of these characteristics alone seems to be sufficient for community. In particular, shared interests alone do not make a group of individuals into a community (an interest group is not a community). Salient communities like the 'gay community' will not necessarily be coincident with a clear geographical location; and if they are, they will almost certainly not have a monopoly on use of the area in question. However, a subjective identification on the part of those who share interests, occupation, culture, tradition or norms, of themselves and others as co-members, does seem to be necessary.

But communitarianism and associated social theories often propose that one particular element is considered a necessary and sufficient condition for community: shared symbols, common meanings, a common language, or at least common understanding. It is said by communitarians that two or more individuals constitute a community when they share a common conception of the good and see this as partly constitutive of their identities (Sandel, 1982, p. 150, 1984, pp. 86–7; MacIntyre, 1981, p. 146). In sociolinguistics the idea of 'speech community', although regarded as problematic, still retains a central place (Alladina and Edwards, 1991). In legal theory, Ronald Dworkin elaborates the idea of the 'community of principle' that alone can generate the stable set of legal meanings which can give body to the idea of law as integrity (Dworkin, 1986, p. 244). And, in political theory, we meet the idea of 'the political community'. This implies that, actually or ideally, the polity is a community, and that citizenship is properly constituted by membership of it (Mouffe, 1992a; Selznick, 1987, p. 562; Dworkin, 1986, pp. 206–15; Sandel, 1984, p. 93; Walzer, 1983, p. 300; MacIntyre, 1981, pp. 253ff.).

These ideas are thought to be attractive in theoretical terms because they capture the connectedness of members, the sharing and therefore the relative stability of meanings, norms and practices, which in turn offer a grounding for claims about the legitimacy of particular institutions and social arrangements. However, they are theoretically problematic in a number of ways. First, the stability of meanings is overdrawn in this theoretical scheme. Linguistic research emphasises the indeterminacy and wide variation in language use; with growing interest in conflict and intertextuality, 'speech community' is much too restrictive a notion (Alladina and Edwards, 1991). It has been argued that Dworkin's 'community of principle' is not based on any actual system of exclusion or inclusion – it is therefore no more than an intellectual fantasy (Lacey, forthcoming). The sharing of an articulated conception of 'the good' is a criterion difficult to meet in sociological reality.

Second, the normativity of these usages of 'community' is odd. There is no straightforwardly prescriptive recommendation that we try to build or rebuild communities – because the shapes of the communities in question are so vague, and it is difficult to give any substance to them beyond an attendance to the connectedness of people. Third, the rhetorical power of the term seems to thrive on the gaps and slippages in its reference. It has been suggested that one particularly rhetorically productive element of its meaning is the suppressed reference to boundaries and processes of exclusion. On the surface, appeals to community – the inclusion of 'us' – articulate a manifest anxiety about the atomism proceeding on the loss of old communities. But equally, of course, they can be seen as articulating a deep anxiety about and a deep desire to reject 'others', to maintain boundaries that exclude 'the other' (Lacey forthcoming; Salecl, 1994, pp. 21–30, especially elaborate this sort of theory). That is, the inclusionary surface of the vocabulary of community masks (but not wholly successfully) a more or less violent process of exclusion and rejection.

Fourth, the invocation of community is reductive. Just as market liberals and rational choice theorists attempt to reduce all social relations, political, legal, cultural and kinship, to exchange and consumption relations; and Marxists reduce all social relations to relations of production, so communitarianism reduces all social relations, political, economic, legal, and kinship, to cultural relations. Fifth, and most salient for the purposes of this chapter, the usage is sociologically naïve – a mistaken view of the nature of the associations and social relationship which constitute society and polity. I shall be returning to these latter two points in the section below entitled 'Problems with community'.

Community and locality

We have seen that locality is not a necessary feature of community. None the less, it is arguable that the rhetorical power of the vocabulary of community, and the recent uptake of communitarian ideas, are connected in part with the push towards regionalism and localism that is being felt with the break up of the Soviet Union and challenges to existing nation states elsewhere. The theme of locality is pervasive in the communitarian literature, where there are strong, and, in some cases, explicit suggestions that strengthened local government would have to be a feature of a reconstituted polity. In a good deal of communitarian writing the emphasis, although rarely made completely explicit, is on small-scale local communities. Elsewhere, this is not a strong implication, and for some the community in question seems rather to be the political community on the scale of the nation-state.

MacIntyre's normative presumption of complex but stable communities and social roles, in which values and practices are shared and public, and an articulated tradition lends authority to practices, strongly suggests relatively small-scale social organisation, as does his commendation of a republican polity (he has the 'city state' in mind, seemingly) (MacIntyre, 1981, pp. 236–7). Taylor discusses politics as such, arguing (against liberal individualism) that public freedom requires a strong identification with the political community (Taylor, 1989, p. 508). This argument suggests, of course, that citizen relations must be intra-community relations. However, Taylor is cautious in insisting that he does not believe that a straightforward retreat from liberal values would unproblematically restore lost meaning to life, nor that we can, or should attempt to, escape from the value plurality of modern society. This is compatible with his commitment to the integrity of a plurality of communities – presumably within the political community, although the analysis is vague. The institutional upshots of all this are not made clear.

Sandel is one of the key participants in the recent upsurge of 'new republicanism', and has done much to bring this thought to the attention of political theorists. He argues that the 'procedural republic' – the set of institutional arrangements that has emerged as value consensus has broken down – in fact functions to crowd out democracy, to undercut the very community on which it depends; and, even more devastating for the liberal, to undercut the individual freedom in whose name it acts by enmeshing the individual in an array of unchosen bureaucratic and impersonal dependencies and expectations (Sandel, 1984, pp. 93–4; Taylor, 1989, p. 508). Again, the institutional upshots of this are not clear – but the emphasis on embraced rather than imposed relationships, on duty and obligation in personal relationships, and on the maintenance of community all conduce to a picture of relatively small scale social organisation.

Selznick too mentions resonances between communitarianism and civic republicanism, with an emphasis on duties as well as, if not before, rights. However, against the recent new right version of republicanism he argues that a simple assertion of people's duties (for example, as a precondition to receipt of benefits) will not do: people need resources if they are to be duty bound, membership of the community must be genuine; and therefore community is a precondition of republicanism. Community must be built first (Selznick, 1987, p. 456).

Walzer is clearest in mentioning the importance of local government, although the reference is tantalisingly brief. In his prescriptive analysis of the polity he defines the political community as a common enterprise, carried on in a genuine forum within which all are equal – political equality must be uncontaminated by any other social inequalities (Walzer, 1983, pp. 300–4). He also discusses the republican tradition, acknowledging that this has been based on the needs of small homogeneous communities, where civil society is relatively undifferentiated, but arguing that perhaps 'the doctrine can be extended to account for a 'republic of republics' . . . a considerable strengthening of local government would then be required in the hope of encouraging the development and display of civic virtue' (Walzer, 1990, p. 20).

There are more or less clear hints, then, that communitarianism flows into localism. However, on closer inspection, the flows are not very strong. For example, the maintenance of a culture or set of traditions across large spatial distances (for example, people travelling from all over the world to a clan gathering in Scotland once in ten years, or for an individual perhaps once in a lifetime) is an obvious possibility. As has been remarked, many individuals consider themselves to be members of 'communities' – for example, the gay community – which are not geographically located. The maintenance of collective values and a public culture are compatible with geographical distance, in the modern age at least – from the eighteenth century onwards newspapers constructed a forum that transcended locality, and recent and current developments in communications have made a further qualitative change in the relationship, from the point of view of social subjects, between space and time (Dahlgren and Sparks, 1991, introduction; Harvey, 1989, pp. 285ff, pt. III).

A fundamental plank of communitarianism is the principle of social constructivism – that we are made in a social context, in our relations with others. But this is quite clearly compatible with non-local contexts, with identification with people who are close socially but distant geographically, and, indeed, with diaspora. Walzer emphasises the desirability of community self-regulation (Walzer, 1983, p. 304). Again, as the example of many self-regulating associations, voluntary, commercial and professional, shows, this does not require locality. Many viable associations are comprised of memberships linked by mail and other communications technologies. That is, the building and maintenance of communities – collectivities of individuals who are tied by shared interests or shared meanings, language, culture and traditions, and who feel that their relationship with one another is one of co-membership – does not entail that these individuals share a location. All that is needed is a means of communication; although it is worth emphasising that for many individuals a powerful allegiance is that with a community in diaspora. That is to say, co-members can even be denied a straightforward means of communication, yet enjoy community.

Problems with community

The most potent image of community and locality seems to be the dwindling number of occupational communities – mining, fishing, agriculture – where participants in the primary occupation are tied to a geographical area, and where a more or less bounded economy of goods and services in exchange for the prime product is bound up with social networks, cultural traditions and so on. Alternatively, there are relatively well defined geographical areas whose population constitutes 'a community' and perhaps shares language, or culture, or interests. However, consideration of these two empirical possibilities immediately suggests problems and issues that have been evident to community workers within educational and social services, and that are made clear in critical examination of recent government policies and pronouncements about 'community care', 'community policing', or 'community development' as well as being discussed at length in the critical theoretical literature on communitarianism (Frazer and Lacey, 1993; Benhabib, 1992; Young, 1990; Friedman, 1989).

These are, first, the problem of divisions and antagonisms within communities, the problem, from the standpoint of individuals, of whether their membership of a community is elective or non-elective, whether they may exit, and whether they have voice within a community. As community workers know, 'community leaders' may be unrepresentative in critical ways – because they are middle-class and articulate, or because they are middle-aged, or because they are men. Work with and for young people, or women, or the poor and disadvantaged will often bring to the surface deeply structured antagonisms and clashes of interest and power within what is thought of as 'the community'. Second, there is the problem of allegiances and antagonisms between communities. Where genuinely common interests and cultural allegiances are articulated by some community, these may well clash with social justice, a greater economic good or efficiency, or at least with the equally valid interests and goods of other communities or individuals. Third, there is a clear ethical question, to say the least, about the desirability of privileging individual people's identification with any community, rather than encouraging a sense of allegiance with people different from oneself, encouraging ties and commitments which challenge the maintenance of stable boundaries, with exploiting to the full the ethical possibilities of unstable identities and relationships.[4]

It is not fair to say that communitarians have wholly neglected these questions. Selznick, for example, argues that within communities we shall find plurality (Selznick, 1987, p. 449). Walzer begins his paper on communitarianism by acknowledging both value pluralism and the social and geographic mobility of the individual person in modern societies (Walzer, 1990, pp. 11–12). Taylor is committed to the ethical and political relevance of the plurality of, and indeed conflict between, goods (Taylor, 1989, p. 506). MacIntyre acknowledges that our social identities are complex; although the final picture of individual social identity that can be drawn from MacIntyre's work is that we have complex, nested identities – he tends to underestimate the amount of conflict between aspects of our identity felt by many people (perhaps especially women) (MacIntyre, 1981, p. 220).

These theorists acknowledge, then, that we participate in a variety of institutions, act in or embody a number of roles, negotiate with clashing and competing ties and allegiances to others, are mobile in a mobile world. In practice, the community and our community identities will not trump other imperatives. This is not to say that there will not be situations in which they might – situations in which individuals will put the interests of their community and its well-being before the interests they might have as women, individuals, professionals, workers, or any number of other social roles and identities (see Kymlicka, 1989 for a normative argument to this effect). It is also incontrovertible that some individuals, residents of particular neighbourhoods, members of particular organisations or associations, professionals such as the clergy or community workers, will take it as their purpose to attempt to build community in a particular setting. These considerations conduce to a sociological analysis that pays close attention to the actual institutions and settings in which people are implicated and bound up, and which contribute to their social identities and allegiances. They also imply a prescriptive analysis that focuses on the individual's integrity in a range of collective settings (Frazer and Lacey, 1994; Young, 1990; Benhabib, 1992, for the beginnings of this kind of analysis).

The suggestion here, then, is that community as an analytic category and as an ideal generates a number of substantive problems, and in any case takes its place as only one kind of social formation and site of allegiance for people. But it is striking that although communitarian theorists themselves set out the fundamentals of this position – looking at the facts and ethical pull of pluralism, and the complexity of the social reality we seek to render in prescriptive terms – they nevertheless revert unerringly to community as an ideal, in seeming denial of the very problems they outline. Again, this points to the rhetorical and perhaps deep-seated fantasy structure of the term's connotations.

Equally striking is the way practitioners, theorists and commentators who are themselves not in any sense committed members of the communitarian tendency will also use the term, deploy the ideal, and invoke the reality, of community.[5] It is only rarely that such usage has a genuine community as its referent: it usually has a more contentious meaning. For example, the people who use a particular service and therefore are perceived, from the supplier's point of view, as having particular needs and interests in common – disabled people, the users of particular sports or recreational facilities, hospital patients, for example, – are referred to frequently as 'the community'. Second, community is used to describe the people who live in a particular neighbourhood, notwithstanding the lack in many neighbourhoods of any of the other characteristics and qualities that are necessary for the correct application of the concept. In this formulation, locality alone is community (Mayo, 1994, pp. 170–87). Third, it is used to describe people who share some aspect of social identity and interest, whether or not they are clustered geographically. So we conceive of national communities (for example, Chilean exiles in London), ethnic communities (African Americans), cultural or religious communities (Hassidic Jews), or people who share a particular aspect of lifestyle and the political interests that follow from it (the gay community) (Mayo, 1994, pp. 187–90). The identification of these collectivities and groupings as communities has had concrete enough effects in local authority policy in the UK – for example, with the provision of resource centres and community centres, and with the designation of areas of cities as 'Chinatown' and so on (Cooke, 1990, p. 42). Finally, of course, the term is used as a rhetorically acceptable and attractive way of referring to people in their many and varied groups, divisions and collectivities. It is as though other sociological categories have a rather nasty flavour. Community, by contrast, does all the ideological work of expressing cosy inclusivity, while also carrying the unspoken connotations of exclusivity that give subtle articulation to our fantasies of rejection and violence.

Local government and community

References to both the sociological existence and the value of community are evident in recent work on local government. For example, Desmond King argues, in defence of constitutional entrenchment for local government in the UK, that local governments are, at least in part, manifestations of local communities. The territorial division of power has a communal, as well as a purely geographic, basis. Political boundaries should take account of communities (King, 1993, p. 217). A very significant aspect of the recent changes in local government is the shift from an idea of local government as representing a local community and tradition, to an idea of local government as a service provider within a given area. The current crisis of local democracy can, in large part, be traced to this shift (Cooke, 1990, p. 41).

By contrast, John Stewart is at pains to avoid the dubious presumption that there are genuine and strong communities that will generate local autonomous governance and local democracy. That is, he rejects one aspect of communitarian theory – that which insists that the bases of legitimacy for the arrangement and exercise of power are the values, traditions and established practices of the community at issue. He nevertheless argues that local government should take on a new role as community government – meaning that local authorities' primary role would be a concern for the problems and issues faced by local communities. This picture is compatible with the existence of differing interests and values, and even conflicts, within and between communities (Stewart, 1989). We can note that it is also compatible with the fragmented and complex nature of individuals' social identities, and their multiple memberships of plural and even incompatible groups and collectivities, discussed in the previous section.

But as my sceptical argument so far will suggest, I believe that it is not helpful to base a normative theory of local government or local democracy on community, whether as an ideal or as a sociological analysis. I am more sympathetic to John Gyford's suggestion that a new normative function for local government might be as the 'orchestrator' of a decentred public sphere (Gyford, 1991a, p. 30). I shall discuss this conception in more detail in what follows.

Beyond community

At this point I want to make clear that I believe there to be a good deal that is helpful in the 'communitarian' perspective. For example, it does seem to follow from the powerful arguments that the individual's social identity is based in her or his relations that cooperation, reciprocity and trust are important values; ones which, furthermore, should be at the centre of social theory. It also seems to follow that the public or collective provision of a wide range of goods is desirable – not only the goods about which economists have long been agreed, such as clean air, or policing, but other worthy goods such as leisure resources and other sites for civil life, childcare and educational facilities, health care and transport. The public provision of such goods is tied up intimately with the promotion and practice of civic values; and civic values must necessarily be practised and promoted if we are to have enjoyable and safe lives.

Another way of putting this is to say, as have many others, that neither market relations nor economic relations more generally are exhaustive of social relations. But as I have argued, it is unhelpful to slip into an alternative position, as communitarianism does, suggesting that cultural relations are primary and key – that all kinds of social relations are, or should be, analysed as community relations based on shared values, traditions, non-contractual commitment and so on. In this connection, the idea of the 'political community' lacks analytic clarity. In this conception, the relationships between state and citizens or subjects, and citizens and subjects with each other, are conceived as the sharing of political values or political culture, and the sharing of particular interests (a crucial one of which would be the interest in the stability and success of the political order in question). Here once again, it looks as though the work 'community' does in this formulation is overwhelmingly rhetorical – for this conceptualisation adds nothing to, and indeed detracts from, the analytically precise but neglected term 'polity'.

Political membership is different in relevant respects from community membership – we must keep the specificity of political relations firmly in our sights. A polity consists of individuals tied by the relationship of authority through which they participate (or not, depending on the kind of polity in question) in the contest for the power to govern and influence government. If we do not maintain the analytic distinction between political relations and institutions, and economic, cultural, kinship and political ones, how are we adequately to explore the relations between them? This enquiry is important if we are successfully to revitalise democratic political life in which the contest for the power to govern is open, and in which government is accountable to the people; and if we are to recognise the 'ethical pull of the political' over other procedures –

for example, the use of military or economic power – for conflict resolution, distribution of goods, and allocation of power and authority (Philp, 1994).

The primary focus for political theorists and scientists must be political relations, including civil relations. Important civil relations at issue for those considering local government and democracy might well be the civil relations between social groups including communities, kinship groups and associations. Equally important will be civil relations between strangers in the public sphere – meaning those spaces that are occupied by economic, voluntary and government organisations (Roche, 1987, pp. 375–7). That is, communities cannot be taken to be the primary constitutive elements of the polity. It may be that local and national governments find themselves treating with communities from time to time: actually existing communities may seek to be heard, or seek to be represented in political institutions, or even to seek political power. But so might a range of political parties, social and political movements, pressure groups, voluntary associations, economic organisations, and neighbourhood or other local associations. Local and national government cannot take it to be definitive of their role that they look out for the interests of communities.

Arguments for locality

However, the existence of local interests and local people's identification with, and commitment to, their area can be seen as the focus for local government and the basis for its legitimacy. But neither of these straightforwardly delivers a robust normative theory of local government. First, because the same problems arise with the notion of a local interest as arise with the 'public interest' – namely that it is likely to be indeterminate, internally inconsistent, or internally conflict-ridden. Second, the strength and salience of people's identification with their area varies across the life cycle, between birth cohorts and between social classes. There will also be disagreement between people who live closely together about the boundaries of the area they 'identify with'. In any case, these boundaries will not necessarily coincide with political boundaries (Rallings *et al.*, 1994, pp. 13–16; Parry *et al.*, 1992, pp. 336–44; Bulmer, 1986, p. 20).

So we can no more rely on the givenness of localities and the existence of local interests than we can on the presence of local communities which generate their own values, social goods and forms of governance. We need, therefore, to develop a distinctive argument for locality as a value, and for local democratic government. That is, we need to develop arguments in favour of building and promoting local people's identification with their area, and for the significance of specifically local government in this process.

We can begin with the empirical fact that in the course of the life cycle, as well as due to the exigencies of class and welfare, many individuals are immobile and many are, frankly, stuck. Children in their educational years, young people prior to full adulthood, adults with caring responsibilities, and older people, are situated in a particular place, without the practical option of exit, and their well-being and welfare is crucially bound up with the health of their area. In particular, their immobility must not be in any way detrimental to their ability to live full and worthwhile lives. This means that relatively circumscribed geographical areas must have a full range of facilities and opportunities for work, leisure, and civic participation.

This immobility is an empirical fact, notwithstanding the high rates of geographic and social mobility which are undoubtedly a feature of modern societies. It is clear that many individuals' allegiances and relationships will transcend locality. We can be members of national and international organisations with headquarters and co-members distant from where we live and work. We may identify with an ethnic or cultural diaspora, and feel solidarities that are global. We may consume goods by post, bought via our TV sets; and we may conduct our friendships and work relationships by e-mail. But even the most thoroughly post-modern individuals must also spend a great deal of time on the ground – the places where we live, work and visit. And this ground must be civil – that is to say, safe, pleasant, and such as to promote citizenly relations between persons.

It is also relevant that in 'new forms of politics', many active groups and campaigns do not focus primarily on the nation-state. The diffuseness of social and political movements, a reluctance to take the route of pressure on national governments via the established channels for legislative reform, and an emphasis instead on practical changes in civil society and in personal life, as well as pressure on government by disruption, is now a familiar feature of

Western politics (Kaplan, 1992; Melucci, 1989; Dalton, 1988; Offe, 1985). The exploitation of local authority programmes and grants by groups who had set their sights elsewhere than national legislation – campaigns and projects by black people, feminists, gay people – in the 1970s and 1980s is well documented. So too are the problems that some of these projects and local authorities ran into, and in some cases their eventual defeat by state and ideological power (Lovenduski and Randall, 1993; Gyford, 1991; Stoker, 1991; Boddy and Fudge, 1984). These relatively fluid forms of political association are still significant, and still hold out considerable hope for the revitalisation of public and political life, the democratisation of civil society and state–society relations. The provision of public goods at the local level is likely to be a concrete aim for such movements and campaigns.

This, then, is the sociological context for consideration of a normative argument for locality as a value. At the heart of this argument is the principle that one key way in which individuals should enact their responsibilities for others is by way of care for the environment. In this connection individuals have particular relationships with particular areas by virtue of their habitual location there – for example, workplaces, residential neighbourhoods, leisure places and the routes between these. People are not relieved from the obligation to care for other locations too – places they may visit or pass through; but *living* in a particular place generates a special relationship between an individual and that place.

This value, the value of commitment to being where one happens to be, at a given moment, has been neglected and denigrated in a great deal of modern Western thought. Particularly notable are libertarian varieties of liberalism, existentialism, and the kind of romanticism that emphasises 'transcendence'. In rather different ways these traditions of thought emphasise the individual's need to consider his/her inner self rather than the social context, to dwell on his/her ability to rise above the present context, to be detached from ties, and to transcend the present moment. The value of care for place is a significant corrective to the tendency to social atomism that is connected with this philosophy.

Feminist critics have associated these traditions and themes with 'masculinity', as have many of the protagonists of these positions (Lloyd, 1984; Elshtain, 1981). By contrast, feminist theorists have made positive attempts to expound and develop an alternative philosophy and ethics of care, with an emphasis on the value of commitment and attention to the present context (Noddings, 1984; Ruddick, 1984). The tendency to associate women in particular with rootedness, attention to others, and commitment to the here and now has in turn inspired a critical reaction (Benhabib, 1992; Young, 1990). Care and commitment, it is argued, are crucial to human society, and should not be the particular responsibility of any one section of the population.

Youth and community workers, and local government officers and elected representatives have, of course, long had the value of care for place at the centre of their practical efforts. From the youth and community work point of view, this is a response to the relative immobility of young people, and the need to encourage and foster a sense of efficacy and empowerment of the individual vis a vis those institutions and sources of power which determine her environment (British Youth Council, 1986, p. 4).[6] It also ties people into reciprocal, reponsible relationships (Paley *et al.*, 1986, pp. 30, 37). Working on local projects with fellow citizens and in association with other social groups not only encourages an appreciation of civil relations, but also contributes to the construction of cared for social and public spaces. Of course, lasting and effective improvements to public spaces are not possible without governmental administration and resources; and the local youth club cannot work miracles in areas where social relations and institutions are damaged, or where flawed architecture and damaged infrastructure deplete the quality of life. Groups which come together to try to act in and for their locality need advice, resources and project management. It is difficult to see that there could be a more efficient provider of these goods and services than local government.

The facts of social immobility and the value of commitment to place, together conduce to a number of institutional recommendations. First, an emphasis on the use of local knowledge in the design of special projects – in education, training, community and youth work, social services, leisure provision, planning, employment policy and so on. As others have pointed out, although the wider national and global contexts mean that many decisions cannot be made meaningfully at the local level, and although considerations of social justice and fairness in the relationships between groups of people and localities may make pressure against local decision-making, consultation or autonomy, there are still many issues that are genuinely local (Phillips, 1994). A second institutional prerequisite for the commitment of local people to their locality is a mechanism for collective choice (as opposed to individual 'market' choice or choices made by professionals, managers or bureaucrats) in respect of public and some worthy goods.

Third, the value of civil relations between strangers, and the fostering of healthy public space, means that the local administration of public and quasi-public spaces would have to be much more vigorous than is currently the case. Further, inequalities in provision (relatively clean town centres and tourist sites, and litter-strewn residential estates and streeets) would have to be corrected. This would not just be a matter of having high standards of cleansing and maintenance, but a constant process of checking on the match between space and use, the competing demands of different kinds of users, the adjudication of conflicts and so on. The maintenance specifically of civil relations means that provision of police and security guards would have to be bolstered and supplemented, if not replaced, by civic positions such as caretakers, wardens, and the equivalent of park keepers.

I am aware that a number of objections might be levelled at this argument and the institutional recommendations I have sketched. They can invoke an unattractive picture of wardens dispensing summary justice to children; the exclusion or harassment of homeless people or ethnic minorities or young men. There is a danger that proprietariness about spaces can militate against civic values – for example, housing developments can become inward looking and physically cut off. Small enclaves with hostile or distrustful attitudes to the outside will not enhance the quality of civic life; the value of locality can threaten to usher in the same problems of exclusion and coercion that we met in connection with the value of community.

But we are better off, theoretically speaking, with locality than we are with community – for there is no suggestion that a single set of values, norms, preferred social identities or tastes is privileged. Within the framework of social justice, the needs of existing users (residents, workers, visitors) in a place would all have to be considered if the value of democracy were to be realised. This means that questions of what counts as, say, social disorder, would always have to be on the agenda for critical debate and discussion. There could be no question of keeping particular kinds of people out of a public space. It is precisely the reclamation of public spaces (including quasi-public ones such as shopping centres) for the public that is important if civic life is to be possible.

Second, it might be objected that individual well-being would be better served by investment in the means of geographical mobility. However, given that even the most mobile people have an interest in the physical, and especially the built, environment offering the possibility of civil relations, the question is begged of *how* it is to be cared for. Local services – cleaning and maintenance – might be delivered by non-local, even international, firms. However, both the direction of services and the regulation of public spaces rely on local knowledge and demands, and crucially therefore on local organisation.

Lastly, it might be objected that the subjective and indeterminate nature of 'localities' makes them an unlikely basis for the peculiar ethical relationship I have been sketching. But it is precisely the overlapping and indeterminate nature of localities, the importance of routes and communications between them – their contingency – that is a crucial ingredient of a normative theory of local democracy and civic life, and more particularly a theory of the political and social processes by which we might construct localities that will support civic values. It is quite clear that just as the existence of a 'community' or many social collectivities such as 'nation', is partly a matter of the imagination of its members, so a 'locality' is not a naturally-existing entity (Anderson, 1991). This means that the argument for the value of locality is not an argument for rooting procedures and institutions in a given set of social relations. Rather, if local government addresses itself to the maintenance of localities, a process of the making and unmaking of identities and relationships will occur.

Localities are contingent on a number of factors. First, and most obviously geographical or topological features are worked on by political and economic decisions: to draw boundaries in a particular way, and to site a city at a particular point, to build suburbs in particular patterns and directions, for example. That is, the exact shape of a locality will be contingent. Second, individuals will differ one from another as to their understanding of the shape and boundaries of the locality. These differences will be due to people's peculiar material circumstances – for example, their shopping habits, their routes to and from work, their habits of visiting friends or attending leisure facilities in one direction rather than another. That is, locality will be subjective. [7]

Locality is also contingent in another important way. How people relate to each other depends on what resources are available and where those resources are coming from. For example, people living on a particular estate will set up a tenants' association not only when they identify themselves as co-residents with interests and capacities in common, but when they perceive opportunities to obtain the necessary resources. As another example, the organisation of rape crisis lines was conditioned in many cases by the perception that particular local authorities could be persuaded or shamed into giving grants; resource centres for groups such as ethnic minorities, gay people or neighbourhoods arose out of the strategic perception that resource centres were the kind of thing that money could be raised for. In this connection, the kind of social relationships that proceed from, for example, the projects and activities of, say, a housing association, is a supremely political matter.

What this means, of course, is that the shapes and aims of local organisations will be conditioned by local and national government priorities and programmes. Availability of funding from central agencies and departments will undoubtedly call forth organisation in response; organisations that might deliver services into localities but equally might not be rooted there. However, if the arguments in this chapter are persuasive we have grounds for emphasising the potential for groups who are located in a particular area and involved in production, distribution and consumption in that area to foster the kinds of practices, relationships and values that are necessary for civil life. Local government will have the crucially important task of ensuring that civil relations between these groups are maintained. In this case, the provision of local funding, and the calling forth of local initiatives, must be the preferred way forward.

Notes

1. I am grateful to Mark Philp for a very helpful discussion about the argument in this chapter.
2. Avineri and de-Shalit have collected together the main contributions to the 'liberal–communitarian debate'. For discussion of 'communitarian-

     ism' in mainstream political debates, see the *Guardian* tabloid section, 8 October 1994, *Sunday Times*, 9 October 1994.

3. It is important to note that John Rawls, who is generally taken to be the main liberal individualist target of the communitarian critique, fully accepts this latter point, and in his most recent work it has a central place (Rawls, 1993).

4. As Seyla Benhabib says: 'Communities tend to constitute themselves by excluding difference, but . . . the task of a philosophical politics is to conceptualise new forms of association which let the different appear in their midst' (Benhabib, 1994, p. 23).

5. For example, in discussions and presentations at the St John's College, Oxford seminars on Law and Citizenship April–July 1994, participants from a variety of professional backgrounds referred unproblematically to 'the community' while acknowledging that one of the issues that had generated the seminars themselves was the perception that communities had been destroyed (and therefore, strictly speaking, do not exist to be referred to using the definite article in this way). Similarly, at the ESRC conference 'Rethinking Local Democracy' held at St John's College, Oxford, September 1994, for which the first version of this chapter was prepared, participants discussed the widespread attachment to the vocabulary of 'community' that is evident in local government officers' reasoning, and found it difficult to think of a suitable substitute term where they themselves were inclined to talk about 'the community'. Why is it so difficult to speak of 'constituencies', 'interest groups', 'occupational groups', 'the population of particular neighbourhoods', 'social networks' and the like? It is not as if sociology has not provided a rich and subtle descriptive vocabulary for referring with some precision to the variety of social collectivities with which contemporary societies are furnished.

6. However, 'changing society at a local level . . . by lobbying a local council or meeting a social need in their area' is only one of a range of focuses for young people's attention. The British Youth Council (1986) also emphasises working against racism, building international bridges (especially within the European Community (EC) and with people in Eastern Europe, and solidarity with the third world (that is, allegiances and solidarities that transcend the local context). Working with and for girls is also emphasised (note that this will rarely be affirming of traditional communities); as is political participation at the national level – for example, taking issues to Parliament.

7. A third factor is less significant for the main thread of this chapter, but important for social scientists – localities are likely to be 'constructed' (as objects of research) by researchers. When they find there is disagreement and difference in their subjects' understandings of the shape of a locality researchers will nevertheless make their own decisions about what and whom to include in and exclude from a 'locality study'.

6 Feminism and the Attractions of the Local

Anne Phillips

Is there a feminist case for local democracy? Does the way that power is distributed between central and local government have any consequences for sexual equality? Are women more likely to participate as equals when political power is dispersed through autonomous local institutions? Are such institutions significantly more open to women's issues or a women's agenda? Can one say, with Patricia Hollis, that 'the most effective way of strengthening women's participation in politics may be to devolve power to where women are, that is to local government, rather than to seek to bring women to where power currently resides, at Westminster' (Hollis, 1987, p. 484)? Does 'the personal is political' mean that politics should be brought closer to home? Do women have particular reasons to favour local democracy, or the further decentralisation of political power?

My starting point for considering these questions is a paradox. As Hollis's comment indicates, women are often assumed to have a special affinity with local government or local democracy. This suggests a relationship between decentralization and sexual equality, because if women are more likely to engage in politics at the local level, or more likely to concern themselves with the kinds of decision that are made in the locality, then shifting the balance between central and local government could well help shift the balance between men and women. But as Elizabeth Fraser's contribution to this volume (Chapter 5) demonstrates, feminists have also been prominent in criticising the coercive implications of 'community', and the way that invocations of a local community can mask major divisions between women and men. This suggests a far more troubled experience of the local, and it points, if anything, towards larger units for political action and political change. On the face of it, at least, feminism can look in either direction: towards strong support for local-level institutions and more radically decentralised

111

power; or away from the locality towards the regional or national level.

The paradox is not unique to local democracy, for even when special affinities do exist, we cannot assume that feminists will want to sustain them. Women are usually thought to have a special affinity with the family, but feminists have taken the lead in criticising family relationships. Women are usually assumed to have special responsibilities for children, but feminists have been the first to argue that these responsibilities should be shared equally between women and men. Feminist thinking on local democracy is, to some extent, a subset of more general issues that arise whenever there is a sexual division of labour, because where history has decreed a gendered distribution of roles and responsibilities, this usually provokes debate between those who seek to raise the value of the (typically subordinate) 'women's sphere', and those who want to challenge this very division of labour.[1] If local government or local democracy is indeed more accessible to women's issues or women's participation, this might well be an additional basis for arguing its importance. But the greater accessibility could also be taken as evidence of a homeliness many feminists would prefer to avoid. A 1975 Conservative Party handbook took pains to establish women's special relationship with local government: 'Women are extremely well-equipped for local government. They have a vested interest in, and immediate knowledge of, the schools, services, housing, care of children, and the environment, which are the responsibilities of the local government' (cited in Hollis, 1987, p. 479). It is easy enough to turn this around, and see it as confirming women in a subordinate, separate sphere. The greater attractions of the local would then be something for women to resist.

Women and local democracy

The supposed affinity between women and local democracy is relatively easy to establish – though also, perhaps, easy to exaggerate. Women have a considerably longer history of involvement in local politics and local government than they do in national politics: as much as anything, because women were allowed to serve on school boards or as poor law commissioners long before they were allowed near national institutions, and because women ratepayers got the right to vote in municipal elections fifty years before any of them was allowed to vote or stand in parliamentary elections. Opponents of women's suffrage (including, to her later embarrassment, Beatrice Webb) often regarded local government as an eminently suitable field for female activity; and the arch-anti-suffragist Mrs Humphry Ward went so far as to set up a Local Government Advancement Committee in order to deflect suffrage activity on to a more appropriately local terrain (Hollis, 1987, p. 471). The number of women elected to local office had already reached 1800 by the outbreak of the First World War, and by the 1930s, the proportion was settling down to a steady 12–15 per cent of the total. Though women over thirty won the right to vote and stand in national elections in 1918 (a privilege not extended to younger women till full enfranchisement occurred in 1928), women continued to find local government a more accessible avenue: for obvious reasons, including the ostensibly part-time work of being a councillor, and the greater difficulties women encounter in persuading their entire family to move home because of their job. The proportion of women serving as local councillors has consistently exceeded the proportion elected as MPs, and even with the recent improvements in the number of women elected to Parliament, the proportion serving on councils is roughly double the number in national office. The scale of this advantage should not be overstated. Even now four out of five councillors are male, and the obstacles that keep women out of political élites still retain their considerable force. But local government *has* proved itself significantly more open to women than has national government, and this provides one part of a feminist case for local democracy.

The association between women and local democracy is further cemented by the division of labour between local and central government, because the functions delegated to the locality have come to overlap quite remarkably with traditional areas of female concern. The historical connection between women and public housing is now largely forgotten,[2] but outside this major area of local government responsibility, local councils have come to simulate much of what was previously provided (if at all) by women inside the home. A substantial proportion of local government activity relates in some way to the needs of children: education, most obviously, but also provision for children in need; regulation of fostering and adoption; provision of libraries, playgrounds and swimming pools; and all those other leisure activities that are so important to parents and children. Local government has also assumed responsibility for many of the routine social services for the sick or the elderly: home helps, for example, and meals on wheels, both of these being activities that simulate what might previously have been provided by women in the extended family. Studies of male and female politicians often reveal a distinctly gendered distribution of political interests, with women expressing their concerns about education, welfare or the environment, and men staking their claim to the economy, industry, energy and foreign affairs.[3] As the comment from the Conservative Party handbook reminds us (see Hollis, 1987, p. 479), the current division of responsibilities between local and central government fits this rather neatly. Women's relatively high profile in local government hardly needs to have any further explanation; what is odd is that men still remain so dominant.

One implication from this second point of affinity is that current moves towards user control of services could have particularly far-reaching consequences for women. Women figure prominently in the statistics for council employees, but they also do much of the work in negotiating the services provided by councils. They are usually the ones delivering and collecting children from school. Outside Sunday morning sessions (when fathers seem to come into their own), they are usually the ones taking children to parks, libraries or swimming pools. They are also likely to be the ones raising routine complaints or queries over the management of council housing estates. In a period when local councils have either chosen, or been required, to draw the users of local services into more direct management of their delivery, women's position as major users might well be turned to their advantage. Current indications, it should be said, are not too encouraging. The local management of schools, for example, increases the importance of locally-elected school governors, but women are still far more visible in the fund-raising activities of parent–teacher associations than as chairs of school governing boards. The kind of decentralisation that is implied in user-management will not of itself increase women's power; whether it does or not may depend on the status of a third affinity that is often claimed between women and the locality.

The evidence of women's greater involvement in local government is frequently reinforced by an additional correlation between women and community action, which suggests that local politics is more open to women as *activists* as well as to women as elected representatives. Women are said to have a high profile in campaigning organisations that deal in more immediate neighbourhood concerns: as members of tenants' associations, for example; as the mainstay of groups campaigning for better childcare provision; as key activists in campaigns for road safety and against new traffic schemes. But outside the campaigns for nurseries, women's refuges or rape crisis centres (many of which are co-ordinated at national level), the evidence for this tends to be impressionistic (see Randall, 1987, pp. 58–60), and it rarely establishes a higher profile for women than men. Women are marginally more likely than men to be involved in the non-party, voluntary sector (Rallings *et al.*, 1994, pp. 29–31), but on the evidence collected by the British Political Participation Study, men still slightly out-participate women in most areas of local activity (Parry *et al.*, 1992, pp. 143–53). The main exception, interestingly, is campaigning for political parties, where women members are almost as active as the men. When people talk of women's higher profile in local politics or community action, the implied contrast is with their low profile in national or regional politics; it is not that women are more likely than men to participate in local politics, but that when women *are* involved in politics, it is more likely to be at local rather than national level. This is true, on the whole, of everyone, so its implications cannot be taken too far.

In the course of the 1980s, the affinities between women and the locality entered more directly into local council practice, with the creation of women's committees in a significant number of Labour councils (Goss, 1984; Edwards, 1988a; Coote and Patullo, 1990). That this occurred at local rather than national level was partly historical accident: in Australia, by contrast, much of the innovative work around gender took place in the framework of federal government (Watson, 1989); and the decisive factor determining where such initiatives develop may be less the level of government and more the preoccupations of the party in power. As Goss (1984) has noted, the development of women's committees reflected the more general progress of the women's liberation movement as well as national-level struggles within the Labour movement to achieve greater prominence for feminist concerns; at a time when central government seemed particularly impervious to these, local government offered a more promising arena for developing what were not exclusively local concerns.

But those involved did claim a particular connection between feminist goals of sexual equality and political activity at the local level, and many of them drew their inspiration from the decentralised democracy which had characterised the women's movement. Most of the committees made efforts to co-opt community representatives who could convey locally identified needs and concerns; in addition, many experimented with open meetings through which local women could be drawn into the policy-making process. Underlying much of this activity was a critique of existing conventions of representation, and a belief that major areas of importance were being sidelined in the standard oppositions between political parties. The agenda was being set in ways that excluded a whole complex of experiences and priorities, and empowering local women to make their wishes better known was seen as a crucial way of combating this. Much attention was then given to new ways of articulating what would be different kinds of policies and demands, and the more 'face-to-face' participation of decentralised democracy became an important element in the practice of the women's committees.

The connection this implies between feminist goals of sexual equality and increasing the opportunities for political engagement at local level is more important, in my view, than the relatively high profile of women in local government, or the close relationship between women and local government concerns. Local government may be more open to women only because it is less powerful; if so, the relative openness could easily dissipate if local councils had their powers enhanced. In their more cynical moments, Scandinavian feminists used to argue that the rapid feminisation of their national assemblies had coincided with a transfer of the power elsewhere: that the women had been let into Parliament only when Parliament no longer ran the show. By the same token, one might argue that the relative (if still mild) feminisation of local government has coincided with its most marked period of impotence and decline, and that if the power of local councils were later restored (or even increased), this might well remove women's relative advantage.

Feminism and the politics of change

A more theoretically significant connection lies in the presumed association between feminism and popular involvement, and this in turn is grounded in analysis of the kind of changes feminism has to bring about. Feminist politics has always been about transformation: about articulating previously unheard voices, exposing previously unchallenged bias, recreating the political agenda. It is always, in the process, a matter of bringing something new into existence, for the policies most appropriate to sexual equality have to be formulated and developed against a background which has denied the pertinence of any such concern. It is for this reason, more than any other, that feminists have developed such a strong commitment to participatory democracy – and by extension of this, to more decentralised units for political control. The 'interests of women' are not transparent: they do not lie around in the rubble of political discourse to be picked up by discerning activists and built into their programme for political change (Sapiro, 1981; Jonasdottir, 1988; Pringle and Watson, 1992). A great deal of hard work is required to disentangle what is natural from what is social, or what is possible from what we have been told is the norm, and this work always takes place under pressures that would otherwise re-impose the more established conventions. The enfranchisement of women was a crucial starting point in this, but giving women the vote was never enough to feminise the political agenda. When what is at issue is the creation of something new, there has to be a process of sustained discussion and debate.

We might think, in this context, of the seemingly endless explorations that feminists have embarked on to identify the difference gender should make to various areas of policy and theory. After a century and a half of women's self-organisation – and a more modest couple of decades in which women have been interrogating the bias of academic disciplines – feminist theory still gives the impression of trying to work out what difference gender makes. This can be a source of considerable irritation (don't these people know what they want by now?), but the open-endedness is intrinsic to the feminist project. Outside the most overt examples of inequality and subordination, feminism is by definition a matter of exploration: hence the otherwise odd phenomenon of women 'discovering' that they have been oppressed. Women's needs, interests or perspectives do not come to us in ready-made form, for the ready-made versions are too deeply embedded in existing hierarchies of power. Preferences, interests and goals are inevitably shaped by the circumstances out of which they arise, and the human propensity to make sense of the most nonsensical conditions often leads people to adjust their expectations downwards in order to conform with what is currently on offer (Sunstein, 1991). The representation of women's needs or interests is then particularly unsuited to the kind of politics which takes our preferences as given. It is particularly unsuited to that narrowing of participation which reduces democracy to the casting of the occasional vote.

If the field of politics were already clearly demarcated, with all needs and interests already in play, we might not so much need that discussion-based politics that has been associated with local or neighbourhood democracy. But when the possibilities have been constrained or excised by a dominant consensus which puts them almost beyond articulation, this puts a high premium on developments that increase opportunities for participation. The point here is not to privilege 'direct' over 'representative' democracy: representation is itself a form of political participation, and the increased opportunities for popular involvement might well come through developing the different contexts in which we elect representatives, as suggested in David Beetham's contribution to this volume (Chapter 2). Exponents of direct democracy often regard decision-making through open meeting as superior to the more distanced mechanisms by which we elect others to represent our views, but the claims made on behalf of the open meeting stand or fall by whether those who attend and participate are themselves 'representative' of the constituency as a whole. Since this is notoriously far from the case (this was a perennial source of anxiety over the open meetings held by women's committees), we cannot fall back on direct democracy as the ideal to which all politics should aim. But neither can we rest content with what Beetham calls the 'crudeness of the electoral mechanism', for the very crudeness delimits the full range of options, and reproduces the standard exclusions.

Feminist politics – by extension, the politics of any group that has been defined out of a dominant consensus – provides us with two key principles that should underpin further moves towards democratisation. One is that those who have experienced inequality, marginality, or exclusion are likely to be the best judges of what now needs to be done: as David Donnison puts this in a more general argument for local action, 'the people who experience the hardship and difficulties . . . are expert about them in ways which no-one else can be' (1994, p. 14). The other principle is that excluded groups have to be enabled not only to articulate, but also to expand and refine their areas of priority and concern. To put this second point in terms that have become particularly influential in American political theory (for example, Cohen, 1989; Mansbridge, 1992; Young, 1993), feminist politics implies more of that transformative politics of deliberation which enables us to reassess our initial preferences and get beyond what we might have registered in an anonymous vote. The problem with the vote is not just that it happens too infrequently, or that it fails to capture all the nuances of political choice; the vote also has a built-in bias towards whatever is currently on offer. Failing that more engaged interaction which allows us to explore as-yet-unvoiced possibilities, it is all too likely to reproduce some version of the existing political agenda.

The association between feminism and local democracy is best understood in this light. The presumed affinity is not just a reflection of local government's greater accessibility to women, or the way its areas of policy responsibility have overlapped with traditional areas of female concern. More fundamental than either of these is that feminism looks to a more involved and participatory democracy as a way of transforming the political agenda, and sees the articulation and refinement of previously unspoken needs as a crucial part of this process. The locality has always figured largely in this: partly for obvious and practical reasons (how are women to speak in politics unless that politics is brought closer to home?); and partly because the very immediacy of locally-based concerns has been seen as an important counter-weight to the abstractions of political life. Women's relative exclusion from political life is not just a matter of numbers: too few women on the council or too few women in the House of Commons. Almost equally powerful are those definitions of the political which reduce so-called 'women's issues' to a footnote or separate appendix. Rewriting that agenda is never an exclusively local prerogative. But when feminists ask us to consider what society would look like if we observed it from the perspective of mothering rather than from that of 'economic man' (Held, 1990), or what our scale of priorities would become if we put the needs of children at the centre of the picture, part of what they are doing is inserting the real live person into an over-formalised political agenda. The new perspectives that might emerge from this are not particularly local in their scope, but the famous insistence on 'the personal as political' has usually been taken as implying a preference for political action at a more local level. The attachment to participation is then linked typically to strategies of decentralisation – a notion that the politics must be brought closer to home.

This is the point, however, at which some feminists have sounded a warning note over the potentially stifling nature of local communities, and the way these can reinforce relationships of subordination. The equation between participation and decentralisation encourages a belief that democracy is best fostered in small units. But small communities are not necessarily the most democratic, nor are they necessarily the most tolerant of people who want to challenge their current conditions. Through centuries of both literature and life, dissident individuals have felt themselves hemmed in by small, homogeneous communities – or by small communities which imagined themselves more homogeneous than they really were – and the anonymity of the big city has offered the classic escape route to those at odds with dominant conventions. Here they can participate in what Marilyn Friedman (1990) calls 'chosen' rather than 'found' communities: instead of being bound to an involuntary community of place, people can create or join new communities based on shared preferences, goals or ideals.

As Friedman goes on to argue, this option is particularly compelling for those who query existing social or sexual arrangements, for these people are often constituted as 'deviants and resisters' by their communities of origin (Friedman, 1990, p. 158). Radical politics sometimes takes the form of defending existing community traditions against forces that threaten their destruction (much of nineteenth-century radicalism could be said to follow this pattern), but feminism has no such tradition of sexual equality that it can set itself to defend. Feminism is necessarily critical. It seeks to reverse current patterns of sexual subordination, and in doing so, it challenges what may be deeply held preferences and opinions on the relationship between women and men. The radicalism is always in potential conflict with the communities from which it has emerged, and feminists must then seek or create alternative communities that can provide them the necessary support.

To put this in more general terms, a movement which aims at social equity or justice – against a background of unjust conditions – often has to reach outside existing localities to forge appropriate alliances and develop appropriate conditions. This perception is reflected in recent feminist writing that celebrates the cosmopolitanism of the city as a potential haven for diversity and difference, and contrasts this with closer confines of suburban or rural life. This has become an important strand in feminist theorising, and it crystalises a number of reservations about the coercive nature of 'local communities'. In Iris Young's *Justice and the Politics of Difference* (1990), for example, the argument becomes the basis for an explicit critique of decentralisation, which has, she believes, been dangerously over-emphasised by traditions of radical democracy. Democratisation, Young argues, 'does not entail decentralization into small units of autonomous local control. Governmental authority should become more empowering but also more encompassing than municipal government is now' (Young, 1990, p. 251). Smaller is not always better; indeed, when issues of social justice are involved, increasing the power and autonomy of the local community will often do more harm than good.

Consider here the experience of those 'black urban regimes' that have developed in many of America's largest cities. The boundaries of these cities typically map on to areas of both relative and absolute deprivation, with much of the personal wealth of the city dwellers lying outside, in the affluent (and predominantly white) suburbs. The black American population of the cities has increased, while the white population has declined: partly through the more general phenomenon in which the middle-classes move out of older city centres; more specifically and depressingly, because property values fall when there is increased black migration, and white city dwellers then flee to the ghettoised safety of the suburbs. Black administrations have been elected to power at a moment when the welfare pressures on the city are going up and the tax receipts from its inhabitants going down: as Adolf Reed puts it, 'the dynamics that make possible the empowerment of black regimes are the same as those that produce the deepening marginalization and dispossession of a substantial segment of the urban black population' (Reed, 1988, p. 148). One way out of this would be for city governments to expand their boundaries to incorporate the richer suburbs. This would be contested vigorously, however, not only by middle-class residents in the suburbs, but also by the existing or aspirant black American politicians, who are 'understandably loath to annex pockets of potentially antagonistic white voters' (Reed, 1988, p. 141), and would see this as threatening their power base. In such a context, even city government is not on a large enough scale to achieve a just distribution of life chances and resources; the problems are too great for any strictly local solution.

Such examples form the background against which Iris Young argues the limits of local autonomy. Social justice is not always well served by strategies that decentralise power to autonomous local communities; on the contrary, Young (1990, pp. 240–55) suggests that social justice can best be realised through the creation of large regional governments, which might have a city or cluster of cities as their nucleus but would also span the less densely populated suburban and rural areas. The smaller the unit, the stronger the tendencies towards an exclusionary consensus; the larger and more diverse the unit, the more chances for accommodating diversity and difference. As applied to women, the argument then reinforces the points raised by Marilyn Friedman. Those whose politics involves a critical challenge to existing traditions or existing distributions of resources may be better served by the larger than the smaller community.

Escaping localism

So how are we to disentangle these competing approaches to feminism and local democracy? One the one hand there is a strong association between feminism and more extensive political participation – an association premised on the role of discussion, deliberation and debate in the development of new agendas, and the need to draw previously excluded groups of citizens into the process of identifying what is desirable and possible. On the other hand, there is a powerful warning about the dangers of too much decentralisation, dangers grounded in the potential intolerance of smaller, more homogeneous communities, but also in the difficulties of achieving social justice without redistribution across larger areas. There *is* a tension here, but it is made more stark than it has to be by the slippage from participation to maximum decentralisation, a slippage which in turn derives from the false equation of participation with

direct democracy. When participation is identified with the kind of
face-to-face democracy that characterised the early years of the
contemporary women's movement, it implies a degree of decentralisation that would radically disrupt the framework of existing local
government; local government is almost as weak as central government where this kind of participation is concerned, and almost
equally wanting. The units appropriate for face-to-face democracy
are by definition tiny – and they are very likely to fall foul of that
intolerance of difference which often thrives in smaller and more
intimate communities (Phillips, 1991, ch. 4). But if participation and
deliberation can be detached from this excessive localism, the
tensions between the two positions may prove more apparent than
real.

One point of clarification is that this is not really an issue of the
city versus the country. Those of us who have chosen to live in cities
probably have an exaggerated notion of the closed intolerance of
smaller and more rural communities: communities which we may
conceive as expecting a much higher degree of conformity to existing
social norms than could ever be imposed in a city; communities in
which anyone at all peculiar or dissident would find it particularly
hard to live. But Marilyn Friedman's 'chosen' communities are
often more intrusive in their expectations than the accidental communities of place – friends can be more critical than family just
because friends will expect you to agree. The coexistence of multiple
communities or ways of life inside a large city does not necessarily
release people from pressures to conform: indeed, the city that is
large enough to sustain numerous subcultures may require *more*
homogeneity within each community than the inevitably disparate
collection of individuals who are gathered together in a small village
or town. Cities permit a greater degree of segregation by class,
ethnicity, occupation or belief than is conceivable in less heavily
populated areas, and within each of these subgroups, the 'community' can exert considerable coercive power. What is at issue here is
not really the city/country axis, because cities do not necessarily
dissipate the more negative elements of community.

The real significance of the Friedman/Young position is that it
makes us think twice about associating 'true' democracy with small
units. Radical democrats – including many feminists among them –
still have a tendency to equate size with degree of democracy, and to
presume that the more decentralisation, the better the democracy.

Most of these are realist enough to recognise that contemporary politics is not going to be reorganised on the pattern of self-governing localities, and that some settlement will have to be reached with more distanced layers of local and central government. But this settlement is typically viewed as a compromise, a poor approximation to what would ideally be set on a much smaller scale. This privileging of the local has, I believe, only one solid point in its favour: that when decisions are made on a very local basis, a larger proportion and wider range of people will feel they have some competence regarding the issues and will be physically able to contribute. Other than that, there is no particularly compelling reason in favour of maximum decentralisation. Some issues are better dealt with at local level, but other issues are better dealt with at regional or national level; the importance we should attach to political participation and deliberation does not translate automatically into a preference for decentralised local democracy.

I have argued that feminist goals of sexual equality add extra weight to the case for increased popular participation in the process of refining political agendas, and since most of us remain tied to particular localities, this has to say something about the importance of democracy at the local level. The argument does not, however, carry any clear implications about the particular level at which decisions should be made, nor does it say very much about the current distribution of power between central and local government. We might say that more people have access to political discussion and decision-making in local than in national government. This is undoubtedly true, but as much as anything, because of the rapid turnover of local councillors, which in other situations would be regarded as a problem. We might also note the various efforts towards involving local citizens in some consultative if not truly decision-making processes: through the women's committees, but also through a variety of experiments in neighbourhood forums and other ways of increasing local people's input into political decisions. It does seem significant that these initiatives have occurred at local rather than national level – but since most of them coincide with a lengthy period of Conservative Party dominance over central government and a reasonably lengthy period of Labour or Liberal-Democratic dominance over local government, they may tell us more about the priorities of different parties than about what is most suited to different levels of government. The local has not necessarily got a monopoly over avenues for increasing popular involvement, for while there is clearly more ease of access to discussion when this takes place near one's home or one's place of work, this does not mean that decisions must be located in a local neighbourhood. We could equally well look to the kind of roadshow consultation that is more widely employed in Canada or Australia, where roving bands of commissioners hold hearings throughout the country, and often see themselves as explicitly charged with empowering previously silenced voices and formulating new political agendas. This final point seems particularly conducive to what I have outlined as feminist concerns, but it employs the locality to formulate recommendations on national policy, and it does not define itself in terms of locality.

What is at issue is perhaps the ambiguity in the term 'local democracy'. Democracies need to draw more people into the process of defining political priorities and agendas, and since we can only participate where we find ourselves to be, this implies more opportunities within each locality for people to influence the policy process. In this understanding of 'local democracy', feminism adds extra weight to the other arguments that can be marshalled in favour of local democracy, because in exposing the conservative nature of ballot-box democracy – the way this tends to reproduce more traditional priorities and concerns – it confirms the importance of accessibility in deciding how any democracy is arranged. If all the activity takes place at the centre, and all our representatives then disappear out of range, our impact on the political agenda is more inherently limited. We can help decide who our representatives are, but not so much what our representatives do. One of the strengths of local government, even in its current (not so very responsive) guise, is that it operates at a level which makes it more open to the influences around it. It is harder to immunise yourself from others when you are required to share the same space.

Local democracy is also, however, taken to mean that local people should assume more control over affairs within their locality, and while there are all kinds of reasons for supporting this, these may not be so specifically feminist. Most of the changes that would be necessary to establish genuine equality between women and men are on a scale that far exceeds the resources of any local community; and while much of the innovative work in developing programmes for change might take place at local level (this has indeed been the pattern in the recent history of British politics), their implementation then becomes a matter of national concern. To take one obvious and simple example, we may well look to local initiatives to develop better patterns of nursery education or more imaginative play-schemes for children in school holidays. But we wouldn't (at least I wouldn't) want to concede as a corollary of this that other localities could opt out of any nursery provision. If democracy is to be extended, it has to have a local basis; in that sense, if no other, there is a feminist case for local democracy. But to say this is not necessarily to say much about local autonomy, nor about whether the issues discussed in the locality are of exclusively local concern.

The preference for the local potentially elides these different meanings of local democracy. Feminism does, I have argued, have something to say about political participation and, more specifically, about the importance of developing avenues for popular involvement in identifying and refining political agendas. None of this depends on exaggerated expectations of people flocking to neighbourhood meetings: much can be achieved through more imaginative mechanisms of representation and consultation which draw people other than elected councillors and MPs into the formulation of needs and objectives, and enable groups whose concerns have been previously under-represented (hardly even articulated) to contribute their voice to the policy process. Some of this must surely take place at local level – otherwise all the opportunities go to those who live closest to the centres of power – and to this extent it implies an increase in local democracy. It is far easier to see how mechanisms for wider consultation, for example, can develop at local rather than at national level, though this may reflect the accidents of British politics, which have generated an increased interest in such developments among local councillors over the period in which national government seems to have given up on the idea. It also seems reasonable to assume that a plurality of centres of power will open up more opportunities for previously excluded groups: the more sites there are for political contestation, the more scope for transforming the political agenda.

These sites for contestation must also be sites of effective power, because people are far too rational in their allocation of time to devote it to centres of impotence. To that extent, the case for democratic activity at the local level also tells us something about the importance of local autonomy. Feminism is engaged in a transformative project which depends crucially on empowering the previously excluded, and this is not an ambition that could be realised in a framework of centralised power. But the feminist project is also about freeing women from the constraints of their immediate communities, and it involves a degree of redistribution of both work and resources that cannot be delivered at local level. Considerations of social equity set limits to local autonomy, so while the argument for more extensive citizen involvement in the formulation and development of policy provides a strong basis for local democracy, it still leaves us with a relatively open question about the level at which final decisions should be made. It is hard to conceive of a feminisation of politics that did not depend on democracy at the local level, but feminism remains more ambivalent over the precise extent of local autonomy. This is an agnostic, rather than a final position, for there are all kinds of additional considerations that have to be brought to bear on this issue.

Conclusion

I have argued in this chapter that there *is* a feminist case for local democracy, but that this should be distinguished from the case for decentralisation *per se*. Many of the problems that confront women are not available to solution by local action: the sexual segregation of the labour force, for example, the sexual division of carework, female poverty, and violence against women. Each of these certainly offers scope for local initiative – and local councils have, indeed, set up training programmes to encourage more women to enter traditional male trades, and financed refuges for women escaping domestic violence. But sexual inequality is too large a subject to be dealt with in a piecemeal way, and if a strong insistence of local autonomy reduced the chances of national action, women would have good reason to resist the attractions of the local.

Local democracy still remains crucial for feminism because of its role in redefining political agendas. Part of the revolution associated with feminism is the reversal of older priorities which always put 'high politics' above social movements, or make social policy an appendix to economic policy or foreign affairs. This reversal must eventually extend to the national stage, but the preliminary challenges are most likely at local level. Local councils have often played an innovative role in developing new possibilities for public action: the provision of public housing, for example, or early experiments in public ownership of water, electricity or gas. In our own time, local councils have often been at the forefront in developing strategies for a work-force composed of both men and women. While these strategies will have limited purchase if they are not taken up at national level, local councils have accumulated considerable experience of what can be done – and what best to avoid.

Councils have much experience, for example, of implementing equal opportunities in education and work, and their mistakes as well as their successes provide invaluable material for future development. Some have experimented in the introduction of job-sharing, so as to open up a wider range of work opportunities to those whose care responsibilities require them to work part-time. Many have introduced children's play-schemes in school holidays, and play-centres for children outside school hours. All these are important building blocks in a strategy for sexual equality; and all of them have developed at local level.

Some of this can be attributed to 'historical accident': the particular parties that controlled local government, and the policies these parties have pursued. Some of it can be attributed to the high proportion of women among local council employees, and the necessity then laid on employers for addressing the double burden of work and care. But even allowing for these elements, the locality has served as a testing ground for a different political agenda. Councillors have been less able to immunise themselves from new pressures and new proposals; activists have been less hampered by conventional notions of what counts as a 'political' concern. The results are piecemeal and patchy – they hardly qualify as a fully-fledged alternative approach. But local politics has retained a marked capacity for innovation, for redefining priorities and concerns.

The attractions of the local lie primarily in this, for any politics that seeks to subvert existing agendas will get its first breaks at local level. The weight of existing priorities lies less heavily on local politics, for even when local elections turn into a vote of confidence in national governments, the newly-elected councillors are less constrained by their party lines. They are more varied in their origins, and more susceptible to pressure from outside. Local activists are even more unpredictable, and while all this contributes to the reservations about local autonomy, it also confirms the possibility for new ideas. A vibrant local democracy is a crucial component in any politics of innovation, for without its explorations, its experiments (and its failures), we may remain stuck with priorities as traditionally defined.

For this reason, more than any other, there is indeed an affinity between women and local democracy. Feminist politics is about transformation, and not only transformation of existing power structures, but transformation of our very notions of what needs to be changed. The process depends on participation; it depends on opening up possibilities that had been previously foreclosed. The strategies that emerge from this may well require implementation at national level; I am not arguing that decentralisation should be the favoured option, whatever the issues at stake. But the initial openings and explorations are most likely to occur in the locality – and this implies enough power to local democracy to sustain an active politics at local level.

Notes

1. A division often theorised as the tension between equality and difference. For a fuller discussion of this, see the essays in Bock and James (1993)
2. I am thinking here of the role women have played historically in organising and sustaining rent strikes in the private sector, and the way this contributed to the development of municipal housing.
3. See Skjeie (1991) on differences between Norwegian politicians. Transport was the only policy area on which men and women were equally likely to express an interest, though inevitably for different reasons. Men like trains, while women worry about how to get about with babies and buggies.

7 Green Arguments for Local Democracy

Hugh Ward

> Our policy is a policy of active partnership with nature and human beings. It is most successful in self-governing and self-sufficient economic and administrative units, of a humanly surveyable size. . . . . We want a society which is democratic and in which relations between people and with nature are handled with increasing awareness. (Die Gruenen, 1983, p. 7)

The political thought of the Green movement has potentially profound implications for rethinking the role of local government and, indeed, the conception of local political processes. Greens argue that the decentralisation of economic, social and political processes is a key to achieving sustainable relationships with nature and satisfying forms of life for humankind. Ultimately, individuals' lives would be grounded in self-sufficient communities with highly participatory political processes. Communal living and grassroots democracy cannot be achieved overnight, however. As we move towards the ideal, political power and economic processes would gradually be devolved to the local level. This implies that the importance of local government will increase and the importance of central government will decline.

One of the main functions of local government in the nineteenth century was care for the environment in the sense of public health issues. Environmental services were among the earliest provided. Arguably, the perceived importance of the environment to local government grew in the 1980s and 1990s, partly as a result of the rise of the environment on national and global agendas (Stewart and Hams, 1992, p. 5). For instance, the Agenda 21 document which emerged from the United Nations Conference on the Environment and Development at Rio in 1992 identified local authorities as being critical to achieving sustainable development, with popular participation through local government being the key to education, mobilisation and many areas of implementation (Gordon, 1993; Mills, 1994, p. 7; Roddick and Dodds, 1993, pp. 242–3; Stewart and Hams, 1992, pp. 13–14). Despite doubts about the commitment of the national governments to its principles, Agenda 21 has been important in stimulating local authority thinking (Roddick and Dodds, 1993, p. 248; Stewart and Hams, 1992, p. 22; Young, 1993, pp. 26–9). Many within the world of local government itself see the need to develop a holistic, long-term approach to local environmental issues (Stewart and Hams, 1992, 12 and pp. 25–6), to be embodied in environmental charters, audits and action plans (Ward, 1993, p. 1). There is enormous variation in what has actually been achieved (Gordon, 1993, 143–50; Ward, 1993, pp. 5 and 12–13; Young, 1993, p. 1); integration across different environmental functions is often still poor (Mills, 1994, pp. 6–8); and there is no well-defined and stable environmental policy community (Stanyer, 1994, pp. 6–8). With expenditure under tight central control, the focus has been on preliminary planning and local consciousness-raising. Nevertheless, this activity is important to local government: an increased environmental role represents an alternative to the Conservatives' minimalist vision of local government and gives a new basis of legitimacy in a period when older legitimations are under constant attack (Mills, 1994, p. 3; Ward, 1993, pp. 14–17). Beside this, environmental activity is seen, perhaps somewhat un-realistically, as a vote winner (Ward, 1993, pp. 21–2) and as a way of attracting and keeping modern 'clean' industry and skilled workers (Young, 1993, pp. 2–3). Some local government officers were also quick to appreciate the career advantages of belonging to the small groups of policy entrepreneurs who were pushing the environment on to the local agenda (Mills, 1994, p. 9). Without wishing to deny the real concern of many of those involved, much of the increased interest can be explained in pragmatic terms – if not in terms of self-interest. This is why the Green arguments are so significant here: if they were valid they would provide a much stronger set of normative foundations for devolution of environmental powers to local level. At the same time, they call into question the conceptions of local democracy which currently underlie much of what local authorities are doing in the environmental area.

My focus here will be upon the normative justifications for the decentralisation of power from central government to the local level which derive from what many take to be the moral imperative to achieve a sustainable relationship with nature. It has now become something of a convention to make a distinction between Green arguments and those which express 'shallower' environmental concerns. The basis for the distinction is to ask whether there is a demand for a change in consciousness to a world view which sees humankind as part of the overall ecological web of life, internally related to it, and neither above nor 'outside' nature (Naess, 1989, ch. 2; Dobson, 1990, ch. 2; Eckersley, 1992, chs 2, 3). Approaches like this, notably deep ecology, imply more thoroughgoing change in our relationship with nature, because human interests are not seen necessarily as being paramount. We may conserve nature because it has inherent value rather than instrumental value to humanity. I do not find this way of distinguishing Green arguments from other environmental arguments appealing, partly because I do not believe that deep ecology and related perspectives are coherent, and partly because many people who call themselves Greens do not adhere to them. Rather, Green arguments suggest that only radical social change will allow us to achieve sustainability, and it is this which distinguishes them from the arguments of environmentalists, who believe that it is possible to achieve sustainability through marginal reforms to society as we know it. No doubt there are differences of interpretation over what is and is not radical, but this move allows me to consider the arguments of the eco-socialists, who are an important force within European Green parties, and eco-anarchists, who present the most thoroughgoing case for decentralisation.[1]

Green arguments are often extremely hard to evaluate because they rely so much on the assumption that major changes in consciousness have already occurred, so that self-interest and materialism are less of a problem. Even the historical record, which Greens rely on so much and which suggests to them that human nature is not inevitably self-interested and materialistic, cannot give us sure guidance about a future which will derive from roots in modern industrial – and capitalist – societies. One thread that runs through this paper is that it is highly relevant to ask 'Are Green arguments valid in the worst case that substantial numbers of people are rational egoists?' The precautionary principle has most commonly been applied by Greens and others in relation to potential environmental harms: assume that a new pesticide, say, is harmful until it can be proved that it is not. Here I am merely advocating the extension of this idea to the assumptions we make about human beings. This suggestion is in line of descent from a tradition of thinking about constitutional and institutional design going back at least as far as the eighteenth century. As Madison puts it in the Federalist Papers No. 72, 'the best security for the fidelity of mankind is to make interest coincident with duty'. It might be thought that this move would lead to a straightforward rejection of Green arguments. However, as we shall see, this is not the case.

Because the precautionary principle is an important organising device here, and because many will find it highly contentious, it is worth saying something more in justification of it. First, Green arguments need to be alert to difficulties experienced in the transition to sustainability. The rational pursuit of self-interest seems to me to be a crucial proximal cause of our environmental dilemma and one which would cease to be important only after major structural change. As individuals we often act in what we know are environmentally damaging ways. We feel that changing our own actions would make for little, if any, improvement in our own quality of life in the short term while having significant financial and other costs (Olson, 1965; Hardin, 1968). If we do change our ways for ethical reasons it is often where the costs of doing so are low. Even if a growth of Green consciousness is experienced through time, during the transitional period we should assume that self-interest will remain an important motive.

I accept that there is typically an important moral dimension to even the most narrowly economic interactions, and that without a surrounding moral order capitalist market systems would long ago have collapsed (Etzioni, 1988). However, I would argue that Greens should not rely too heavily on normative attenuation of self-interest in the transition to sustainability or, indeed, in the steady-state society they seek to achieve. One reason for this is that strong normative pressures to act in benign ways have often failed to work historically – a point I will return to below. Besides this, if achieving sustainability is a moral imperative for Greens, it would be wrong for them to take a substantial risk of their proposed solutions unravelling because of the effects of residual or re-emergent self-interest. Greens should attempt to design social institutions, including local government institutions, which provide incentives for rational egoists to act in more environmentally benign ways.

It might be objected that there are forms of human motivation even less favourable to the achievement of sustainability than self-interest. Strictly speaking, egoism excludes all forms of concern for the well-being of others', including envy; and envy may generate more environmental harm than strict egoism via status competition and the consequent production of goods unnecessary to meet basic needs. However, the conclusions I shall draw from formal models of collective action still hold so long as individuals are somewhat concerned about their own absolute payoff as well as their relative payoffs, although increased envy leaves less room for co-operation.

I break down the arguments presented by Greens into the following categories: those which relate decentralisation to the shift to a Green consciousness; those which argue that the corrosive effect of self-interest on the environment is best controlled by political processes operating at the community level; those which suggest that smaller scale economic processes, centring on relatively self-sufficient communities, would be of lower overall environmental impact; and those which argue that grassroots democracy is a necessary condition for sustainability.[2]

Decentralisation and the development of Green consciousness

Greens generally argue that the shift in consciousness towards a thoroughgoing awareness of ecological interrelatedness, with humankind being placed within rather than above nature, is crucial to achieving sustainability (Naess, 1989, chs 1, 4; Devall, 1988, ch. 2). Some Greens see this shift as most likely to occur if there is a simultaneous movement towards decentralisation of economic, social and political life. Perhaps the most fundamental arguments here are those of the bioregionalists.

Bioregions are defined territorially by natural characteristics of geology, climate, and localised flora and fauna, all of which interact within an ecological subsystem. In turn, bioregions contain ecologically defined subregions. From this perspective a bioregion forms a boundary round a set of human communities that are closely related ecologically (Sale, 1985, pp. 55–62). It is argued that 'dwellers in the land' whose lives become rooted is a specific community located within a bioregion come to understand and to identify with the bioregion, to know its ecology, the rhythm of its seasons, its ecological limits, and the extent to which nature may sustainably be used for human ends (see Devall, 1988, p. 47; Sale, 1985, pp. 42–4).

Through understanding and identifying with their own locale, individuals may develop a wider ecological consciousness, too. Furthermore, a return towards community-based living might start to erode important aspects of the cultural hegemony which lies at the base of consumerism. Locally-based grassroots cultural initiatives can provide a counter-balance to the dominant, centrally-produced cultural forms. By eroding the dominant mode in which we consume culture produced by others, wider forms of consumerism may also be called into question (Die Gruenen, 1983, p. 49).

Bioregions are very difficult to define clearly, given the very high degree of interconnectedness we now know exists on a world-wide basis in relation to problems such as atmospheric pollution. Even if bioregions can be defined sensibly in terms of ecological subsystems, they are likely to cut across existing social boundaries defined in terms of language, history and ethnicity (see Eckersley, 1992, pp. 167–70; Wall, 1990, pp. 52–3). This would make the formation of a bioregional consciousness difficult and might prevent the Green movement from making links successfully with social movements for regional autonomy.

Bioregional arguments often rely on evidence about indigenous peoples living in particular geographical regions in a set of small, loosely interacting communities. The argument is that the religious traditions of such groups were bound up with the local ecology, and that they tended to discourage unsustainable practices. However, it is far from clear from historical records that such forms of consciousness always override the material pressures to change the local ecosystem drastically. To take one example, the Celtic religions of many tribes in pre-Roman Britain seem to have taken the approved Green form, according to Roman and archeological sources. However, the evidence is that much of the de-afforestation of lowland Britain was carried out by these people.

While the hope is that problems of co-ordination between different relatively autonomous communities or regions can be overcome by the development of a global sense of identity with the 'world spirit', Gaia, some Greens are also aware that community living could, at least potentially, lead to a form of inward-looking parochialism (see Porrit, 1994, pp. 164–5). The danger is that this might allow environmental problems to be externalised on to other communities, the standard scenario of freeriding on others' provision of environmental public goods (Hardin, 1968) being displaced to the intercommunal level. For instance, unpleasant forms of economic activity which are nevertheless important to achieving sustainability might be kept out – a version of the 'not in my back yard' syndrome. It may be that the ability of modern information technology rapidly and cheaply to disseminate information and to facilitate co-ordination would dispel tendencies towards parochialism (Porrit, 1984, p. 166; Sale, 1985, pp. 94–6). However, the precautionary principle discussed above means that Greens ought to think about how freeriding by communities could be overcome.

The immediate implications of these arguments are that an important role exists for local government in building communities grounded in their locale, sensitive to their local environment, aware of the global implications of local activity, and ready to make sacrifices to achieve environmental ends. This adds a new twist to the old consensus-building justification for local government. However, I will suggest below that the current ways in which community and consensus building are conceived within local government are not necessarily well adapted to the task in hand.

Freeriding within and between communities

While some Greens see freeriding as a danger, the general argument is that, in the long run at least, it can be contained more successfully at the community level than by external regulation by the nation state. In the difficult period of transition to sustainability there will be a need for self-restraint backed by informal social sanctions to enforce a general will mandating 'environmentally sound' forms of behaviour. The argument is that effective social sanctioning is more likely in small communities than in the unstable large communities of the modern world (Editors of the *Ecologist*, 1972, pp. 50–1). One ground for this belief is that communities in traditional, stateless societies were able to make use of social sanctions effectively in this way without the need for hierarchy and the imposition of solutions from above (Editors of the *Ecologist*, 1972, p. 115).

Another argument is that freeriding is less likely when problems impinge directly on the lives of individuals. In these circumstances people see that it is desirable for them to act and that their acts are locally efficacious. In contrast, individuals feel powerless in relation to spatially and personally distant environmental problems and relate to them, if at all, only at an abstract, ethical level with few direct consequences for action (Sale, 1985, pp. 53–4). This argument lies behind the Green slogan 'Act locally think globally': where many global environmental problems are concerned, the assertion is that the key to successful resolution is to change individuals' everyday behaviour and consumption patterns, something best done through local initiatives and intercommunal processes.

Finally, some Greens suggest that communal living will encourage people to be less egoistic and materialistic, which ought to discourage freeriding. Greens assert that the natural, historically normal, and most individually satisfying scale for human lives has been in relatively self-sufficient and autarchic communities of some 500 to 1000 people (Sale, 1985, p. 65). In small communities individuals can be truly themselves within the context of meaningful social relationships and without experiencing a conflict between themselves, conceived of as an isolated 'social atom', and the wider community. More satisfying interpersonal relationships will help to compensate for any loss of material consumption associated with the move to sustainability (Editors of the *Ecologist*, 1972, pp. 52–3).

There are good theoretical and empirical grounds for suggesting that the communal processes Greens identify can help to ameliorate localised environmental problems if communities are small enough, even under the worst case assumption that people remain self-interested materialists. Because the games being played here are repeated over time, conditionally co-operative solutions based on strategies under which an individual only co-operates if enough others have done so in the past, may be viable if individuals are far sighted enough and the short-term gains from freeriding are relatively low (Taylor, 1987). Such conditionally co-operative strategies only work effectively when the numbers of individuals concerned is relatively small, because it must be possible to identify freeriders effectively, something which gets more costly and more difficult as numbers increase (Taylor, 1987, p. 12). As Greens suggest, small communities have used social sanctioning and heavy socialisation to reduce the incentives to freeride and to encourage far-sightedness, and this helped to cement conditional co-operation (Taylor, 1982). These sorts of processes have not always contained freeriding at a community level where specifically environmental problems are concerned (Ostrom, 1990, ch. 5). Nevertheless, a number of long-

standing and successful examples of communal control of environmental common property issues are well documented (Ostrom, 1990,
ch. 3). The key to success may be long-term continuity in local
institutional structures which facilitate definition of property rights,
aid in monitoring freeriding, and encourage reciprocity (Ostrom,
1990, ch. 2).

This evidence certainly undercuts the case made by some neo-
Hobbesian environmentalists that the only viable solution for
environmental problems is the concentration of coercive power in
the hands of an 'environmental sovereign' – perhaps a world
government, or a national government of experts under little, if
any, democratic control (Hardin, 1968; see also the critique by
Walker, 1988). This argument seems invalid even in the weaker
form, that pluralistic democracy could flourish in all areas except
those relating to the environment (Ophuls and Boyan, 1992, part 2).
However, it cannot plausibly be concluded, as some eco-anarchists
have suggested, that there is no role for the nation state and little, if
any, role for local government as currently understood.

The first point is that the size argument in rational choice theory
is a two-edged sword for Greens. On the one hand, it helps to
sustain their claim for the potential of community-based solutions.
On the other, the scale at which the theory suggests these solutions
will work is very small indeed in relation to the population sizes of
even the smaller conurbations in Britain. Greens provide little
guidance about how cities might be split up, or 'artificial' human-
scale communities recreated. I will suggest below that we need to
reorientate Green arguments away from geographically-defined
communities and towards the associations that sometimes act as
surrogates for community in the modern world.

Legal structures operating on a wider scale than the community
seem to have provided very important backing in relation to many
of the examples of communal solutions discussed by Ostrom (1990).
Also, there are arguments which suggest that under conditions of
less than perfect information, total reliance on communal processes
for the solution of collective action problems may not be optimal.
As the number and size of communities grows, the probability of
accidental breakdown of all-round conditional co-operation
through informational failures becomes higher and higher. Under
conditions where, without outside intervention, this would lead to
complete failure, this possibility may be prevented if there is another

set of incentives to continue to co-operate generated by some centralised authority which punishes *communities* within which conditional co-operation breaks down (Bendor and Mookherjee, 1987). Finally, not all environmental collective action problems can be solved via conditional co-operation within communities. Where the conditions for co-operation are absent and cannot be created locally, the Green position demands external solutions such as state power (Goodin, 1992, pp. 156–68). The implications are that: even if community processes can help to regulate environmental harms, they need support by the state; and the state should act as a backstop when community processes do not work.

Greens often favour the idea of repeating the pattern of conditional co-operation at intercommunity level, interregional level, and in the end, at global level. The idea is that individuals co-operate conditionally in communities; communities co-operate conditionally in regions, and so on. The belief is that solutions can eventually be achieved without the need for national or international legal regulation, although this will be important in the interim. However, the problem of information is crucial here, too: in relation to problems such as global warming the number of interacting communities and regions involved would be enormous, and the chances of identifying free-riders correctly extremely low. The transaction costs of achieving solutions would surely rise very rapidly once we moved beyond environmental problems of purely (bio)regional significance. This seems to sanction the nation-state as a bargaining unit. The counter-argument is twofold: first, states have not notably been successful in co-operating to solve global environmental problems; second, the very arguments which sustain the belief that states can co-operate conditionally in the absence of a 'global sovereign' to keep them in awe also sustain the belief that communities and regions could co-operate conditionally without central government interference (Paterson, 1994, pp. 5–9). But this seems to neglect the size principle that conditional co-operation is easier if the number of units is smaller, which applies equally to conditional co-operation between individuals and social units (such as states) acting as if they were single unitary actors. It also neglects the transaction cost argument. Besides this, time is of the essence when dealing with global environmental problems (Meadows, Meadows and Randers, 1992, ch. 4) and we may not have time to create the structures that the Greens want (Eckersley, 1992, p. 174).

To summarise, Greens have a case for saying that if small, geographically-defined communities could be recreated, then informal social processes at the community level would be important to control freeriding. However, the question of how such communities could be created is hardly answered. In any case, communal processes would need to be supported by a broader structure and this is most naturally provided by the nation-state and by formal local political institutions. The strongest counter-argument the Greens might bring against this conclusion is that states erode the capacity of communities to come up with solutions to environmental problems, because they destroy informal political processes operating at the local level (Editors of the *Ecologist*, 1972, p. 122; Taylor, 1987, ch. 7). I will return to this point below.

Do these arguments have anything to say about local government in the here-and-now? In considering this I hope to suggest a way through some the difficulties we have encountered with the idea of community. Recent discussions of associative democracy picture individuals as belonging to a multiplicity of associations relating to work, social welfare provision, leisure, religion, and other needs (Hirst, 1994). Individuals' sense of belonging is not to a geographically-defined community, as in eco-anarchist and decentralist arguments; and it is not to a single social group such as a class. Rather, individuals relate to a multiplicity of groups which are liable to spill over local boundaries as well as having local structure, and which have potential to become associations. Even if the individual does not identify with the metropolis, s/he can have multiple senses of belonging to a particular small locale, a church, a local sports club, a union branch and so on.

The associational vision sees democratic participation as taking place fundamentally within the multiple associations to which individuals belong. It does not neglect the organs of representative democracy, however. The state provides the framework within which associative democracy works, and acts to patch up its failures. One mode is for the state to broker deals between associations when their common interests are imperilled. Tripartite corporatism is a familiar, although for associationalists a limited, example. I suggest that there is potential, even as things stand in the mid-1990s, for local government to act as a broker of environmental deals between associations conceived of in this way. This way the strengths of the communal solution can be made relevant without destroying the current spatial structure of human settlement, which has some environmental advantages.

While the number of individuals affected by most environmental measures is enormous, even in a small conurbation, the number of relevant associations would be much smaller. Even if conditional co-operation between individuals is unthinkable currently, conditional co-operation between associations might be feasible, so long as the consent of their members can be achieved (see Hirst, 1994, ch. 3). Take the pressing need to discourage people from driving to work. The relevant associations would include major local employers (perhaps associated within local chambers of commerce), local unions branches, and employees' associations. The deal might take the form 'organisation X will discourage driving to work so long as organisations A, B, . . ., N continue to do the same'. For employers, conditionality means that they will not be disadvantaged in the job market because other employers implicitly pay higher real wages by allowing their employees to externalise their travel costs. For workers' associations and the workers within them, conditionality guarantees that their sacrifice will not be rendered pointless by others continuing to drive to work. (If others do not act to, you are free to go back on the deal.)

I have assumed that associations can deliver the consent of their members to the deal. However, the social pressures within communities and size arguments eco-anarchists rely on to bolster their case would work within the local structures of associations, so long as these come to resemble the strong communities of the pre-industrial era (Taylor, 1982). All the arguments which suggest that democratic participation attenuates self-interest in favour of a discursively-arrived-at conception of the collective good (Dryzek, 1990, ch. 2) would come into play to the extent that democratisation of associations increased participation.

Many will be sceptical of arguments which seem to rely on associations becoming strong communities, and on high levels of participation within associations (see Hirst, 1994, pp. 63–4). They might consider the pressures that leaders could bring to bear on members whose participation was limited to occasional voting through their narrowly-defined material self-interest. Alongside the public goods they offered, associations typically would provide services to their members that were private, or semi-private goods. For example, housing associations would provide loans, and health associations would provide individual care, alongside public health functions such as immunization. Such goods can be seen as selective incentives for contributing to the solution of collective action problems around the provision of the public goods, such as improved environmental quality, which the associations also supply (Olson, 1965). Such selective incentives could be wholly or partially withdrawn from members who did not consent to the environmental deals that their association had entered into. Associationalists picture associations as being key providers of goods and services important to members' lives, which could be used as selective incentives in this way, giving a great deal of power to offset incentives for environmental freeriding. Inevitably, this suggestion raises its own problems: could associations monitor realistically individual compliance? Where the selective incentives are important to the individual and the association had some monopoly power in their provision, there are questions about whether the individual would be free, in any meaningful sense, to exit the association if s/he did not like the environmental deal, yet, for associationalists, freedom of exit is a crucial bottom-line guarantee of democracy within associations (Hirst, 1994, pp. 51–6). If it is recognised that the leaders of associations need individual incentives for developing a new area of activity (Hirst, 1994, p. 62), there is the question of what they would get out of participation in environmental deals, too. One answer is: votes and legitimacy. It might well be rational for an individual member desiring environmental improvement to vote for associational leaders promising 'mutual coercion mutually agreed' (Hardin, 1968, p. 1247), even though s/he would also freeride rationally in the absence of incentives to stick to deals: so long as enough others are also so bound, this is merely a form of self-binding to ensure a higher payoff.

Local government would play the same role as the local institutions to which Ostrom (1990) refers, or the regimes of co-operation which some hope will cement international co-operation (Young, 1989): agenda setting; building trust that others will not go back on deals; monitoring deals and providing feedback to participants about whether they are being adhered to; cementing all-round conditional co-operation by making side payments to co-operators and imposing penalties on defectors. The crucial advantage of this method can be illustrated by reference to my example. It is very difficult to envisage local government being armed with enough penalties and powers to stop individuals driving to work when the social structures those individuals are set in are left out of the equation. However, making use of those structures, far more could be done with given resources, partly through conditionality of co-operation, partly by relying on participatory democracy in reinvigorated associations to socialise members, and partly by relying on selective incentives provided by associations.

My example suggests a form of local environmental corporatism. However, as I have said, associationalists envisage a plethora of cross-cutting associations. For instance, Hirst advocates the decomposition of the National Health Service through the formation of non-profit-making and heavily locally grounded health care associations, run democratically by citizens and professionals (Hirst, 1994, chs 6, 7). Leaving aside the case for this in health terms, there might be environmental advantages. The unionist unwilling to give up his car *as a unionist* would be cross-pressured if he were a participant in a health care association which offered him more favourable terms if he walked or cycled to work. Local health care associations could be cut into the deals brokered by local authorities by, for example, ploughing some of the financial savings made on road provision back into the associational welfare sector.

Local government has always fostered civic associations, but a new rationale for a much broader conception of what it could do in this area can be given: the consent of individuals is more likely to be delivered for environmental deals, to the extent to which they feel a sense of belonging to multiple associations and those associations sit at tables where environmental deals are brokered. Local government should help to create the local dimension of the flourishing, democratic civil society which associationalists desire (Hirst, 1994, pp. 37–8). The attempts to forge a unitary local identity among individual citizens working from the top down, which constitute the accepted norm for community building within local government, are neither especially successful nor particularly democratic. Working through associations would: recognise the reality of fragmented identities; avoid parochialism because of the way associations typically extend over local government boundaries or are federated into national and international associations; and potentially be more democratic.

The argument here is in no way inconsistent with the view that sustainable development at the local level can be fostered by local participatory democracy: rather, it represents a fleshing out of one dimension of that process and an expansion of the stakeholder notion so as to acknowledge the crucial importance of internal democracy within stakeholding associations. I see no reason why local environmental corporatism should not be viable now, albeit that it should develop towards full environmental associationalism: it would simply represent the continuation of a war already being fought by local authorities on the terrain of conventionally defined economic development on to the new terrain of sustainable development. The argument is not inconsistent with the precautionary principle: collective action theory suggests possibilities of co-operation in the sorts of nested or federal structures discussed here even in the worst-case assumptions that communal processes do not alter individuals' hearts and minds (Olson, 1965, pp. 62–3).

Economic decentralisation and the reduction of environmental impact

Greens often argue that by decentralising economic processes back to self-sufficient communities, overall environmental impacts can be reduced. Again, the presupposition is that the communities will be small. Some Greens see cities as being parasitic on their hinterlands for resources. Cities lead to high concentrations of pollution (Sale, 1985, p. 65). The long term aim, at least, ought to be to break them up into more manageable components, reintegrating the components into their former hinterlands. Within communities, some envisage a blossoming of small individual or family-owned enterprises (Dauncey, 1986), while others envisage co-operatives in which workers have a say (Ekins, 1986; Wall, 1990, p. 57). Either way, there would be dense social networks between productive units so that the economic model is based less on competition and more on co-operation (Phillips, 1986, pp. 278–9). As part of the delinking of the local economy from the global economy, there would be a growth of unpaid work and bartering (Sachs, 1986, p. 333). The division of labour would be much less intense, and the associated reduction in alienation would reduce pressures for compensatory gratification by wasteful consumption (Wall, 1990, p. 23).

The environmental impact of transport can be kept down if production is for local use (Editors of the *Ecologist*, 1972, p. 51). By integrating home, work, recreation areas, and other services spatially, the need to travel is reduced and environmentally benign forms of personal transport such as cycling and walking are encouraged (Die Gruenen, 1983, p. 20; The Green Party, 1992b, p. 8). Similar arguments apply to other forms of infrastructure: levels of provision – and hence environmental impacts – go up more than linearly with the size of the population in the urban area, implying the need to break up the metropolis into units of more appropriate scale (Editors of the *Ecologist*, 1972, pp. 53–4).

Where production is for local use and there is a degree of local democratic control over economic life, a much tighter relationship between supply and demand can be achieved, so that less waste is generated, and the creation of false needs through national and global advertising is reduced (Editors of the *Ecologist*, 1972, p. 51). It has often been argued that local government is potentially more responsive to citizens' demands than is central government. Here the argument is set in the context of minimising environmental impacts and wasteful production. Of course, it should be acknowledged that major changes would be needed to realise this potential.

Large units producing for national or global markets generate very high degrees of local dependency for employment, posing the 'jobs versus environment' trade-off in a way that would be far less intense in a diversified local economy producing for a relatively self-sufficient community (Editors of the *Ecologist*, 1972, p. 52; Dauncey, 1986, p. 265). Indeed, some Greens suggest that the exclusion of economic giants would lead to the local economy having a far greater degree of economic stability (Sale, 1985, pp. 79–82). Within a locally-based economic order, stability of employment and local prosperity may be created, which allows greater weight to be given to environmental quality (Dauncey, 1986, p. 268). The general empowerment of individuals and groups that goes with successful local economic initiatives may encourage them to feel that their actions influence global environmental outcomes, so that they act in more responsible ways (Dauncey, 1986, pp. 264–5). By decentralising economic processes to the local level, the political pressures for damaging forms of growth which arise from competition between nations can be weakened (Sachs, 1986, pp. 336–7).

International free trade is seen as leading to the externalisation of costs on to other nations, future generations, or the biosphere (Daly, 1993, p. 26). As with any other form of market-based system, there is no guarantee that it will lead to production at a scale consistent

with the finiteness of the biosphere (Daly, 1993, pp. 27–8). Furthermore, it is associated with inappropriate development in the South,
which has damaging local and global environmental effects (Trainer,
1989, chs 4, 5 and 6). Within a locally-based economic order these
problems can be addressed: pressures to cut environmental corners
for comparative advantage would be lessened; the scale of production sustainable at local level could be decided democratically; and
exploitation of others and their environment through trade would
cease.

The implications for the long term are that economic intervention
by central government would be much reduced – if it was necessary
at all. There would be political intervention and, indeed, planning,
but this would take place at community level (Die Gruenen, 1983,
p. 20), implying a significant strengthening of the economic functions of local government (Dauncey, 1986, p. 270). As we shall see
below, Greens also argue that local economic planning would have
to become much more participatory than at present. However, it is
by no means obvious that smaller-scale economic processes will
have a lower impact once we aggregate all the communities concerned. Moreover, there may be environmental advantages to much
more extensive intercommunal and, indeed, international trade than
is implied by Green accounts of self-sufficiency. This reopens a
space for economic intervention by the nation-state.

It is not clear that breaking up cities is desirable from a Green
standpoint: some Greens object to the spreading of human habita-
tion into pristine areas that would result (Paehlke, 1989, pp. 244–
50); the environmental impacts of relocation would, themselves, be
enormous. In any case, many standard products that would be
important in a Green society are arguably better produced on a
larger scale than would supply the needs of the sorts of community
that Greens want to see. Steel would, no doubt, still be a crucially
important material, albeit that demand would be lower and recy-
cling more intense. While some see the future of steel-making as
being based on much smaller productive units than the enormous
integrated plants of the post-war period, the scale of production
envisaged is still large. In order to minimise energy inputs, it might
well be better to continue to produce on scales where good use can
be made of waste heat. Besides this, a given form of production will
have different overall impact depending on where it is located. A
process which requires large volumes of water, such as steel-making,

will have a lower impact where water is more abundant. A brief consideration of other areas of production also suggests that impacts are often likely to be lower on a larger scale, and that a regional or even international division of labour might be a more sustainable way to produce what is necessary to meet basic needs.

While it is logically possible that management of environmentally desirable large-scale production could be shared between the communities, the problem of intercommunal collective action reappears. We are dealing here with monopolies and quasi-monoplies that are natural from the perspective of minimising the impact of meeting basic needs. There is just as good a case for state intervention to regulate such natural monopolies as there is in relation to standard cases; and some would argue there is just as good a case for state ownership. Again, if some international trade were environmentally desirable, it is hard to see environmental efficiency being achieved without international economic institutions, which have typically been associated with interstate co-operation (Young, 1989).

It is clear that decentralisation of economic life and a higher degree of self-sufficiency could result in a great deal of inequality across communities and across nations, since the carrying capacities and population levels of areas differ considerably. Eco-socialists have rightly drawn attention to the fact that inequality generates environmental problems: where inequality is associated with poverty, the environment may be overstressed merely in providing the bare minimum of subsistence; inequality generates envy and status-competition, with the possibility that those living in less-favoured areas will attempt to keep up in life-style and status terms, at cost to their local environment. While traditional communities typically had social mechanisms for maintaining internally high degrees of equality and a right to a basic income (Sale, 1985, pp. 82–7), there is little evidence to suggest that redistributive mechanisms between communities were well developed. Indeed, there was a tendency to exclude outsiders wishing to move to more favoured areas. These arguments suggest that central government would need to play a redistributive role between communities and between nations. One method would involve progressive taxation of whole communities, with redistribution from the centre to the local level, together with international transfers. Another, possibly complementary, approach would be to follow André Gorz's suggestion that central government should provide access to a basic income for all citizens in return for an appropriate individual-level work contribution, leaving considerable time available for individuals to interact communally to produce other goods and services (Gorz, 1980, pp. 42–55).

It is a very difficult task to carry out a case-by-case assessment of the most environmentally appropriate scale and location of economic activity, and the proper location of the accompanying political powers, especially given that there are considerable ecological differences even within a country the size of Britain. In my view, Green arguments about economic decentralisation, self-sufficiency and smaller scale do apply to some areas of economic life, but they hardly support the view that the role for state economic intervention and activity will be minimal in the long run. We might conclude that where it is environmentally defensible, local government should promote local production for local use and infrastructural changes which minimise environmental impacts. Greens would suggest the need to democratise local economic planning, however.

Grassroots democracy and sustainability

The argument of Greens in relation to democratisation is that, 'The ecological, economic and social crisis can be countered only by the self-determination of those affected' (Die Gruenen, 1983, p. 8). Greens see the concentration of power, in all its forms, as being unnatural. Hierarchies of the sort that exist in modern societies do not exist in nature, where the pattern is one of mutual interdependence. Institutionalised, permanent concentration of power did not exist in human societies until some time after the Neolithic agricultural revolution. Some Greens argue that the emergence of hierarchy in human societies preceded, then mutually reinforced, the emerging conception that humankind should be the dominant species, separate from and above the rest of nature (Bookchin, 1989, chs 2, 3 and 4).

From a Green perspective, the state is as much an independent cause of environmental degradation as part of the solution (Carter, 1993, p. 45). This is exemplified by the modern nation-state with its penchant for large-scale, environmentally problematic technologies and for weapons of mass destruction which may yet devastate the biosphere as a whole. It may be that national governments are too distant from ecological realities – and hence from an understanding

of natural principles – to do anything effective to solve environmental problems (Sale, 1985, p. 91).

Participation in representative democracies is seen by Greens as
being largely empty, whether it be at national or local level (Porrit,
1984, p. 89). Indeed, there is a tendency for democracy to be even
further eroded: local democracy is replaced increasingly by local
administration, with key decisions being made at the centre and
articulated through control over spending (Porrit, 1984, p. 90);
excessive bureaucratisation and hierarchical administration thwarts
the attempts of citizens to take the initiative (Die Gruenen, 1983,
p. 36); and state secrecy blocks citizens' attempts to inform themselves about environmental problems (Porrit, 1984, p. 167). Unless
the battle to enforce and to extend democratic rights is won, it is
impossible for citizens to resist politically the destruction of the
environment and to improve their working and living conditions
(Die Gruenen, 1983, p. 36).

Although, as the environmental crisis looms, the temptation is to
opt for centralisation of power in the hands of experts who can deal
with the dangers, Greens argue that such a pattern of rule is
unsustainable, because powers would be abused in a way that offset
any positive effects (The Green Party, 1992b, p. 16). The belief is
that the decisions which are most likely to benefit people and the
environment are those made by the people who will not only live
with the consequences of that decision, but also pay for it (The
Green Party, 1992b, p. 17). The need is for decentralised human-
scale political units based on communities and districts with extensive autonomy and rights of self-government, and citizens participating directly in decision-making (Die Gruenen, 1983, p. 8).
Decentralisation of power has the implication that there will be
more experimentation with solutions to social and environmental
problems, and more scope for emulating what turn out to be
successful adaptions, than in a relatively monolithic political system.
Also, if a development turns out to be maladapted, this matters less
if it has only been tried on a local scale (Editors of the *Ecologist*,
1972, pp. 122–3). Decentralisation gives the opportunity to learn
locally before acting locally for global ends (Stewart and Hams,
1992, p. 28).

For eco-anarchists, the implication of these arguments is that the
nation state will have to go, and sooner rather than later (Bookchin,
1989). Other Greens envisage a much slower process of transition,

using existing political mechanisms to decentralise powers gradually
back to regions and communities (Porrit, 1984, pp. 167–8). Many
Greens recognise that national governments will have important
functions for the foreseeable future, even though their powers will be
reduced. In the interim, the guiding principle – difficult though it is
to put into operation – ought to be that nothing should be done at a
higher level that can be done at a lower one (Porrit, 1984, p. 166).
Green arguments are echoed in the demands by local authorities
that the principle of subsidiarity should be applied when dividing
environmental regulatory powers between central and local levels
(Stewart and Hams, 1992, p. 9; Ward, 1993, p. 2).[3]

In summary, the broad Green argument is that movements
towards participatory democracy would allow for the expression
of citizens' environmental concerns. There is an implicit assumption
that existing institutions and procedures block the expression of
these concerns. There is considerable evidence from opinion polls
and environmental pressure group membership figures for such
concern (Ward and Samways, 1992, pp. 121–2). Nevertheless, some
suspect that the attitudes being expressed here are often relatively
shallow: when faced with major costs in terms of other values such
as material consumption, many would not emphasise the environment. This calls into question whether democratisation to the local
level would lead inevitably to greater environmental quality, as
Greens seem to assume. The key question is whether the local
democratic process would generate a widespread consensus that
major costs should be born. Such a consensus need not develop
inevitably in all communities.

The Greens' agenda for constitutional reform is similar to that of
many other groups. To accompany the gradual devolution of power
there should be: electoral reform to institute some version of
proportional representation, both at national and local level; the
setting-up of elected regional assemblies; and the dismantling of
official secrecy (Porrit, 1984, pp. 167–8; The Green Party 1992a,
p. 11). The scenario many Greens hope might arise, drawn from the
West German experience in the 1980s, is that constitutional change
might give the Green Party a chance of holding office as part of a
coalition government at regional or national level.[4] The evidence is
that Die Gruenen had little power even to prevent sensitive construction projects going through when they formed part of coalitions
at city and *Laender* level. The reason is that their bargaining power

was low, given that they could not play off potential coalition partners to the right and to the left against each other. Despite the protestations of some members that they were neither to the right nor to the left, their ideology was too distant from that of the Christian Democrats to make a stable coalition viable. Similarly, the bargaining position of the British Greens would be weak unless they were willing to drop themes and ideas that alienate Conservatives, such as social justice, the democratic regulation of markets, and the decentralisation of power. Moreover, the danger for the Greens is that constitutional reform, together with the promotion of decentralisation, might lead to the fragmentation of existing national parties. One result might be political gridlock, preventing policy initiatives on the environment. Many Greens hope to use community politics as a launchpad into national politics, in the same way that the Liberal Democrats have done (Wall, 1990, pp. 66–7). While constitutional reform might make this strategy more viable in the present political conjuncture, it can hardly be justified normatively by a tactical argument so tied to the present.

While Greens would reject the traditional argument that participation in politics is currently more extensive and meaningful at the level of local government, they suggest that it could be made *more* meaningful. Besides advocating constitutional reform, Greens place particular emphasis on increasing citizens' direct participation. Elected representatives should act in a way that is consistent with the mandate of the citizens who vote for them, and these respresentatives should be subject to recall by voters if they fail to do so (The Green Party, 1992a, p. 11). Current empty forms of consultation of citizens should be replaced by participatory planning boards having joint responsibility over key matters such as the budget together, with elected political authorities (Die Gruenen, 1983, p. 37). Citizens' initiatives, whereby groups of citizens can themselves propose new laws and policies, should be encouraged (The Green Party, 1992a, p. 11). For this to work there would have to be a very high level of participation and awareness among citizens, backed by strong participatory norms (Sale, 1985, pp. 101–7).

An obvious worry here is that current rates of participation in local politics are low, albeit that people are more likely to participate locally about a local issue, and that some local authorities have fostered participation. Mechanisms which aimed at increasing participation might simply be misused by vociferous and well-organised minorities. The precautionary principle suggests the need to plan on the basis that these problems remain troubling. A traditional justification for representative democracy at local level is to attenuate the influence of vociferous minorities by balancing their demands against some broader conception of the public good. This rationale would continue to be weighty even if participation at the local level were much higher.

Green arguments focus too closely on the geographical dimension of community. There is a greater prospect of meaningful participation within associations and their local branches than in the relatively large-scale forums that Greens propose; and there is more plausibility to the idea that representatives of local branches of associations would participate in Green forums than there is that individual citizens would participate. Of course, we need to be realistic about the idea that overall participation would be higher if local politics was more democratic and more grounded in associations, especially in the light of what is known about participation rates at present: currently the proportion of individuals involved in organised groups is lower than the proportion of individuals who have used the conventional local channels of participation of contacting a local councillor, although the number of individuals who have attended a protest meeting is not many fewer than the number who have contacted their town hall (Parry *et al.*, 1992, p. 319). However, rational choice arguments suggest that participation will be higher if individuals believe there will be more chance of their swaying the outcome, and more is at stake if they get their preferred outcomes. This would favour participation in local branches of radically empowered associations over bigger local forums, on two counts: the chances of altering outcomes rise in smaller groups such as local branches of associations; and participation in associations would increase as more was at stake in their successful operation.

The associational model consists of associations involved in the implementation and monitoring phases of the policy cycle, as well as in decision making. Why should cyclists be reliant on local government officers, ignorant of their needs, to build and maintain cyclepaths? To devolve this function and its associated funding to cyclists' rights groups – with the help of local officials and the cyclists' own national associations – would arguably be a move towards greater efficiency and democracy. The possibility of giving residents' associations the resources to traffic-calm their own streets again raises the possibility of externalising (traffic flow) costs on to others, and underlines the need for democratically elected local government to prevent associational special interest leading to pathological results. Greens wish to extend local democratic control to the economic sphere as well. Without planning and other forms of political intervention, revitalisation of the urban environment will go by the board, and solutions to the growing social problems of urban areas will not be found (The Green Party, 1992a, p. 7). However, planning must be carried out at a local level and must be participatory rather than technocratic (The Green Party, 1992b, p. 8). Citizens should have the authority, through economic and social councils, to control business activities, with a view to promoting a regionally specific economic mix compatible with ecological and social ends (Die Gruenen, 1983, p. 11). Community based banks, local employment training schemes, and community-based housing associations might be set up to promote environmentally-sound local economic activity (The Green Party, 1992a, p. 7).

Conceptions of economic democracy which focus on empowering workers omit crucial stakeholders in economic decision-making – consumers for one. Greens acknowledge this implicitly when they conceive of democratising local economic planning. They fail to get to grips with the dangers of low participation on the worst-case assumptions of the precautionary principle. In contrast, an associational conception of local economic planning would seem to be more workable and potentially democratic.

The idea that considerable economic power might be devolved to the local level might seem utopian to some, given the realities of the operation of global markets and the structural power of capital at a national level. Greens reply that a high degree of economic self-sufficiency within a bioregion would free its people from such constraints (Sale, 1985, p. 47). But, once again, we have the problem of what would happen in the interim. National governments do have some powers that countervail the structural and other powers of capital. The fragmentation of authority might simply allow capital to use 'divide and rule' tactics, playing on perceived trade-offs between economic security and environmental clean-up at regional and local level. It seems to me that economic democracy at a local level is highly desirable, but that it will only start to flourish if it receives some degree of political shelter from national government.

Indeed, there is a strong case for saying that the changes Greens want constitute an economic revolution which would be strongly resisted by capital, leading to a battle that could only conceivably be won within the context of national politics.

Greens are generally committed to the idea that diversity within and between communities and bioregions is both natural and desirable (Sale, 1985, pp. 107–10). One favoured argument is that diversity in ecosystems promotes stability, although this rests on an extremely tenuous analogy between ecological diversity and social diversity, and a misreading of the science of ecology itself. There are other problems, too. First, small communities are typically rather intolerant of diversity and only work successfully if there is a highly-embedded normative order which allows only minor forms of deviance. As I suggested above, the communal solution to collective action problems may rely, in practice, on such a normative order. Second, Greens clearly could not tolerate large numbers of individuals holding religious or other cultural beliefs which led them – to take the most obvious example – to have large families. There may be a partial way out of this dilemma, but it certainly suggests that formal government legal structures at both national and local level would continue to play a key role. One might envisage communities being rather homogeneous, but with some diversity between communities. Then those under unacceptable pressure in one community could exit to another, more congenial, one. To make this operational, though, the overall size of the polity would have to be reasonably large, and some institution would have to protect the human rights of individuals (and perhaps of quite large groups) to move or to set up new communities. In the interim, before sustainability was achieved, 'ecologically unsound' religious and cultural practices ought to be protected, too, the hope being that the numbers of individuals involved would diminish gradually. It is very difficult to see how existing structures of national and international law articulated through local enforcement agencies could be dispensed with here. If my suggestion that Green arguments about democratic participation in the community need to be recast in associational terms is taken, state guarantees of the right to enter and exit from associations (Hirst, 1994, pp. 49–56) become all the more crucial.

Despite their emphasis on decentralisation, the reality that many environmental problems exist on a world scale forces Greens to be internationalist in orientation. The argument is that loose international federations of communities may come to replace the existing international structures. For example, the European Community (EC) should be replaced by a confederation of European regions, the regions being based on ecological and cultural boundaries, and an attempt being made to achieve consensus within, and then across, regions. This is in line with the view of many Greens that there is an excessive concentration of power in the hands of the EC and the European Commission. Although the EC has been a force for tighter environmental regulation in Britain, Greens argue that the EC's economic agenda derives from a focus on world markets and economic competition. This causes environmental deterioration and the economic marginalisation of the poor (The Green Party, 1992b, pp. 16–17). There may be major problems with the conception of a federation of communities and regions in terms of transaction costs. More workable ways of democratising the EC need to be considered. Because associations have local roots but are already somewhat organised at the European level and could become more organised, they provide one attractive way forward (Hirst, 1994, pp. 139–42). However, the representative dimension of European democracy also needs to be enhanced.

Greens are right to suggest that the major changes in lifestyle necessary for sustainability cannot be thrust on citizens. Local participatory democracy provides one path to legitimacy, albeit that the case for important powers of environmental regulation and taxation to remain at the centre is compelling. The democratic deficit at the local level needs to be addressed. However the Greens' model of participatory democracy based on geographical definitions of community is less workable than the associational model. At present, local government should start to pay even more attention to associational representation and begin to exert its influence to democratise associations.

Conclusion

Green thought generates a case for decentralisation of power and grassroots democracy which has to be taken seriously in any attempt to rethink local governance from a normative perspective. However, I have suggested that both on the road to sustainability and in a society that has achieved sustainability there would continue to be a significant, though diminished, role for central government and for some forms of conventional local government. By way of conclusion, I wish to return to the argument that the very existence of significant powers in the hands of central government would inevitably undercut the basis for communal democracy, and communal solutions to environmental problems. I do not believe this argument is valid in this strong form. However, if I am correct to conclude that there will still be a significant role for central government, a new agenda for discussion opens up. Besides firming up ideas about what is best done centrally and what is best done locally, we need to pose the crucial question of how the balance of power between community, region and national government should be maintained in dynamic equilibrium. The inevitable question for those who accept the use of the precautionary principle is how would we stop central government expanding its powers outwards, eroding communal politics in ecologically inappropriate ways? This vital question has hardly been posed in Green theory or in the related literature (but see Gorz, 1980, pp. 34–53; Illich, 1973, ch. 3). Certainly, the potential utility of conventional constitutional limitations on central government and divisions of powers within central government should not be neglected by Greens. But such an institutional fix has insufficient credibility, and Green theory desperately lacks other answers!

Green arguments do have a bearing on local government in the here-and-now. First of all, they call into question environmental rationales for further centralisation of powers. Indeed, they tend to reinforce the desire of many local authorities for an expanded environmental role and to sanction much greater backing for this by central government. They have distinctive things to say about the role of local authorities in brokering environmental deals between associations, recreating old communal solutions under modern conditions. They suggest a new thrust for local economic planning: an orientation towards local production for local consumption *when* this is environmentally the best way; widening participation beyond business and trade unions to include other stakeholders; weaning the local economy away from dependence on international capital in order to lessen the jobs versus the environment trade-off; and a focus on creating less alienating work as an antidote to consumerism. Finally, they suggest a move along associational lines towards the participatory end of the democratic spectrum, both in relation to policy-making and implementation, with the boundary between local government and associations becoming increasingly blurred.

Notes

1. Inevitably in a piece of this sort, I have done some violence to the very real disagreements which exist among Greens.
2. Critical surveys of the sorts of themes discussed here are also presented in Dobson (1990, chs 3, 4); Eckersley (1992, ch. 7); and Goodin (1992, ch. 4).
3. Other echoes of Green thinking can be found in such documents as the Local Government Management Board's submission to the Rio Earth Summit (Stewart and Hams, 1992): local government is closer than central government to everyday problems such as energy efficiency (Stewart and Hams, 1992, p. 9); because it is close to such problems it has higher capacity for correcting its mistakes and achieving the diverse solutions tailored to local circumstances that are necessary for sustainability (Stewart and Hams, 1992, p. 10); given the major changes in lifestyle necessitated by sustainability, popular participation is crucial to legitimation and to implementation, and participation can be expected to be greater at the local level (Stewart and Hams, 1992, p. 12).
4. British Green Party members are divided internally over the issue of whether their party should enter coalitions, and there is some evidence in Britain for a negative correlation between activism and support for the coalition strategy (Bennie *et al.*, 1993, p. 17).

8   Theories of Local Democracy in the United States

Harold Wolman

Theories of local democracy and local government vary from country to country and are embedded in each country's history and political culture. In this chapter I present and discuss theories of local democracy in the United States and contrast them to theories of local democracy in Britain as set forth by Stoker in Chapter 1 of this volume. My primary concern is with the fundamental values that underlie the practice of local democracy and local government. I argue that American theories of local democracy reflect both the American emphasis on individualism and localism in their concern with participation and local government as a vehicle for democratic decision-making. British theories, on the other hand, reflect the development of the unitary state in their preoccupation with local service delivery.

American theories of local democracy

American theories of local democracy reflect several strands of American political thought. Some of the theories discussed below reflect widely held popular beliefs about American local democracy, while others are more the subject of academic discussion. None-the-less, in both cases it is well to start with a firm base – the strong disposition on the part of voters, politicians and theorists to espouse the values of local autonomy and localism (even though this commitment does not always guide political behaviour). So strong is this commitment to localism that debate over the role or importance of local government in the United States is rare.

This commitment to localism exists within a formal constitutional context that is not unlike that of Britain. Although there is no constitutional relationship at all between the federal government and local government, local governments are legally creatures of the fifty state governments. Dillon's Rule, the most widely cited constitutional dictum related to local government, states that local governments are creatures of the state and can engage in no activities that are not authorised specifically by the state. This rule presents a situation not unlike that of the *ultra vires* rule in Britain with respect to the formal relationship of local government to the state. Despite Dillon's Rule, many states have voluntarily granted their local governments a degree of general competency ('home rule') by specifying that local governments have the ability to engage in activities not expressly prohibited by state constitutional or legislative provisions.

Individualism and individual participation

In the United States, as Sharpe (1973) points out in his insightful essay on American democracy, all authority resides in the people. The bedrock of American local democratic theory is that the role of the local government is to reflect the will of the people, and that direct individual participation in local government is the best means of achieving this end.

Thomas Jefferson's 'sovereignty of the individual' was the animating force behind early American municipal government. Jefferson's concern for direct democracy and individual participation as primary values led him to advocate a system of 'little republics' (which he termed a 'ward system'). Wards were to be small enough to enable every citizen to attend ward meetings and 'act in person' (Syed, 1966, p. 39). The New England township governments were celebrated by Jefferson as the perfect manifestation of the principle of sovereignty of the individual:

> These wards, called townships in New England, are the vital principles of their governments, and have proved themselves the wisest invention ever devised by the wit of man for the perfect exercise of self-government and for its preservation. (Quoted in Syed, 1966, p. 39)

Indeed, it is Jefferson's sovereignty of the individual that is reflected in De Tocqueville's classic description (1954, p. 64) of New England local government, written in 1835:

> In the township, as well as everywhere else, the people are the source of power; but nowhere do they exercise their power more immediately. In America the people form a master who must be obeyed to the utmost limits of possibility . . . in the townships, where the legislative and administrative action of the government is nearer to the governed (than at the state level), the system of representation is not adopted. There is no municipal council; but the body of voters, after having chosen its magistrates, directs them in everything that exceeds the simple and ordinary execution of the laws of the state. (De Tocqueville, 1954, Bk 1, p. 64)

The individual participation celebrated by Jefferson and De Tocqueville is justified by the fundamental tenet of republican government that all authority resides in the people: the people should rule. The Jeffersonian tradition lives on, not only in deeply-held and expressed populist values about the role of the individual and local government, but also in the widespread use of institutional mechanisms that are found in few continental systems of local government – the referendum and the initiative (a device that allows the people, by petition, to place an issue on the ballot for decision). In addition, city institutions to promote citizen participation – a by-product of the 1960s – and neighborhood decentralisation – to the extent the concern is participation rather than efficient administration – reflect a Jeffersonian concern.

Pluralism: local government as a vehicle for democratic decision-making

In the pluralist vision, local democracy consists of the expression of and conflict among diverse views and values held by contending groups attempting to shape local government decisions to meet their ends, with all-important groups having the ability to gain access to and exercise some degree of influence over decision-makers. Local government's role is to serve as the vehicle through which group conflict occurs, and through which this conflict is resolved. Local government is thus concerned with, in Easton's terms, the authoritative allocation of values, or, in Lasswell's classic language, 'Who gets what, when, and how.' Local democracy is thus the free flow of group political conflict, and local government is its arena. In the introduction to their classic book, *City Politics*, Banfield and Wilson (1963, p. 1) argue this point of view:

> The day to day workings of city government in the United States are best understood by looking at the differences of opinion and interest that exist within the cities, at the issues that arise out of these differences, and at the ways institutions function to resolve (or fail to resolve) them. It is based, in short, upon a view of city government as a political process.

The critical role of participation in American local democracy remains in pluralist theory, but the emphasis has shifted from individual to group participation. Pluralism and group participation reflect the influence of Madisonian and representative thought placed on top of Jeffersonian individualism. Thus the Madisonian emphasis on limiting government power through separation of power and checks and balances (as reflected in the Federalist papers, particularly Nos 10 and 51) is reflected in the separation of executive (mayor) and legislative (council) power characteristic of American municipal government as it developed beyond New England township government in the nineteenth century. In addition, Madison's focus of attention was on interest groups ('factions') rather than individuals: 'All civilized societies are divided into interests and factions' (quoted in Abbott, 1991, p. 84). The structure of government, under the Madisonian system, must serve both to moderate and to control factional conflict, but also to provide for adequate representation of group interests. In the context of representative rather than direct democracy, the relevant unit of participation shifted from the individual to the group and focused concern on the representation of the interests of various groups through local government.

The pluralist normative theory of local democracy deriving from Madisonian thought is that all groups should have the resources necessary to enable them to gain access to local decision makers and to influence public policy. Dahl (1961) argued that, in practice, the conditions of local democracy were met if all major groups had some resources that permitted them some access to the political process on issues about which they felt strongly. During the 1960s and 1970s the Pluralist–Elitist debate that preoccupied American political science revolved around the question of the extent to which the normative conditions of pluralist local democracy were, in fact, empirically present and, indeed, whether the normative conditions posited by R. Dahl and his followers were appropriately stringent in terms of the extent of group access and influence required for local democracy to be present.

Within the pluralist theory of local democracy, the role of local government is to be the political vehicle through which contending groups at the local level reflect and resolve their differences over local issues. Local government is responsive to group interests and is a resolver of group conflict. Local government itself is not necessarily neutral; elected office-holders and bureaucrats may themselves reflect specific interests, but local government is none the less the forum through which contending interests in society are resolved.

Local government as service provider: economy and efficiency

In the early part of the twentieth century municipal reformers advanced a theory of local democracy that focused on local government's role as a service provider and on the values of economy and efficiency related to service provision. These values were a reaction to machine politics and the corruption that frequently accompanied it. Arising as a product of the Progressive movement in the early part of the twentieth century, the role of municipal government was defined to be primarily that of the efficient delivery of local services. As the National Municipal League (1939), the primary advocate of municipal reform, saw it:

> Local government exists to perform functions and render services which the people of the community demand and which can be performed more cheaply by government than any other way . . . the citizen's questions should be 1) Am I receiving all the services which government should, by reason of economy and convenience, rightfully perform? 2) Are these services being efficiently

rendered? and 3) Is government sufficiently subject to democratic control, sufficiently responsive to public opinion, in performing those services?

The reformers drew the analogy to the business corporation which pursued economy and efficiency through application of experts and scientific techniques rather than through 'political' considerations. A typical expression of this view is displayed by an early reformer, John Patterson, who wrote:

> A city is a great business enterprise whose stockholders are the people . . . Our municipal affairs would be placed upon a strict business basis and directed, not by partisans either Republican or Democratic, but by men who are skilled in business management and social science; who would treat our people's money as a trust fund, to be expended wisely and economically, without waste and for the benefit of all citizens. (Quoted in Stillman, 1974)

The advocates of this conception of local government proposed a series of structural changes as the best means of implementing these values: a council–manager form of government (the manager to be appointed by the elected council and to be the source of expertise on the efficient delivery of services); non-partisan elections (to reduce or eliminate the influence of parties and politics); and at-large rather than ward elections (to eliminate the politics associated with small area interests and to encourage the council to focus on the general good of the community). As Richard Childs, the 'father of the manager plan', wrote:

> The position of city manager of course is the central feature of the council–manager plan and the ultimate theory of the scheme contemplates that he should be an expert in municipal administration, selected without reference to local politics. (Written in 1915 and quoted in Stillman, 1974, p. 5)

> This . . . plan corresponds to the general manager under the board of directors in a business corporation. It gives the stability of the combined judgment of many men on matters of policy, but leaves execution to a single-headed controlled executive establishment. (Written in 1913 and quoted in Stillman, 1974, p. 8)

Concerns with group representation and checks and balances, the Madisonian tradition in American local government, are absent from the reform ethos (though the Jeffersonian value of direct democracy lives on in the progressives support for the referendum, initiative and recall). In the reformers' conception, the primary role of the citizen is that of voter, the source from which the elected council members obtain their legitimacy and from which they derive the values local policy should embody. While this reflects back to the republican value that 'all authority resides in the people', it does not require the individual or group-level participation of either the Jeffersonian or pluralist theories of local democracy. Indeed, municipal reformers' emphasis on economy and efficiency of service delivery tends to go hand in hand with a distrust of and distaste for group politics and the role of interest groups (and political parties) in public affairs.

Localism and public choice theory

Although public choice theory is an academic construct rather than a popular set of beliefs about local democracy, its premises and findings correspond closely to many popular beliefs about local democracy. Public choice theory's emphasis on the value of localism, the individualist utilitarianism which is at its core, and the focus on the views of individual citizens rather than 'government' as the core of political legitimacy all resonate with public views about localism.

Public choice theory as it applies to local government was developed by Tiebout (1956) among others to address the question of how the optimal level of public-good expenditure can be determined in a non-market situation. Tiebout's setting was the metropolitan political economy, and he and his colleagues attacked the conventional wisdom that reform of the local government system within metropolitan areas required consolidation and metropolitan-level governments. Public choice theorists suggest that fragmented metropolitan areas consisting of many small units of local government, supplemented by larger single-function districts for government services that had true economies of scale, would yield a more efficient solution.

Public choice theory builds, to some extent, on the efficiency values inherent in a 'local government as a service provider' theory of local democracy, but goes far beyond this to construct a positive theory of local government structure for local democracy. The core political value of local democracy is the accurate representation of individual tax and service preferences necessary for an efficient allocation of resources. Efficiency is defined, in a welfare economics sense, as that allocation of resources that best reflects the aggregated preferences for goods and services of local citizens, given their willingness to pay for them. Efficiency thus implies maximisation of social welfare.

In order to maximise social welfare, individual preferences must be expressed accurately. In the private economy, individual preferences are expressed through the market mechanism. When public goods are provided, tax and service packages should reflect as accurately as possible the aggregated preferences of community members. For a variety of reasons, this situation may not occur. Public choice theorists tend to distrust the representative process as distorting the true preferences of local residents. For reasons of status enhancement, local public officials tend to favour higher levels of public spending than local public preferences would in fact justify. Thus, direct democracy, in the form of referendums on fiscal issues, is preferred to the extent possible, as are tax and expenditure limitations which serve as counterweights to the inherent tendency of government officials to spend in excess of public preferences.

The most controversial result derived from public choice theory is the preference for a fragmented system of local government as yielding the most efficient (in a social welfare sense) structure for local service delivery. Because individual preferences for public goods differ, there will inevitably be some divergence between the preferences of individual community members and the tax and service package adopted reflecting aggregated community preferences. It is likely that the average divergence of individual preferences from the tax and service package adopted by the community through its government will be less in small communities of relatively like-minded individuals than it will be in larger, more heterogeneous areas. As a consequence, the larger the population (that is, at the metropolitan level), the greater will be the average divergence of the preferences of individual residents for public goods from the tax and service package actually adopted, and the lower will be the resulting degree of allocative efficiency and social welfare.

By contrast, if political decision-making is decentralised among many small units of local government, each unit can more easily tailor its tax and service package to the preferences of its citizenry. As a result, the average divergence of the public-goods preferences of individual residents from the actual tax and service packages will be reduced. This logic implies that the *greater* the number of local governments in an urban area, the lower will be the average divergence of individual preferences from actual tax and service packages. This is because large numbers of local governments are likely to imply many small units of like-minded individuals. Efficiency and social welfare are thus, it is argued, maximised under a decentralised structure of many local governments.

Efficiency is also furthered by the mobility of residents – the ability of residents to 'vote with their feet'. As a consequence, residents can sort themselves out by moving to those communities whose tax-service packages best correspond to their own preferences. The realisation that residents have this option will force local governments to compete against each other, both by offering different packages of services and by attempting to offer similar types and quality of service at lower costs (the more traditional management or *x*-efficiency).

Comparing American and British theories of local democracy

In comparing American theories of local democracy to those in the United Kingdom (see Stoker's presentation in Chapter 1 of this volume), it is useful to begin with L. J. Sharpe's threefold classification of arguments: liberty (local government as a counterweight to national government); participation; and efficiency in the delivery of local services (Sharpe, 1970).

With respect to the liberty argument (dismissed by Sharpe as unconvincing), the argument of local government as a counterweight to centralised power is one rarely heard in the United States (although it is the argument of Madison in the Federalist Papers). The participation argument in British debate is usually expressed in terms of the role of participation in promoting civic education or as a training ground for local politics (after J. S. Mill, 1962, pp. 286–7;

see the discussion in Stoker, Chapter 1 in this volume) than as, in American discourse, an expression of the sovereignty of the individual and of the right of the individual (or group) not only to participate in but also to determine local affairs.

The efficiency argument is, as Sharpe notes, the predominant one in British theories on local government and democracy. He refers (Sharpe, 1970, p. 159) to the 'Benthamite tradition' that sees local government primarily as a series of agencies for providing services as efficiently as possible to national minimum standards. The efficiency theory, with its emphasis on value for money, seems reasonably similar in both countries (except for national minimum standards which, of course, are quite contrary to American localist traditions), but its institutional manifestations (council–manager system of government, distrust of political parties, and non-partisan elections) have been radically different in the United States. Public choice arguments, reflecting the value of allocative efficiency, again are relatively similar, but have had a much greater practical impact in the highly fragmented metropolitan areas in the United States (although the abolition of the metropolitan authorities in England during the 1980s perhaps owes something to the rising influence of the public choice theory of local democracy).

What appears to be missing from the traditional British context is what I have termed above the 'pluralist theory' of local democracy, with pluralism implying local government as a vehicle for group participation in the political process and for resolving political conflict among groups. What appears to be present in the British debate, but absent in the USA is the sense that local government is, in fact, a vehicle for accomplishing public purposes. Sharpe (1973, p. 130) refers to this property as 'functional effectiveness'. He argues that:

> The link between functional effectiveness and democracy rests on the simple proposition that the right to choose presupposes the possibility of action on the part of those chosen. If government cannot act because it is too weak – because it is not functionally effective – then democracy ceases to exist.

Sharpe argues that functional effectiveness, thus defined, is a concept central to the notion of representative government, 'but one that seems to be largely ignored in the American tradition.'

The pluralist tradition: critiques and prospects for local government theory and practice

Does the pluralist conception of local democracy have any relevance for British local government theory and practice?

First, let us consider the possibility that the two concerns of pluralism and functional effectiveness discussed above are linked inversely to one another. It has been argued by many that American government lacks functional effectiveness, in Sharpe's terms, precisely because of its pluralist nature. Large numbers of groups contesting with one another in a framework of divided powers and checks and balances are more likely to produce stalemate than effective policy. The clearest argument for this point of view with respect to American local government is presented by Douglas Yates in his aptly titled book, *The Ungovernable City* (1977), an analysis of the paralysis that gripped New York City's government in the 1970s. However, Yates's analysis has been criticised as both time- and place-bound. More recent works by Jones and Bachelor (1986) and by 'regime theorists' such as Stone (1989) argue that cities are able to accomplish important public purposes by assembling coalitions of political (particularly the mayor), business and community élites. But this suggests that, to some extent, the stalemate producing tendencies of pluralism can be surmounted only by moving beyond pluralism to decision-making by élites, a situation that has important normative implications.

In addition to stalemate, pluralism at the urban level in the United States has also been criticised for leading to excessively symbolic politics (as contesting groups seek – or are bought off with – symbolic rewards rather than substance), lack of competence (as group representation rather than professionalism is emphasised in filling high appointed positions) and corruption. But it is difficult to sort out whether these attributes, like pluralism itself, merely reflect the nature of American local political culture or whether they instead *result from* pluralism and thus whether the widespread participation of groups in local politics would have similar consequences in Britain.

In academic debate, the primary criticism of American pluralism has been that the empirical reality of group participation does not meet the normative requirements of the pluralist creed, even in the fairly loose terms set forth for it by its foremost adherents such as Polsby and Dahl. This normative theory of pluralism stipulates that all important groups should have sufficient (but not equal) resources and ability to gain access to the decision-making process and to exercise some influence over decision-makers on issues important to them. It also assumes that local government and locally elected officials are important actors in decisions affecting the local citizenry.

In the United States there has been a long tradition of community power studies that have argued that pluralism and local democracy are illusions and that important local decisions are, in effect, made largely behind the scenes by an élitist power structure isolated from the local electoral process and local public opinion. Floyd Hunter's work on Atlanta (Hunter, 1953) initiated a long debate on the reality of democracy in American local government and, while Hunter's work was vigorously attacked for its methodological shortcomings (see Judge, 1995 and Harding, 1995 for a review of the resulting Pluralist–Elitist debate), it was followed by a set of studies (primarily by sociologists) that also found élitist power structures. It was also followed by a large number of studies, largely by political scientists, that found 'pluralist' power structures that were more consistent with traditional theories of local democracy, particularly the pluralist version discussed above (see Dahl, 1961). As Judge (1995) notes, British studies, particularly Newton's influential study of Birmingham (Newton, 1976) also rejected pluralism as an adequate description of British local democracy, though the findings and critique were less surprising and met with less opposition, since pluralism as a theory of local government did not, as we have seen, underlie the normative foundation of British local government.

More sophisticated versions of the élitist argument stressed that if actual decision-making appeared 'democratic', important – sometimes the most important – issues were effectively kept off the agenda by the real wielders of community power (see Bachrach and Baratz, 1962). Bachrach and Baratz termed this hegemonic control over agenda setting the 'second face' of power, while Lukes (1974, p. 22) described a 'third face', arising out of 'socially structured and culturally patterned behavior of groups, and practices of institutions'. Stone's argument (1980) about the 'systemic' power of business in community decision-making – itself similar to

Lindblom's argument (Lindblom, 1977) about the privileged position of business in market-based democracies – is closely related to this third face.

Other attacks on pluralism have come in the form of critiques of the concept of local democracy from those concerned with 'local autonomy'. It is argued that local governments, whatever their decision-making structure, are increasingly irrelevant (except, perhaps, as a deliverer of routine local services) because of their lack of effective discretion in making important decisions. This argument gained political currency in the United States during the expansion of federal programmes and the federal role associated with the Great Society period of the 1960s and 1970s, then receded with the federal cutbacks and decentralisation thrusts of the Ronald Reagan and George Bush Administrations. In Britain, it arose as a concern during the late 1970s, when central government began to impose increasing fiscal constraints on the ability of local governments to tax and spend from their own resources. Indeed, the centralisation of authority and the effort to delimit the effective autonomy of local government served as one of the major themes of the Margaret Thatcher era. The result was, according to Newton and Karran (cited in Gurr and King, 1987, p. 180), 'Britain stands within sight of a form of government more highly centralized than anything this side of East Germany.'

In the United States the most important challenge to local democracy in terms of local autonomy came from Paul Peterson in his influential book *City Limits* (Petersen, 1981). Peterson argued that, because of structural constraints, cities had an overriding (unitary) interest in development policies and were unable to engage in redistributive policy-making. The inability of North American urban governments to engage in redistributive policy resulted from the mobility of both residents and business within the jurisdictionally fragmented metropolitan areas in the United States. To put it simply, efforts by a city to tax the better-off to redistribute to the poor would only result in the better-off moving outside the city limits to other local jurisdictions in the same labour market, with a resulting decline in the city's fiscal capacity. In effect, Peterson was saying that, in an area of what many considered critical economic and social policy, local governments simply were not players. Although Peterson was arguing that local governments *could* not, rather than *should* not, engage in redistributive policy-making, he was interpreted by many readers as advocating developmental rather than redistributive policies. (It is worth noting that Peterson's argument does not export well to Britain, where larger local authorities and redistributive grant systems – and what is effectively a national business tax – largely sever the link between local policy decisions and local fiscal consequences.)

Gurr and King (1987) set out a more thoroughgoing analysis and critique of the extent of local autonomy. They begin by identifying two separate dimensions of local state autonomy. Type I local autonomy concerns the extent to which local government can 'pursue its interests without being substantially constrained by local economic and social conditions' (p. 57). In particular they identify three types of constraint facing local governments:

1. Limits on the revenues that can be extracted from the local economy;
2. Resistance of dominant local interests to the policies of the local state; and
3. The activities of locally-based (or focused) political organisations and social movements which aim at reshaping the content of local public policy, or at thwarting its implementation.

Type II local autonomy is the more traditional conception and relates to 'the extent that it (the local state) can pursue its interests without substantial interference by the national state'. Gurr and King conclude that local autonomy of both types is declining in both Britain and the United States, but that 'local states in Britain have considerably less autonomy than do their American counterparts'.

Wolman and Goldsmith (1992) bring a similar challenge to theories of local democracy. They argue that the real concern of urban politics ought to be with the well-being of residents in urban areas, and they pose the question of the extent to which this well-being is affected by the activities of local government. In order to answer this question, they first examine other major determinants of the well-being of urban residents, particularly the operation of the private market place, the activities of national government, and the functioning of a broad variety of non-governmental institutions (family and personal relationships, church, neighbourhood institutions and so on). They then turn to local government and conclude that, in both countries, local government does have some scope, albeit limited, for affecting the well-being of its citizens. Following Gurr and King, they argue that the available scope – or potential – is subject to the various kinds of Type I and Type II constraints discussed above. They conclude (Gurr and King, 1987, p. 47) that local governments in both countries possess autonomy in limited, but not unimportant, spheres.

Some authors, on both sides of the Atlantic, who have studied the impact of global economic restructuring and change on urban governments are even more pessimistic about the ability of local government (and the relevance of local democracy) to shape its own destiny in the face of these sweeping changes. Others strenuously disagree, arguing (Clavel and Kleniewski, 1990, p. 199) that in both Britain and the United States, 'The space for local response is greater, not smaller, in the 1980s than in previous postwar decades.' Clarence Stone and other proponents of 'regime theory' also argue that local politics – and by extension local democracy – is relevant and can make an important difference.

Of course, even if the results of pluralist participation were meaningless in terms of the relevance and importance of policy outputs – an argument that, as we have seen, is in contention – widespread group (or individual) participation might still be justified in a British context in terms of the intrinsic value of participation as an end in itself (engendering group solidity, the pleasures of personal interaction in group activity and so on), contribution to civic education (in the Millsian tradition) or increased interest in, identification with and legitimacy of the local political system.

It is interesting that one of the leading critics of the traditional British theory of local government as an efficient service deliverer, John Stewart, has advocated the concept of 'community government' that begins to resemble the American version of pluralism. Stewart writes (1989, pp. 240–1):

> If one abandons the assumption that the primary role of local authorities is to act as agencies for the administration of a series of separate services, then a new basis for the future of local government can be explored . . . As community government, local authorities' primary role is concern for the problems and issues faced by local communities. They are the means by which communities confront and resolve those problems and issues that are

beyond the scope of individuals or other modes of social action. The concept of community government is not based on the idealistic picture of local communities. It recognizes within communities many differing interests and values. Conflicts exist as well as shared purposes. Community government is achieved through political processes that express different interests and values and seek their resolution is political action. A local authority is a political institution for the authoritative determination of community values.

What is clear is that the development of a pluralist rationale for British local government – a set of values underlying and justifying widespread group participation in local politics and a justification of local government as something other than solely a provider of local services – will emerge, if at all (and evidence does suggest a substantial increase in group participation) from a specifically British context. The American experience is instructive for the light it throws upon the unspoken assumptions and beliefs of Britain's own experience, and not because it suggests an implausible transplantation of political values and traditions.

9 Normative Theories of Local Government: A European Comparison

Mike Goldsmith

It would be strange indeed if other countries adopted similar traditions and values to those the British have applied to the institution of local government, however true it may be that people everywhere would expect their system of local government to be both democratic and efficient. The simple reason is that democracy and efficiency are often given different meanings or interpretations. This chapter examines the way in which local democracy has been interpreted in Western Europe and suggests that European local government follows a number of different practices. In particular, it draws attention to differences between northern and southern European experience, and the ways in which countries have responded to the fundamental dichotomy involved in reconciling the competing claims of local government to be both democratic and efficient.

It is helpful to take as our starting point the distinction made by Hesse and Sharpe (1991a, pp. 606–7), suggesting that there are three broad types of local government. The first is the Anglo group, in which local government is a creature of statute, but enjoys a high degree of day-to-day autonomy from central control. Hesse and Sharpe suggest that such a group would include, as well as the United Kingdom, countries such as the Republic of Ireland, Canada, Australia, New Zealand, and with some qualifications, the USA. For most of this group, we should note the limited legal and political status of local governments, notwithstanding the wide discretion they may enjoy on a day-to-day basis.

The second group is called the Franco group, in which:

> local government more or less follows the French, or Napoleonic, model. In its purest form, local government enjoys constitutional

status, but, for service delivery, it is usually dependent on the assistance and direction of deconcentrated central field agencies. The *raison d'être* of local government is accordingly essentially political rather than functional – local government is primarily about community identity rather than self-government. Constitutionally, all local government units of equal status are in a relationship of tutelage to a 'common general superior' . . . who exercises formal control in the name of central government. (Hesse and Sharpe, 1991a, p. 606)

Included in this group are France, Italy, Belgium, Spain, Portugal, and to some extent Greece. Again here we should note the limited legal status and apparent limited discretion these systems enjoy, notwithstanding the greater political status they may have.

The third group to which Hesse and Sharpe draw attention is what they call the north and middle European variant, covering the Scandinavian countries, Germany, the Netherlands, Switzerland and Austria – and perhaps beginning to influence the shape of local government in some of the southern European countries and in eastern and central Europe. Within western Europe this group is certainly the largest. Hesse and Sharpe suggest that while this group shares similar features in relation to its pattern of central–local government relations, it differs in terms of the equal emphasis given to local democracy *per se* – in the sense that local government is commonly granted a general functional competence over and above any statutory powers it may be given. This group is the most formally decentralised of the three, and owes much of its form to the nineteenth-century Prussian tradition, which in turn expresses itself 'in the importance attached to strict procedural rules governing intergovernmental relations' (Hesse and Sharpe, 1991a, p. 607), reflecting the operation of the subsidiarity principle so beloved by the European Union. As a result, this group sees local government enjoying high constitutional status, and a relatively high degree of local autonomy and financial independence, as well as being responsible for many of the personal welfare state functions – more so that in the case of the other two groups.

While the Hesse and Sharpe distinction is helpful for classificatory purposes, it provides little guidance as to the fundamental values that underlie the distinction in local government systems. There are some clues – the value placed on local self-government, as expressed by the general competence given to local governments in the north and middle European group, as compared to the value placed on community identity and general central oversight in the Franco group. But, essentially, the distinction depends on a formal constitutional interpretation and less on evidence of an analysis of the different values underlying the three types. Further clues as to these values are suggested by the Page and Goldsmith (1987) analysis of central–local government relations in unitary states in western Europe, and by Page's (1991) further work on the political and legal bases of local self-government in western Europe. Page and Goldsmith adopt a similar distinction between northern and southern Europe, but see the British case as being more in line with the Scandinavian experience. They also draw attention to the high degree of administrative regulation exercised by Scandinavian central governments over their local authorities, which limits the latter's discretion.

Similarly, they draw attention in the southern group to various informal relationships, such as the close working relationship between local mayors and French prefects and the *cumul de mandats* there, or the importance of party linkages in Italian and, more recently, Spanish local government, which in effect increase local government discretion, decreasing the extent of formal central control over them. The creation of the autonomous communities in Spain, as well as greater decentralisation to French and Italian regions in the 1980s and 1990s, has further increased local discretion in the Franco group.

Page and Goldsmith (1987, pp. 162–8) suggest a variety of explanations for these differences. They accept that the Napoleonic tradition is an important distinguishing factor, but also suggest other factors: religious differences (Catholic south/Protestant north); the different processes over time of urbanisation (early north/late south); a similar distinction over the development of the welfare state, and the location of technical expertise (local north/ central south). A major difference between the two groups, however, has been the willingness or otherwise to redraw the map of local government – and especially the ability on the part of central government to abolish local governments – strong in the north and weak in the south. But again, while these factors might help explain the differences between the north/middle European group and the Franco group, they still give us little more than clues to the normative bases of these different local government systems. These clues echo those suggested by Hesse and Sharpe: the importance of political localism as a reflection of community on the one hand, and the need for larger local governments to handle the range of welfare state services on the other. In other words, in these cases the core values frequently used to support local government systems, namely democracy and efficiency, reappear in a different and conflicting guise.

Page (1991) provides a more historical perspective on these differences, and also draws on the work of Otto Hintze[1] as a means of additional explanation. Again, the distinction that Page stresses is the one between functional responsibility – what he calls legal localism – and the persistence of political localism. Legal localism explains why local government has developed in the way it has in northern Europe, while political localism explains the form of local government to be found in southern Europe. Page stresses the importance of forms of clientelism and the special relationships between leaders and led which clientelism produces. Interesting in this context is his discussion of Denmark and Norway which, unlike Britain and Sweden, experienced strong central supervision through the Scandinavian equivalent of the French prefect until well into the twentieth century, an office that has subsequently fallen almost into obscurity with the post-Second World War reforms of local government in both countries.

Unfortunately, Page's analysis excludes extensive discussion of Germany, the Netherlands and Belgium – such discussion being limited to a few pages in examining whether Page's approach would hold for other countries. But if there is a distinct north–south divide within western Europe along the lines that Page and others suggest, then we would expect Germany and the Netherlands to side with the north, while Belgium would exhibit the same characteristics as the south. Indeed, given the fundamental divisions in Belgian society between Flemish and Walloons, one would expect the country to exhibit divided tendencies in terms of the north–south distinction. This view is hinted at on more than one occasion by Sharpe (1988, 1989, 1993) in his discussion of territoriality in western European politics – though he generally places Belgium in the same category as France, Italy and Spain.

Territorial politics in historical perspective

This territorial distinction between north and south follows in the footsteps of Stein Rokkan (Rokkan, 1967; Rokkan, 1970, 1983). Page provides a useful service in drawing our attention to the earlier work of Hintze, for two reasons. First, Hintze makes a similar distinction between core and periphery to that made by Rokkan, except that his core is a European one, by which he means those lands that came under the Frankish empire and which reached as far south as central Italy and northern Spain, while the peripheral areas included both Britain and Scandinavia. Second, Hintze's work is important 'because it links what might be called mere administrative institutions and their structures to the process of state building' (Page, 1991, p. 55). Thus, according to Hintze, Sweden and Britain did not develop the same kind of centralized bureaucratic administration as did the nations in the core of Europe in the eighteenth and nineteenth centuries, preferring instead to rely on local élites or overseers drawn from the ranks of local élites – such as the Justices of the Peace (JPs) in Britain in the eighteenth century, a difference which also contributed to differences in the way in which local government developed within the European core and the periphery over the same period. For Hintze, it was the absence of a feudal tradition and the existence of a local gentry or petty nobility that allowed the peripheral nations at this time to develop a tradition of local self-government, albeit that this pattern was to disappear later, in the late nineteenth and early twentieth centuries. What it meant, however, was that in these northern countries there existed a group of local notables who could be entrusted by the central state to look after the affairs of what J. Bulpitt calls low politics (Bulpitt, 1983), whereas in those countries where a strong feudal tradition persisted and was reinforced by the exposure to the Napoleonic tradition, the development of local government took a different form (Page, 1990, pp. 48–52). We might expect this historical experience and tradition to reveal itself in the way in which the values of local government are currently demonstrated. And if this north–south difference exists, then we would expect the countries making up the two groups to share similar values and beliefs about local government as an institution. How far does this expectation hold up in practice?

The northern group

How far are the values of representative government and of *ultra vires* associated with British local government also carried across to Scandinavia and to the Netherlands? In a simple phrase – not very far. Hulmes (1991) argues that this group, in which he includes Austria, Switzerland, the Netherlands, Belgium and the Scandinavian countries, is much more influenced by the Prussian or German system. Here the values of local governemnt were much more influenced by the writings of Immanuel Kant, Georg Hegel and von Gneist (Hulmes, 1991, p. 8). The result is a system of governance 'emphasizing administrative efficiency in which the sub-national governments exercise extensive autonomy and the local chief executives exert considerable authority' (Hulmes, 1991, p. 8). The principle of subsidiarity operates, in that each level of government relies upon the one below for the management of public affairs; central control is exercised through a Ministry of the Interior or its equivalent; and local governments have considerable discretion or autonomy. As such they conform to Page's expectations that their system of local government would be driven by the ideas of legal localism, and that the value of local self-government would be incorporated into their constitutional arrangements. In Norway, Sweden and Denmark, the centre has conferred general competence powers on local governments, which presumes that local government has a constitutional status considerably different from that in Britain, placing emphasis on the idea of local self-government. Further, the generally consensual and corporatist style of government associated with much of post-Second World Scandinavia presumes that any reform of the structure and function of municipalities will proceed on an agreed basis – yet in all three countries reform of the structure, function and finance of local government has been extensive over recent years.

In the case of Sweden, Gunnel Gustafsson (1981, p. 76) suggests that local self-government enjoys a long tradition, based on its constitutional right to raise finance at the local level and the form of local elections which enhance local responsibility, as well as the extensive functional responsibility it possesses. In addition, Swedish local governments possess both a long-standing general competence which makes them responsible for their own affairs, and which allows them to take 'any appropriate action which is deemed to be in the interest of the inhabitants of the municipality'. This general competence is in addition to the specific authority given to Swedish local governments under central government legislation. As a result, the limits to what can be decided in a Swedish municipality are not clearly defined.

Many of the reforms in Sweden since 1960 have been concerned with the competing demands for efficiency and democracy, and particularly pressure for more participation at the local level. Most recently, in Sweden as elsewhere, it has been the 'free commune' reforms which have attracted attention, and in Sweden at least the impetus came from a desire to improve local democracy on the one hand, and to free local governments from detailed administrative supervision on the other. As a consequence, rather than (re)intro-duce a large number of small local governments to permit greater participation, participation has been accommodated by allowing greater access by local pressure groups to the municipal decision-making process – a development which fits the general corporatist, consensual style of Swedish and Scandinavian politics. Such a view is also supported by Stromberg and Westerstahl (1984, pp. 64–5) in their review of the reforms, though they suggest that the moves towards local corporatism can also endanger representative democ-racy. Furthermore, they suggest (p. 67) that Sweden exhibits a tension or contradiction between local and national democracy – between local self-government on the one hand, and ideas about equality and justice on the other. By contrast, Agne Gustafsson (1983, p. 11) suggests that the local self-government tradition itself is what has made the development of the Swedish welfare state possible. Local government thus becomes the main service delivery vehicle for the welfare services.

Obviously, given the extensive nature of welfare services in Sweden, the division between central and local responsibilities is less than clear. Following the reforms of the 1970s, a more detailed process of central supervision (administrative regulation) of local functions developed (Lane and Magnusson, 1987), and it was this development that the free commune experiments were designed to tackle (Rose, 1990). In so doing, Sweden was reflecting, and to some extent restoring, the long-standing local self-government tradition.

The Swedish case is typical of the way in which Scandinavian local government has developed. Similar pictures would exist for

Norway and Finland,[2] and to a lesser extent for Denmark. For example, all have been through a similar process of reform to that undergone by Sweden in the 1970s, and all have adopted the free commune experiments of the late 1980s and early 1990s.

In the case of Norway, both Hansen (1991) and Kjellberg (1987) stress the competition which exists between the values of local self-government and of others such as equality and justice. Kjellberg (1987, p. 49) says that the Norwegian case 'is almost a blueprint of the Swedish amalgamation reform . . . the underlying logic is strikingly similar'. Hansen (1991, p. 212) saw the financial reforms of 1987 as the last piece in a jigsaw which re-established the long tradition of Norwegian self-government, though he warns that these reforms could worsen a growing local fiscal crisis and raise doubts about the sustainability of the levels of the (Scandinavian) welfare state, a view echoed by Gustafsson (1991, p. 259).

Kjellberg (1987) suggests that Denmark is an exception to the other Scandinavian examples. He suggests that the dominant ideology of local self-government was absent from Denmark, which allowed a more radical reform of local government structure and functions in the 1970s than had occurred in either Norway or Denmark (Kjellberg, 1988, pp. 56–64), and that the consensus in Denmark behind the value of equality was much stronger. Such a view is echoed by Bogason (1987, 1991), who says of Danish local government: 'Though there has not been a British ultra vires clause in Danish local government administrative history, most tasks have de facto been explicitly delegated from the state' (Bogason, 1991, p. 262). He suggests that efficiency and effectiveness (Bogason, 1991, p. 287) have been the guiding values over recent years in Danish local government, and that there is not a strong tradition of local self-government. But Denmark also adopted the free commune experiment, though has been less willing to extend it after the initial trial period.

On balance, Scandinavian local government reflects the dichotomy implicit in the idea of local government – namely between local self-government on the one hand, and demands for efficient welfare services on the other. The stress on equality – implicit in the social democratic consensus upon which so much of Scandinavian politics for much of this century had been based – has supported the moves towards reform and greater efficiency, and allowed for the detailed administrative regulation by the centre. More recently, moves towards financial decentralisation and the free commune experiment reflect liberal and conservative concerns with local-self government – and with the ever-rising costs of the Scandinavian welfare state. To what extent do other countries in the northern group, such as the Netherlands and Austria or Switzerland, share similar perspectives? Morlan (1981, pp. 42ff.) notes that Dutch local government differs from Denmark in that it has a long history of local self-government, and that, as a country, the Netherlands is heavily urbanised. But it shared the same arguments when it came to a broad restructuring in the 1970s, even though by the early 1980s the subsequent process of change had been slower, a result that Morlan (1981, p. 52) attributes to the history of local self-government. Dutch local governments are general purpose territorial governments, in part a result of reactions to French domination in the Napoleonic era (Toonen, 1991, p. 294). Toonen suggests that the key to understanding the development of Dutch local government lies in an understanding of organic state theory as set out by Thorbecke. Thorbecke's point of departure from the French model, which sees local authorities as if they are instrumental creatures of the state, was the independent strength of local governments, meaning that they are characterised by a certain degree of autonomy as organic and evolutionary parts of a larger system. Thorbecke believed that a unitary state 'neither needs nor requires a hierarchically constructed system. State authority is considered to be the result, not the cause of unity among the component parts of the state' (Toonen, 1991, p. 296). Furthermore, Thorbecke took the view that the autonomy of local governments was embodied in the initiative they took to do things – or not as the case might be, and not in their insulation from other levels of government – giving rise to what Toonen (1991, p. 297) calls a kind of 'bounded municipal autonomy'. In effect, this model gives the higher levels of the state – provincial and central governments – blocking powers over the initiatives taken by local government.

The power of local initiative is not guaranteed by the constitution or other legal forms, so that effectively any municipal initiative can be regulated by national legislation, as is the case with Britain. Effectively, in the Netherlands this gives rise to a process described by Toonen (1987, 1991) as one of co-governance (*medebewind*) – municipalities can initiate and move into new areas, but national legislation can require municipalities to implement and deliver policies and services. It is this process that has allowed both the extension of the Dutch welfare state, peaking in the late 1960s and early 1970s, and its subsequent restriction in the 1980s (Toonen, 1987, pp. 114–23; 1991, pp. 311ff.). But these restrictions have brought an increase in both central and provincial supervision of local government activities (Toonen, 1993, p. 145), albeit of a largely indirect kind. In this sense, the provincial governments play a role as a kind of open democratic window in their supervision of municipal activity. Thus while the case of the Netherlands reveals some differences from the Scandinavian countries, it shares with them a stress on efficiency and effectiveness in service delivery, and of administrative supervision of municipal activities. The difference lies in the sense of local initiative that is at the heart of the Dutch municipal system, giving rise to a sense of co-governance not found so strongly in Scandinavia.

The German case is different. The German political system consists of three 'more or less autonomous tiers of government' (Reissert, 1980, p. 159), the federal level, the *länder* or states and the local governments, all based on representative bodies, with responsibilities generally divided 'not by policy areas but by functions in the policy making process' (Reissert, 1980, p. 160). As drawn up under the 1949 constitution or Basic Law, in effect the result has meant that policy formulation, guideline setting and finance-raising functions were essentially centralised at the federal level, while policy implementation and expenditure were the responsibility of state and local level. Local governments were seen as creatures of state government, but were given general competence powers within the limits set by the law – which gave local governments considerable autonomy, both to assume all public activities or else not to undertake them. In this respect, the Basic Law 'restores, formalises and protect traditional autonomy' (Norton, 1985, p. 102), Nassmacher and Norton (1990, pp. 105–10) suggest that local government has three traditional meanings in German – that of local self-government, derived from medieval times, when some cities achieved a degree of autonomy, as noted also by Hintze; that of local administration; and that of local democracy. Taken together, they can be taken as meaning that German local governments have traditional and long-standing inalienable functions of their own. The different occupying powers after 1945, however, added some 'instant tradition' of their own, with the French and

Americans continuing regional traditions from the pre-Nazi era, but adding the 'strong mayor' feature. By contrast, the British-occupied areas followed British ideas, with the stress on representative and responsible democracy. As Hesse (1987, p. 76) notes, clearly the occupying powers 're-established the institution of local self-government to promote a democratic political culture'.

Since 1949, both state and federal legislation has altered the scope and limits of local autonomy (Reissert, 1980, pp. 161ff.), both by the introduction of such things as federal grants in aid, and the spread of the welfare functions. Nevertheless, the principle of subsidiarity of areas remains the operating principle of the German system. Thus, as Hulmes (1991, p. 56) puts it: 'The national government relies upon the states, and the states upon the local governments, for the administration of public services.' At the local level, two tiers of government operate – the county (*kreis*) and the municipality (*gemeinde*), all with wide responsibilities, but with different forms of political executive structure.[3] Regardless of their type – mayor, board, burgomaster or chairman – German municipal executives generally have long tenures and are highly respected – the basis of this position being both the skills of the individuals concerned and their ability to develop political support. State-induced reforms in the 1960s and 1970s reduced significantly the number of municipalities, but at the same time preserved the strong role of local government generally by maintaining the system's capacity for service delivery. On the other hand, a major criticism of these reforms has been that grassroots participation has been decreased.

Overall, the German system is one of joint policy making between the three tiers (Nassmacher and Norton, 1985, p. 110), though Hesse (1987) suggests that there is more fragmentation of power than the joint policy making model would imply. For Hesse, the scope of local responsibilities is a matter of some dispute, and with what is really an entanglement of levels of government and not a collaboration, one that is characterised by 'an intensification of bargaining relations between the different levels' (Hesse, 1987, pp. 71–2). Germany is thus characterised by 'a dynamic intergovernmental process which goes beyond existing constitutional norms' (Hesse, 1987, p. 86) involving both a centralisation of politics and power, and a process of politics from below. The main role for local government is thus 'to serve as key spatial coordinating instruments for *Land* (state) administration' (Gunlicks, 1986, p. 92). But, while local governments carry out many obligatory and delegated functions, many important functions are carried out voluntarily – that is, as local self-government activities: examples would include local transport; care of the elderly; and cultural and sports facilities. As a result, Hesse (1991, p. 377) argues that the 'political importance of local government has grown' because of the vertical division of labour between national and local government; changing value systems, especially the emergence of post materialism; and as this is the level most immediately affected by economic and environmental change. In Hesse's (1991, p. 382) view, local government therefore sees a revival of politics from below in the hope not only of 'greater efficiency, transparency and legitimacy in traditional politics to be achieved by decentralised political processes', but also because of a recognition 'that the relations between state and society in Germany are changing once again'. Local government in Germany is thus seen as a central and important actor in the German political system (Bahrenburg, 1989, Hesse, 1991).[4]

Turning to a brief discussion of Austria and Switzerland, Hulmes (1991, p. 65) suggests that they share many of the features of the German system of government. Such a picture is largely confirmed for Austria by Bauer (1991). He indicates that there is a tradition after the end of the seventeenth century in Austria of local self-government which is carried through to today, in that municipalities continue to have general competencies and a right to self-government. Such local authorities have played an important role in the development of the Austrian welfare state, as well as in Scandinavia and in others among the northern group. Similarly, this increased welfare role has led to more joint policy-making, or joint decision-making – for example, in the co-governance of the Netherlands – though it may involve some subordination of local government. A similar picture exists in the case of Switzerland, where municipalities have an unwritten tradition of autonomy – but not the kind of general competence found elsewhere. In the Swiss case, municipal freedom of action relates to matters that are not the function of either the cantons or the federal government. In the nineteenth century, there was a clear division of power, but Swiss federalism is now characterised by 'a complex network of co-operation' (Linder, 1991, p. 409), even though the system is decentralised (Linder, 1991, p. 427). The co-operation comes about because the higher levels of government deem it necessary to compensate between small and large, and rich and poor municipalities and because common standards have to be set for the main welfare services, reflecting not only efficiency issues, but also issues of equity.

Our review of the northern group of countries suggests a number of key features that distinguish this group from British experience, even though it might be argued that Britain shares many features in common. First, they all expect municipalities to have some sense of self-government, whether it be in the formal constitutional general competence associated with Austria, Norway and Sweden; the sense of initiative, as in the case of the Netherlands; the unwritten but accepted local self-government tradition in Switzerland; or the subsidiarity principle operating in Germany. In some countries, such as the Netherlands, Austria, and perhaps Germany, this principle is also supported by the idea of co-governance – or of strong traditions of co-operation between different levels, as in Scandinavia. Although local governments have been strongly involved in the development of welfare state services in these countries, giving rise to a dependence on local horizontal cohesion through general-purpose area governments, the problems of fiscal stress and overload such developments have brought in recent years have placed these systems under some degree of stress. Solutions to these problems have been sought through such measures as financial changes in Scandinavia; the emergence of stronger provinces in the Netherlands (Toonen, 1993), or discussions about more decentralisation – again the free commune experiments in Scandinavia and similar moves in Austria and Switzerland.

What sets these countries apart is both a general belief in the values of local self-government and decentralisation, which gives local government as an institution an important role in the way in which public services are shaped and delivered on a joint or co-governance basis. Though custom and practice play their part, considerable weight is placed on the formal constitutional and legal basis of local government – reflecting the importance of legal localism to which Page (1991) drew attention.

The southern group

Our introductory review of European local government suggested that the value of political localism would dominate the southern

European countries. As a result, one would expect local government to represent communitarian values quite strongly, with the representation of territorial interests being its main feature. Further, one would also expect strong central supervision of municipalities to be the second feature, with the formal constitutional relationship being more hierarchical. Since the early 1980s, however, many countries in this group have undergone a process of decentralisation, including the strengthening of the intermediate or meso tier of government. The result has been that, unlike among the northern group, local territorial politics play a large part in the political system, thus reflecting a different stress on the meaning of local democracy and consequently placing a different value on the need for efficiency at the local level.

As Mabileau (1989, p. 18) suggests, these features result in France having a system of government in which there are strong political and administrative links between the different levels. And France shares with Britain the legal principle of *ultra vires*, in which municipalities can exercise only those functions given to them by law. Hulmes (1991, p. 26) suggests that French local governments serve a dual role – one as self-governing local polities designed to respond to local pressures and undertaking essentially local tasks, and the second as local offices for delivering certain delegated functions from the central state. But the essential difference between the two countries lies in the Jacobin tradition of France which has 'ensured a centralisation of administrative powers (the one and indivisible state) which has no administrative parallel in Britain' (Mabileau *et al.*, 1989, p. 3).

French local governments (communes) all have equal legal status, expect to be treated on an equal basis, and have a strong sense of common identity. The result has been to preserve the structure of much of French local government (France still has the 36 000 communes associated with the Napoleonic era) whose main function is to represent the *collectivity* of the area.[5] The importance given in the French system to the task of representing the collectivity – a form of territorial politics – results in the concentration of power in the local executive or mayor (Mabileau *et al.*, p. 246). French mayors have a much higher profile than do their British counterparts, the local party leaders, even though they do have to work closely with their deputies and chief officers (Borraz, 1994).

In this context, one has to remember how recently France has urbanised and industrialised. As Mény (1980, p. 53) reminds us, before 1939 only half the French population lived in communities of more than 2000 inhabitants, and one in four of the population was employed in agriculture; it was not until the 1950s that industrialisation and modernisation occurred – and then very rapidly. The strong French state was able to achieve significant reforms, a process which continued largely uninterrupted but at varying speeds right up to Francis Mitterrand's decentralisation reforms of 1981. Those reforms recognised the importance of developing regionalist politics, sometimes based on ethnic or nationalist claims (Breton; Alsaciene or Basque), Another peripheral pressure was the emergence of major urban centres – the power base of the Socialist and Communist parties at the time. Despite the strengthening of the departments and the introduction of the regional tier associated with the Mitterrand reforms, the fundamental unit – the commune – remained largely untouched, though there has been some encouragement (and at the local level, necessity) of intercommunal co-operation. At times, the centre has encouraged the development of regional associations – coalitions of local interests – to promote regional economic and political integration (Mény, 198, p. 61), the overall result being an interpenetration of centre–periphery élites, giving rise to what Mény calls a process of incremental adaptation and democratic integration, which recognises 'local and regional values' and an adaptation by the central state to the demands of territorial democracy. But, Mény claims, the process has not transformed the fundamental characteristic of the French politico-administrative system: the idea of a 'one and indivisible state'. The French local government system remains personalised, but 'change in the élites has not resulted in any substantial modification in the way things are run' (Mény, p. 68). Most strikingly, as Page (1991, p. 59) shows, the penetration of French national politics by local politicians remains high: in the 1980s 75 per cent of French MPs had a local office, while 53 per cent of Cabinet members also held local office – a reflection of the *cumul des mandats*, which recent reforms to limit have done little to change. This interpenetration not only allows the central state to influence localities, but also gives the localities access to the centre on a scale unknown in Britain, for example – meaning that locality matters in French national politics in a way far less common in the northern group of countries. Representation of the collective interest of the locality in French politics is thus simplified. It is largely through one channel, the mayor; it is personalised, and gives the locality the ability to resist central domination of its affairs. This localism means that local political leaders are able to maintain their influence by constantly cashing one of their resources – electoral legitimacy. Being re-elected not only reaffirms that legitimacy, but also increases the basis of their influence accordingly.

Thus the essential value of local democracy as represented in France is that of territorial representation or political localism in Page's sense. It represents a sense of communality or collectivity largely absent from much of English local government and from the northern group, but it also reflects the French tradition of the state. It binds the centre and locality together, ensuring some remaining degree of control for the centre over the locality (the French tradition of the centralised state) while allowing local interests to be represented on the national agenda. It is highly personalised and, as a number of writers (Tarrow, 1977; Kesselman, 1967) note, gives rise both to a kind of ambiguous consensus at the local level and to forms of clientelism.

Italy and Spain reveal similar features. Given the recent emergence of Spain from the shadow of General Franco, it is more difficult to be precise about the main values represented by local government. It remains an under-developed system, and the regional governments or autonomous communities represent the major forces in subnational government (Alfonso, 1991). The essential element of the post-Franco reforms was that the federal government and autonomous communities – the regional level of government – should be the key levels, so that a broad conception of local government at the municipal level is essentially inhibited and its powers largely prescribed.

Having said that, German influences on the new system appear strong, in that municipalities were given powers to tax and to intervene in affairs directly affecting their interests. The 1985 Law precluded the idea of general competencies or autonomy at the municipal level, but, at the same time, required higher levels to legislate in such a way that municipalities would be able to 'intervene in all public matters that affect the community' (Alfonso, 1991, p. 475). While Spanish municipalities could expect a wide range of specific competencies, it remains true that a complete new framework that would endow local government with a wide range of powers, as well as a proper defence of its autonomy, has not yet been introduced (Alfonso, 1991). Though the main constitutional influence has been the German constitution, with its principle of subsidiarity, it was this principle that helped the Spanish to tackle the difficult problem of giving some degree of autonomy to the nationalist regions. What success reform has achieved, at both local and regional levels, involves forms of political localism. Party linkages are important, as is the personality and stature of individual mayors and leaders of regional governments, between whom there is often considerable rivalry. For example, the mayor of Barcelona is often in conflict with the president of Catalonia, and both represent different traditions – one socialist, the other Catalan. So localism and territorial politics, especially in the form of nationalist or regional identity, is again a key value in Spanish local government, also expressed in clientelistic relationships (Clegg, 1987, p. 148). Spain thus shares with the French relatively strong forms of political localism, yet has not developed a form of legal localism that would enshrine local self-government formally as a value of the subregional level.

Unravelling Italian local government, its structure and processes, let alone its values, remains a difficult problem. Tarrow (1977) drew attention to the importance of political localism, and especially the importance of the party linkages as a means by which local élites could negotiate with and extract benefits from the centre, using votes as the trading commodity. Sanantonio (1987) confirms the importance of parties for local government and of the form of clientelism which results, showing some degree of foresight when he suggested that 'The parties are now deeply rooted within the system and pervade public activity to such a point that complaints about a "spoils system" and of parties taking over all aspects of public life are common' (Sanantonio, 1987, p. 125). The result of this system is that well-placed local political élites gain influence through the party mechanism, well illustrated by Allum's (1973) study of Naples.

Putnam's recent evaluation of regional government in Italy, however, suggests that two different civic traditions can be found in Italian politics. His analysis helps explain the persistence of clientelistic politics in Italy, especially in the south, but also offers support for the difference suggested earlier by Hintze, who included northern Italy in his sense of the European core. Putnam suggests it was the persistence of feudal forms of relationship, themselves established as early as the twelfth century. In the north, a communitarian and republican system developed, in which individuals played a role as citizen rather than subject, and the locality had a stronger sense of self-government. By the seventeenth century, however, the North had become more clientelistic in its politics. With the unification of Italy, the old civic communal traditions of collective solidarity and collaboration reasserted themselves in parts of the north, while the clientelistic pattern of relations continued in the south, the differences expressing themselves in different party networks and policies (Putnam, 1993, pp. 121–52), but not eradicating the sense of political localism and territorial politics, and the clientelistic practices so much a part of Italian life.

As far as the formal position of local government in Italy is concerned, Dente (1991) draws attention to the fragmentation and lack of uniformity of subnational government, between regions, provinces and municipalities, which exists in Italy, but clearly sees the municipality in its diverse shapes as being a key feature. But Italian municipalities lack a general competence – indeed 'the powers and tasks are distributed in such a way that more than one governmental level is inevitably involved' (Dente, 1991, p. 531). Dente thus describes the reform of Italian local government as a 'never ending story' (Dente, 1991, p. 536). Clearly, the role of political and party linkages in maintaining governmental services in Italy have been important, though recent corruption scandals, as well as the election of the right-wing central government, may come to undermine those linkages.

What this brief analysis of southern European states suggests is that it is the territorial representation – of collectivity or communality, and of political localism – accompanied by clientelistic practices and relationships, that are the values that come through most strongly. Again, the contrast with Britain and the northern group of countries could not be stronger.

Conclusion

Can we learn anything from this wide-ranging review of European local government and the values that it appears to be based upon? Within the two groups identified at the outset, two distinctive features, identified by Page (1991), are reinforced in this review. First, there is the tradition of legal localism – of local self-government, incorporated into the constitutional and/or procedural arrangements of the northern group, which effectively ensures a role for elected local government in the affairs of state.

Local government in the southern group occupies a similar position as a result of its role as territorial representative – political localism in Page's terms – which, through party and political linkages, ensures that the voice of the municipality is heard at the highest levels. This form of territorial politics can give the individual locality an influence at national level which would not be acceptable in the northern group. Yet this southern group is beset by the problems of lack of clarity of local functions – that is a well-defined legal localism – (Italy, Spain) and by the possibilities of widespread corruption that attend the clientelistic nature of the linkages. By contrast, in the north, the acceptance of local autonomy as a basic value of the political system has not stopped the process of reform essential to the functional development of the modern state. On the contrary, it may well have helped that process by ensuring the place of local government in the continuing structure of the state.

Notes

1. See also Page's (1990) discussion of Hintze's work in *Political Studies*, vol. 38, no. 1, pp. 39–55.
2. For Finland see, for example, Kiviniemi (1987).
3. For a brief discussion, see Hulmes (1991), pp. 62–3; Bulman and Page (1994) for a further discussion.
4. For a slightly contrasting view, suggesting that the (West) German political system is characterised by political immobility see Reissert and Schaefer (1985). Post-1989 the former West German system has been extended to the former East German areas: for a discussion of this process of reform, see Wollmann (1993).
5. An important point to be made here is that French political science appears to have little literature on the concept of community as it might be applied in the Anglo-American literature on local politics: see for example Mabileau *et al.* (1989, chs 1 and Part V) for a discussion of this question.

10   From Theories to Practices: Looking for Local Democracy in Britain

Allan Cochrane

The arguments of this book confirm that local democracy is a problematic concept. It is not enough to follow the 'common-sense' practice in which the words 'local' and 'democracy' necessarily and magically combine to produce something good and wholesome to be defended automatically against all those who seek to undermine it. Yet, conventionally that is just how the notion has been used, since – as Harold Wolman suggests in Chapter 8 of this volume – in Britain the existence (or possibility) of 'local democracy' has been constructed as one of the fundamental justifications for the existence of elected local government. Not only has 'local democracy' been presented as a 'good thing' (particularly in contrast to centralisation or bureaucratic hierarchy) but the equation between 'local democracy' and local government has more or less been taken for granted. The Thatcher-inspired reforms of the 1980s were met with almost universal hostility from within local government and academic communities, on the grounds that they threatened local democracy (Cochrane, 1993, pp. 31–2).

It is important to move beyond this understanding if the notion is to be of any use, whether analytically or as a guide to policy. Otherwise it will remain a confused and unhelpful slogan with a slippery content whose meaning changes according to the person using it. As Gerry Stoker explains in the Introduction to this volume, earlier chapters of this book have set out to explore the normative value of the concept, by interrogating particular aspects of the theories upon which it might have been based – from communitarianism, pluralism and feminism to Green approaches and public choice theory. They have sought to build from the bottom up, asking whether there is a theoretical or philosophical case for something that might be called 'local democracy'. If we did not have forms of local government and other local political institutions with some claims to democratic legitimation, what, if anything, would be the theoretical justification for building them? It is fair to say that the conclusions of the earlier chapters have been equivocal: although there are arguments for taking some decisions locally, there can be no simple presumption that 'local democracy' is necessarily superior to other forms or levels of political decision-making, particularly where localism may undermine equity.

This chapter looks at the case for democratising local political institutions and considers some of the ways in which democratisation might be taken further. It starts from the recognition that local political processes and local political institutions exist – whether or not the justification for their existence is one based on claims that they offer the promise of a more democratic polity.[1] In other words, given the existence of local politics, the question is whether it should be democratised and, if so, how this might be achieved.

More or less democracy?

The dominant model of local democracy in Britain has been an institutional one, in which elected councillors are expected to make decisions about the main direction of policy, which is then implemented by specialist professional officers (see, for example, Byrne 1992). In the Introduction, Gerry Stoker critically explores some of the theoretical justifications of such a system. This model goes beyond the parliamentary one, since, in principle, the committee system within local government also offers councillors the possibility of detailed scrutiny and access to a wide range of decision-making. Committee agendas often stretch from broad statements of policy (and even policy in areas for which councils have no direct responsibility) to recommendations for spending on particular activities. At the same time, it is assumed that councillors act as representatives for their individual constituents on issues that affect them – for example, dealing with individual cases on housing transfer, or disputes with particular service professionals. It goes alongside an understanding of local government as a mechanism for delivering a discrete set of public services (for most of the post-1945 period these have included education, social housing and personal social services).

The broader notion of citizenship identified by Marshall (1950) also finds expression in this interpretation of local democracy. Marshall characterised citizenship in terms of three sets of 'rights'. The first of these related to individual freedom (and included such aspects as freedom of speech), the second embodied the right to participation in public power, as a politician, or, more frequently, as an elector; while the third related to economic and social welfare. These rights helped to define the nature of the welfare regimes that emerged in many 'Western' countries in the first half of the twentieth century, and which were consolidated in the twenty-five years after 1945. The balance between them also helped to define the British version of local democracy in that period, since local government was seen as one of the principal routes to participation and was in practice chosen as one of the key conduits through which social welfare services were to be delivered.

The traditional model may never have been a very helpful way of explaining how local politics worked in Britain (since it under-represented the role of professionals, missed the significance of policy networks, and was uninterested in exploring the operation of local power relations). But its significance as a symbolic repre-sentation should not be discounted, since, in principle at least, channels of political accountability seemed to be reasonably clear, through the electoral process and through the openness of many (although admittedly not all) council and committee meetings, and their agendas. Of course, the extent to which electors could influence directly the operation of councils and their employees was limited, and the extent to which election results bore much relationship to local judgements on decisions made by councillors was limited, too. Gyford's reflections on the weaknesses of municipal labourism neatly sums up the gap between council and elector: 'Usually it did the right things for people; but sometimes it could do the wrong things to people; and only rarely had it previously discussed either of those things with people' (Gyford, 1985, p. 10). Nevertheless, and however self-serving the claims to representativeness sometimes made by local politicians, there was at least a presumption that they were locally and directly accountable to the electorate.

Whatever the past weaknesses of the model, it is no longer very helpful, even as an element of the 'dignified' aspect of the British 'constitution'. Since the early 1980s local politics has changed. In part, this change reflects the force of critiques of existing local government launched from above and below, from 'left' and 'right', by communitarian, Green and feminist. It is important not to exaggerate the extent of popular disenchantment with local government, even in the early 1980s, since surveys continued to show more favourable attitudes to local than to central government, and levels of satisfaction with some services (such as education) remained high. Nevertheless, the political atmosphere was changing. Despite the often dramatic ideological differences between them, the critics all focused on the problems associated with a local government system dominated by bureaucracy and professionalism, which excluded and patronised those reliant on the services provided through it (see, for example, Blunkett and Green, 1983).

If these criticisms provided the backdrop to a changing politics, they were given substance in the wide-ranging reforms introduced by the Conservative Governments of the 1980s and 1990s. Although these reforms were not always directed specifically at local government, they helped to change the context of its operation quite dramatically, and in the process significantly reshaped local politics. Some changes *were* directed explicitly towards the restructuring of local government. This was probably clearest in the setting up of new systems of local government finance and local taxation; in the regulations relating to compulsory competitive tendering; and in the restrictions placed on the political activity of local government officers. Most recently, the local government systems of Wales and Scotland have been completely overhauled in moves towards unitary councils and away from a two-tier system. Although attempts to achieve a similar shift in England have been less successful, there too some county councils are to be abolished (in addition to the metropolitan counties abolished in 1986) and some districts are to become unitary authorities.

Other changes were consequences of the restructuring of services traditionally delivered through local government. In education, not only have there been moves towards the local management of schools and an extension of grant-maintained schools, but further education colleges have been hived off from local authorities, and in higher education, polytechnics were first removed from local government control before being transforming into universities (see, for example, Fergusson, 1994). In social services not only has there been an expansion in the numbers of agencies involved in service delivery, but forms of management have been transformed with an increased stress on interagency working (with networks of accountability confused) and (not always successful) attempts to institutionalise purchaser/provider distinctions (see, for example, Charlesworth *et al.*, 1995; Wistow *et al.*, 1994). Yet other sets of changes appear to be unconnected with local government, but have had a substantial impact on the ways in which it is able to operate. The fragmentation and restructuring of the National Health Service, for example, has helped to create myriad forms of trust and health authority, many of which influence policy areas in which local governments used to be paramount. The formation of Training and Enterprise Councils, and Local Enterprise Companies, has also constructed local political forums whose interests overlap with those on the edges of local government responsibility (and which have been a growing area of interest for many councils).

Meanwhile, broader shifts in social and political realities mean that the electorate itself has changed in ways that make traditional models of democratic accountability unhelpful. It is no longer possible to identify a clear transmission belt linking some more or less monolithic set of 'voters' or even 'ratepayers' to some rational-bureaucratic set of local government institutions. Gyford suggests that local political movements are fragmented, pluralistic and diverse, which implies that new forms of local politics may be needed to respond to them adequately. He writes of 'a proliferation of pressure groups at both local and national level, devoted to the achievement of quite particularised goals in such areas as pollution and the environment, sexual behaviour, media policy, animal welfare, homelessness, transport policy, energy policy and disarmament and defence' (Gyford, 1986, p. 109). While class-based movements, such as trade unions and some community groups, remain important at a local level, it is also clear that they cannot be, and are not, the only political movements that matter. The linkages between trade unions and the Labour Party, which helped to construct the municipal labourist tradition, do not have the significance they once had; and the relationships of respectability and deference which supported Conservative power in the shires has also long gone.

Local democracy and accountability can no longer simply be translated into a series of questions about the operation of local councils. Multifunctional local authorities are no longer the sole agencies delivering a fairly standardised set of services to a relatively homogeneous population. There are other important agencies at local level, whose position needs to be considered, as well as an increasingly differentiated population and sets of political actors whose demands, interests and forms of political intervention need to be taken into account.

Alternatives to local democracy

'Solutions' to the problem of local democracy in the changed world at the end of the twentieth century have been almost as extensive as the ways of analysing it. For some the solution has implied the abandonment of political democracy in any very obvious sense. Marshall's understanding of citizenship has been challenged directly and explicitly, with alternatives which suggest not only that public participation is unnecessary to the achievement of economic and social welfare, but that it may even make it more difficult to achieve. Although the argument has rarely been pursued as consistently as the theorists discussed by Keith Dowding in Chapter 3 of this volume might have liked, one element running through the reforms of the 1980s and early 1990s has been the attempt to rediscover some sort of 'objective' or 'rational' means of determining how (and which) services should be provided at local level. The intention of the overall package – even if different elements of the package have not always been entirely consistent – has been to remove local service delivery from political controversy and, above all, to reduce local pressures to increase levels of spending.

So, for example, stress has been placed on finding ways of standardising types of service to ensure that comparisons between costs can be made in terms that focus on relative efficiency levels, rather than on differences in political approach. Instead of market-ising services so that consumers can make choices between them (for example, in terms of cost or level of provision) the emphasis is on standard contracts made with local authorities for the delivery of particular services. There is a move away from democratic – political or electoral – accountability towards financial, or sometimes technical, accountability (see, for example, Alexander, 1991). The power of the three 'Es' (economy, efficiency and effectiveness) sponsored by the Audit Commission, and value-for-money accountancy is ubiquitous. Sometimes, a fourth 'E' (for enabling) is introduced to the debate with an 'enabling' authority defined as one which delegates responsibility for most aspects of service delivery to others, 'enabling' them to be delivered, rather than delivering them itself. The principles underlying this shift minimise the political aspects of service delivery. The notion that there might be differences of priority, as well as access to power and resources, between different groups is rejected. The search for an overall (accounting) rationality suggests that political conflict is in a sense irrational, even if it is recognised that (supposedly non-political) market forms of allocation are not always appropriate. It is assumed that the only issue is how most efficiently and effectively to deliver a given set of services, even if it is not always clear where and how the decisions to provide them have been made (see, for example, Humphrey and Pease, 1991). Notions of local democracy are, of course, completely over-shadowed by these kinds of approach, except in so far as it is assumed that local electors (in the past frequently represented in the almost sacred category of 'ratepayers') can be mobilised in support of this essentially anti-political model. In a speech made while he was Chancellor of the Duchy of Lancaster (and responsible for overseeing the government's Citizens' Charter initiative) William Waldegrave expressed this view clearly, arguing that the search for democratic accountability was irrelevant to the operation of the local welfare state: what mattered to people was the quality of the services they received (Waldegrave, 1993).

A related – if not entirely consistent – approach uses the language of democracy rather differently, by developing what Phillips (1994) calls the notion of citizen–consumer, linking citizenship to market-based approaches to local service delivery and the allocation of resources at local level. This approach redefines electors as citizen-consumers able to influence resource allocation through their choices (for example, of the schools to which to send their children) and their preparedness to pay for services (whether individually or through tax-benefit packages) (see also Le Grand, 1990). The search for market surrogates, however, has not always been successful (the introduction of the poll tax is perhaps the best example of its failure) and has also fitted uneasily with other attempts to secure change. Market-based approaches should imply a close relationship between consumer and provider, for example, but in practice moves towards contracting have reinforced the position of those engaged in nego-tiating the contracts and monitoring their implementation. The consumer generally remains on the outside looking in, often reliant

on the decisions of professional gatekeepers to get access to whatever resources or services may be available (see, for example,
Langan and Clarke, 1994 for a discussion of the reforms in the
field of personal social services).

The notions of accountability through accounting or through the
construction of the citizen–consumer are ultimately unsatisfactory,
however, precisely because they attempt to depoliticise what are
inevitably processes of political choice. Clarke and Stewart argue
that it is necessary to distinguish between citizens and consumers,
because local government cannot be reduced to a series of straightforward commercial or service delivery transactions. Instead, it is
argued, it must both provide services and be concerned with the
rights of its citizens – it must be concerned with 'equity, justice and
citizenship' as well as with 'responsiveness, quality and customer'
(Clarke and Stewart, 1991, p. 40). As Kieron Walsh suggests in
Chapter 4 of this book, even efficiency may be easier to achieve
through elected local government than other systems of delivery and
resource allocation. Many of the choices made at local level are
choices about the redistribution of resources, and as a result they
need to be made collectively rather than just by the aggregation of
individual decisions.

Reshaping local government

If the role of elected local government has changed dramatically
over the last twenty-five years, that does not mean that local politics
have declined in importance, nor that locally-based institutions of
the welfare state have lost their significance. On the contrary, there
has been a proliferation in the numbers of such institutions and in
the forums in which political decisions about their activities are
made. The role of elected local government has declined – or at any
rate changed – while there has been a substantial increase in the
range of other local state institutions and political arrangements,
whether expressed in terms of networks, partnerships or mixed
economies. There has been an apparently inexorable rise in the
number and range of institutions of non-elected local government
(see, for example, Greer and Hoggett, 1995). At the same time,
British local government has more clearly become part of a wider
European system, with direct links to transnational bodies and

European networks (Benington, 1994). As a result, local politics has in many ways become more complex (and even 'messier'), encouraging a focus on governance rather than government, as Gerry Stoker notes in the Introduction to this volume.

If there has been a process of decentralisation, however, it is one which appears to have made decision-makers less, rather than more, accountable, at least through the traditional forms of electoral democracy. Instead, accountability is fragmented among different groups, some of which have more access to decision-makers than others. Decisions are made within the forums of joint committees or are the result of negotiations between officials (well insulated from public scrutiny) so that when they emerge it remains unclear who is to blame or who should be given the credit for making them. Of course, the forms of electoral democracy have often had more form than content, but the new arrangements are caricatures of a pluralism in which only some carefully licensed participants are allowed to play the political game, while others are left on the sidelines, to be brought in on terms acceptable to the main players. Fragmentation and decentralisation, which promise local empowerment, instead increasingly come to represent new ways of managing those with little power.

Although the direction of these changes points to the possibility of an increasingly local focus for policy-making, it often does so in ways which reemphasise central controls or responsibilities, both through the appointment process and through the centralised allocation of resources, and – more important for our purposes – it highlights their quasi-democratic nature, as what Glennerster *et al.* (1991) call 'small scale semi-representative bodies'. The old models of democratic accountability – however inadequate and misleading – have gone, without any clear alternatives having emerged, or been created. In the remainder of this chapter an attempt will be made to consider what these might be: what might the main features of a new local democracy look like?

One way of approaching this question is to build on existing forms of local government. So, for example, it has become common to borrow from debates within the new public management, which have begun to transform the public sector more generally (see, for example, Cochrane, 1994). There has been a focus on changing structures of local authorities, moving towards more flexible 'post-bureaucratic' forms (Hoggett, 1991) leading to a particular focus on decentralisation, whether expressed in budgets, offices, or bringing front-line workers closer to consumers in practice or rhetoric. Although even the strongest proponents of decentralisation strategies would acknowledge that they do not always deliver greater democracy, it is often assumed implicitly that 'decentralisation' is at the very least a necessary condition for 'democratisation', because it should allow users to gain easier access to professionals and encourage greater openness to community and user pressures.

Burns *et al.* (1994; see also Hoggett and Hambleton, 1987) have taken the lead in presenting decentralisation as the appropriately radical form that should be adopted by local government in the present period. They discuss a range of reforms, particularly drawing on evidence from the London Boroughs of Islington and Tower Hamlets, highlighting the ways in which bureaucratic power was challenged and responsiveness increased. They explicitly consider issues of local democracy in their discussions of neighbourhood forums in the case of Islington, and decentralised town halls in the case of Tower Hamlets. According to Burns *et al.* (1994), neighbourhood forums encourage significant local involvement in consultation over the operation of neighbourhood offices, while the existence of localised town halls encouraged increased attendance and involvement of the public at meetings in at least some cases. In Tower Hamlets in the late 1980s and early 1990s, it is argued, the existence of local town halls also helped to reinforce traditional forms of representative democracy, since it was easier for electors to judge the success of those they had elected, which paradoxically may have found reflection in 1994 in the defeat of the Liberal Democrat Council which introduced the decentralisation reforms. Some of the problems of decentralisation also come out in the Tower Hamlets case: the emphasis on locality enabled some neighbourhood councils to resist pressures to accept their responsibility to house members of the Bengali community.

Moves towards decentralisation should probably be seen as elements within a broader local government based strategy for local democracy. In this context, the approach adopted by Stewart and some of his colleagues is interesting (for example, in Clarke and Stewart, 1988, 1991; Stewart, 1989a and b; and Stewart and Stoker, 1988), pointing increasingly to what is called 'community government' as the way forward.[2] Stewart argues for a responsible and accountable authority which would 'provide services not to the public, but for the public and with the public' and require a more active involvement by its citizens in decision-making (Stewart, 1989b, p. 241). The notion of community government builds on the potentially strategic role left to local government and implies that the powers of local government should be extended to meet new needs. Stewart and his colleagues argue for a much broader definition of local government focused on the needs and problems of the communities – or localities – concerned, arguing for a move to community or local *government*, rather than local administration (Clarke and Stewart, 1991, pp. 1–11).

> Local government is 'about local authorities facilitating the meeting of the needs and problems of their communities in the most effective way. It is an expression of the *enabling* authority, not in the narrow sense of enabling other organisations to do the work of the local authority – that is in its own way another inward-looking approach that defines the local authority not by the communities it serves, but by the services for which it is responsible – but in the sense of enabling communities to define and meet their needs. (Clarke and Stewart, 1991, p. 62)

A key notion upon which much of the argument about 'community government' is based is that of 'empowerment'. The genesis of 'empowerment' as a term in debates about democracy is a rather confused one (with its roots both in the radical language of community action and the – arguably equally radical but quite different – language of popular management theory) (see, for example, Osborne and Gaebler, 1992). Its usage can also often be confusing. Clarke and Stewart distinguish between three models of empowerment, depending on whether the person being 'empowered' is defined as 'customer' (in which case the emphasis will be on individual choice through quasi-markets); 'citizen' (in which case the emphasis will be on rights); or 'community' (in which case the emphasis will be on new forms of democratic arrangement). Their own sympathies lie with the notion of self-governing communities, since a 'local authority as the community governing itself empowers the community and those who live and work within it' (1992, p. 22), but Clarke and Stewart argue that a balance between the different models is required in practice, in what they describe as a pluralistic approach, not least because they recognise that 'actions which

empower some may disempower others' (p. 24). In this context it
becomes necessary to emphasise the role of local government as that
of community government, in ways that are not merely strategic in
the usual sense, but recognisably political so that they involve
campaigning as well as managing and – above all – set out to
rediscover (or create) a representative role for local governments
which allows them to build on notions of democratic accountability,
instead of encouraging democracy be lost in the increasingly confusing networks of interagency working, pragmatic bargaining,
partnerships and appointed boards.

Reinventing local democracy

It is unhelpful to limit debates about local democracy to the
experience of existing forms of elected local government. Nevertheless, some valuable insights can be drawn from a consideration of
that experience. Stewart and others focus on the ways in which local
government can and ought to respond to change, and in doing so
they highlight a role for local government in leading and shaping
change processes. Since, as we have argued, the new arrangements
imply a move away from Marshallian notions of citizenship which
link civil, political and social rights, the call to transform elected
local government into a profoundly political rather than merely an
administrative agency is an important one. But local democracy
cannot be reduced to the existing institutions of local government,
nor to the structures bequeathed by representative democracy. Of
course, those structures remain important. They may be necessary
elements in a broader democratic framework, but they are not
sufficient. The local world in which democracy is to be developed
is one in which the most important decisions are no longer necessarily those being taken by elected local governments. It is a recognition of this which has led to the notion of 'community government'
– that is, government as a political lightning rod or campaigning
body, with the role of enabling or, perhaps better, 'empowering'
groups and individuals to make decisions or to act. But it also
highlights the need to think about other ways in which democratic
participation and involvement might be encouraged or might
develop.

Underlying much of the argument for local democracy or demo-cratisation is a belief in the importance of active involvement by 'citizens'. Participation is itself seen to be a good thing, which encourages the 'empowerment' of those who were previously merely defined as passive recipients of initiatives developed by experts of one sort or another. Empowerment can be viewed from two perspectives. The first implies a 'top-down' approach, in which those with economic or political power license certain groups to represent people who have little power or influence. So, for example, local government departments or other state agencies may delegate responsibilities for some activities (such as housing management) to service users or may develop more or less effective consultative frameworks around particular issues (such as development control). But some have also suggested that more extensive shifts in the operation of local politics might be possible. In exploring what he calls 'initiatives beyond charity', for example, Jacobs raises the possibility of private-sector agencies working with neighbourhood communities to achieve wider social benefits. He sees corporate social responsibility as the way of the future, stressing the value of community empowerment as part of the 'social vision of the free market' (Jacobs, 1992, p. 217). For Jacobs, empowerment implies the bypassing of existing institutions of local (city) government, to the extent that he concludes with the warning that those institutions may 'be seen as an obsolete way of organising human activity' (p. 263). In his model, local communities are empowered to negoti-ate directly with socially responsible businesses, instead of having their welfare needs mediated through state agencies.

Another perspective on empowerment, however, might start from below. Instead of seeing the process as one in which power is handed down from above, it is possible to see it as something that is claimed, or demanded through political action from below. Such a vision immediately implies a revitalisation of local democracy, suggesting that the appropriate arena for political action by citizens is not through electoral politics, but through a range of organisations, some of which will be based in local communities, while others may be based on shared interests as users. Hirst's discussion of forms of associative democracy is one of the most developed versions of this approach, redefining politics in terms which question the centrality of 'governments' and 'states' (Hirst, 1994). Hirst builds on the notion that society is made up of a plurality of associations, through which individuals come together in a complex variety of ways that reflect their multiple identities (at work, in leisure, at home, as a consumer and so on). These associations are not necessarily local. Although some will cut across divisions between localities, however, many of them will be locally-based and come together in ways that help to define places in terms which recognise the importance of local diversity rather than homogeneity. The role of local government in such a model of democracy is to provide the framework in which the associations can develop and interact most fruitfully – as Hugh Ward notes in Chapter 7 of this book, acting potentially as broker between associations where interests overlap or conflict. Hirst suggests that the state needs to be involved in 'orchestration of social consensus' and to regulate distributional arrangements (Hirst, 1994, p. 118).

The power of Hirst's arguments is that they make it possible to imagine a society with widespread participation in decision-making over a wide range of issues. It makes it possible to move towards radical notions of pluralist democracy such as those espoused by Mouffe (1992a). She questions notions of citizenship (such as Marshall's) which are universalist and undifferentiated. Like Hirst, she stresses the importance of differences between individuals and groups, and highlights the extent to which individual citizens themselves have multifaceted political and social identities, which rarely find expression in the formal world of electoral politics. Approaches like these allow theorists to recognise and celebrate the political importance of a range of agencies that are frequently overlooked in more orthodox approaches.

The weakness of Hirst's arguments, however, remains that they fail to deal adequately with issues of power, so that it is not always clear how differences in power between associations will be dealt with nor, indeed, quite what will happen to those whose involvement is likely to be severely limited, whether through choice or necessity. It is possible to present the blueprint of a complex institutional model of cross-cutting representation, as Hirst does, without it ever being quite clear how one might get from here to there.

Evidence (see, for example, Rallings *et al.*, 1994, sect. 4) suggests that professional groups are overrepresented in existing voluntary organisations, while ethnic minorities, the unemployed and working-class people are underrepresented, and women are underrepresented at leadership levels within them. Despite assertions to the contrary, the model suggested is one that suggests rather too rosy a picture of pluralism to be entirely convincing. With only a light hand on the regulatory/distributional tiller, it is assumed that groups can and will work productively together (or, at least, not 'irrationally' against each other). Similarly, although there is some discussion of associations which do not yet recognise themselves as such (presumably their members have some form of false consciousness) and of those who are relatively inactive, the implication is that it should be possible to raise awareness in the former, while helping the inactive into activity. As Anne Phillips suggests in Chapter 6 in this volume, such a vision of permanent mobilisation, as well as being utopian, also rules out the possibility that people may be inactive because they have better things to do and are reasonably satisfied: the important point may be to make it easy for individuals and groups to mobilise themselves on issues which concern them, and for existing institutional arrangements (whatever they are) to be open to the full range of such activity, not just ready to defend the comfortable relationships with organisations to which they have grown accustomed.

One way of building on the associative model is to combine it with the representative democracy of 'community government'. This is essentially the route favoured by Burns *et al.* (1994). They suggest that new approaches to democracy and the public sphere are needed, based around 'a much greater plurality of democratic provider organisations' which are 'collectively accountable or controlled', alongside strong local representative institutions whose purpose is to help overcome the necessary fragmentation of civil society, but not to act as monopoly service provider. Merely chanting mantras calling for decisions to be taken within civil society is not enough. Not only is civil society itself divided, but those divisions reflect highly unequal power relations. The authors argue that, as a result representative government will always have an important and active role to play in seeking to correct these inbuilt inequalities. Geddes similarly highlights the danger of the political and social exclusion of poor people and outlines the possibilities of developing local political strategies to encourage the integration of such groups into the wider political system. He identifies the tensions that are likely to exist, but stresses the need to strengthen grassroots (neighbourhood) initiatives, even where they may challenge formal political structures – local democracy, he concludes, must be 'rooted both in and against the state' (Geddes, 1995, p. 17).

In parallel with such initiatives, a range of other ways of drawing on popular opinion and allowing it to develop through debate can also be identified, rather than leaving them as the responsibility of the local governing class. The available menu of democratic consultation is a rich and – in Britain at least – still barely explored one. Local referenda on key issues have been and are used in some countries. The experience of referenda as a means of extending democracy is, of course, a mixed one. It is possible to list scare stories, in which they have been used to endorse the decisions of dictators (including Adolf Hitler) as the best example of democratic dictatorship, since, instead of reinforcing diversity, they institutionalise uniformity through a yes/no ballot choice. But it is also possible to highlight their value more modestly if they incorporate a range of choices, rather than just one, eliciting a wider range of response and forcing voters to make decisions for themselves instead of leaving it to their representatives. Similar points can be made about the use of market research and surveys: it doesn't take much to construct a survey that will give you the answer you want before you start, but it should also be possible to use surveys more effectively to identify issues that are seen as important locally. This can, of course, be done by unelected as well as elected forms of local government. Unfortunately, although it may be more important for unelected forms, it is also they who have a greater incentive to commission surveys that will give them 'good' news about their successes, since they are unlikely to have to suffer electorally from their unpopularity. In principle at least, one might expect elected politicians to worry rather more about the popularity of their policies.

The idea of a jury-type model for local decision-making on some issues (such as planning) has also been suggested. Utilising such an approach, if the jury were representative in some sense, would allow decisions to be made by 'citizens' on an informed basis without it being left to elected politicians or activists with special interests. In borrowing the jury model from the courts, of course, it might also be worth remembering that there is a risk of leaving the jurors at the mercy of professionals laying claim to technical objectivity able to bury them under mounds of detail (some of these and other possibilities are discussed in Stoker (1994), particularly pp. 14–15). Even the most sceptical of us can begin see the possibilities of wider consultation and participation through the use of information technology, although it is not too difficult to see how they might also be used as means of exclusion if access is restricted to those with the resources to own relatively sophisticated equipment (for a positive discussion of the possibilities, see Percy-Smith, 1995).

Initiatives such as these have paradoxical implications. The arguments in their favour stress their ability to involve a wider range of the population in political decision-making. They suggest the possibility of a wider notion of democracy, the possibility of a more deeply-rooted and extensive popular involvement. Yet they also carry with them rather a different set of possibilities, because in a sense they legitimate inactivity, and the possibility of not having to take serious responsibility. Voters in referendums are minor actors within an impersonal process – individuals whose identity is lost within a collective voice. Whichever way they vote they are not responsible, because a majority only emerges from a mass of numbers. Referendums offer the prospect of power without responsibility – the chance of using the electronic zap button. Implementation is still left to someone else. The use of surveys and jury models can similarly be seen either as a means of increasing democratic involvement – increasing openness and participation, or as a means of avoiding political decision-making through conflict. Like the policies of the 'new right', which emphasise market approaches as an alternative to politics, these proposals also appear to offer the possibility of non-political decision-making, or perhaps more accurately the possibility of a politics without politicians. In attempting to solve the dilemmas of representative democracy these approaches also run the risk of sanitising the political process by removing the possibilities of conflict and masking the unpleasantness of clashes between different interests.

Conclusion

The practices of local democracy are as complex and uncertain as the theories that try to grapple with it. It is, however, possible to point towards features which may come together to help transform traditional understandings and build a more positive way forward.

The role of elected local government is perhaps the most complex, since it cannot avoid combining the role of service delivery and political representative. In its continuing role of service delivery, moves towards local democracy imply that local governments need to open up processes of decision-making through decentralisation, the increased use of neighbourhood forums, and forms of user involvement. Above all, it is important that decision-making is transparent and open, so that it can be scrutinised, even – or perhaps particularly – when it involves contractual deals with other agencies to deliver services. At the same time, however, and this is perhaps the most difficult shift, local governments need to take on the role of active political representation and involvement in areas outside their direct service delivery role. It is this which begins to move them towards 'community government'.

This also implies a commitment to supporting the development of active associations which involve citizens across a range of issues and interests, even when their activities might be embarrassing to the councils that support them. A move in this direction is one away from the view that the role of voluntary organisations is primarily to act as surrogate service delivery agencies under detailed contract to a commissioning agency, since the implicit threat is that campaigning organisations are unlikely to be given contracts once they challenge the agencies that issue them. The danger of this can be seen in the experience of community care legislation, which has resulted in the institution of a purchaser/provider divide, in which the purchaser determines what is provided and is under pressure to limit the costs of what the provider does. The aim may be to diffuse accountability through encouraging active participation by a wider range of groups (including users). But the danger in practice is that relationships become more tightly and more narrowly defined through contracts which promise empowerment but in fact bring rigidity. Questioning such outcomes is vital to any democratic initiative at local level. A wider forum is required in which it is possible to develop more strategic views, generalising from the needs of particular groups and individuals and seeking to integrate what are increasingly fragmented local agencies of the state, quasi-state agencies and the private sector.

From the perspective of community and voluntary organisations, of course, the new world of local politics offers the prospect of careful negotiation, a tightrope walk between satisfying the demands of those who issue the contracts and the demands of their members or those whom they seek to represent. There is a tension between accepting the rules of the powerful to ensure that resources are made available for activities that fit with the aims of community and voluntary organisations, and losing touch with the members or supporters of those organisations. This is particularly the case when levels of activism begin to fade as the work of organisations becomes routinised and professionalised (see, for example, Gutch and Young, 1988; Cochrane, 1986). The possibility of an expanded local democracy depends on the possibility of a continuing process of renewal in which there is always access to the emerging institutions or new ones can be created and recognised relatively easily. In the new world, democracy has to be redefined as a process, not a straightforward institutional arrangement.

The role of elected local governments is changing and has to change in the new context – away from a narrow focus on service delivery (although, of course, some services will continue to be delivered through local government) to one which stresses their political role (as 'community government'). Emphasising this democratic role for elected councils, however, is not intended to undermine arguments for the democratisation of the newly emergent (non-elected) organisations, institutions and arrangements. On the contrary, although the focus has so far been on elected governments and their relationship with locally-based associations and popular organisations, it is also important to transform the state, quasi-state and public–private organisations that have been created since the mid-1970s. Similar demands to those one might make of elected local governments could equally well be made of all locally-based public organisations. The creation of locally-based specialist agencies may offer genuine opportunities for groups to become involved in influencing decisions on issues which concern them. In 1994–5, for example, school governors (including those elected by parents) played a significant part in questioning government policies on funding. Greer and Hoggett (1995) explore some of the differences between agencies usually lumped together as quangos and highlight the wide range of different possibilities that exist, to open them up to democratic involvement. It is legitimate to ask for the opening up of appointments to, and the decision-making processes of, health authorities, training and enterprise councils, and the governing bodies of grant maintained schools and further education colleges.

Questions about how people are appointed to such boards are also legitimate, and unless there are elections of some sort (relating to appropriate constiuencies) then the possibilities of local democracy are always going to be limited.

An openness to the concerns of local residents and service users through a range of consultative and participative forums may provide one way of increasing democratisation, picking up on some of the mechanisms discussed earlier (referendums, user panels, jury models and so on), but that openness is unlikely to be sustained without active campaigning by locally-based groups, or, indeed, without a transformation in the way in which elected local governments define their roles. Local democracy is not something that can be guaranteed, and it will only be achieved through the campaigning of a changing set of activists on a range of issues in the framework of a positive commitment from the institutions of local government. The rise of the 'quango state' does not mean that democratic involvement must disappear, indeed – in principle – new possibilities may open up if there is a concomitant growth of locally- and citizen-based groups alongside them. But the responsibilities of elected local government within the new world not only change, but also become fundamental to the extension and maintenance of a democratic framework. As a continuing presence, it is local government that can provide the context within which the growth of citizen groups may be encouraged and the 'excluded' involved in decision-making. In the past, local government has been an overwhelmingly respectable – even dull – part of the British political scene. In the future, not only will it need to draw on all its powers of imagination in developing its relationships with all the other actors in local politics, but it should also become the base for democratically licensed subversion and the questioning of emergent power relations.

Notes

1. Defining the arena of local politics is, of course, itself problematic: some have attempted to develop structural theories which explain the distribution of responsibilities between levels of government (see, for example, Saunders, 1984); while others have been reluctant to talk of local politics at all, instead using the term 'urban' politics (see, for example, Dunleavy, 1980); some have sought to find 'local' social relations (see, for example, Cooke, 1989); while others have utilised

theories of uneven development as a starting point (see, for example, Duncan and Goodwin, 1988); and the common-sense world of local government studies has in most cases simply taken for granted the structures handed down by legislation (see, for example, Byrne, 1992).

2. The use of 'community' in this context may well be influenced by some of the communitarian arguments criticised by Elizabeth Frazer in Chapter 5 of this book, but the linkages are not made directly. In this context the key contrast being made is between 'community government' and 'local administration', with the former being explicitly political and the latter defining itself solely in terms of service delivery.

11   Conclusion

Desmond King

Normative political theory can be used in two ways. First, principles derived from prescriptive exercises may be deployed as criteria with which to assess the success or failure of political institutions in realising specified aims. Second, scholars may employ normative frameworks to derive principles appropriate for specification in political institutions. In this volume, the contributors have engaged in both exercises with an emphasis upon the latter, which is also my interest. In this conclusion I argue that most recent theorising fails adequately to examine or explain how local autonomy can be combined with the maintenance of nationally-valued rights of citizenship.

The constitutional context in which local authorities operate in Britain sets fundamental limits upon their powers and remit. The position was lucidly, if circumspectly, formulated by the Widdicombe Committee:

> local government has no independent right to exist. Its continued existence is based on the contribution it can make to good government. It needs to be able to demonstrate that it is a more effective means of government than local administration (Widdicombe Report, 1986, p. 55).

This is an uncompromising and unpromising environment in which to formulate prescriptive theories about local government. It sets a constraint upon scholars wishing to design institutions of local government, but need not deter reflective exercises on local democracy. It is a view that is reproduced in a survey of senior civil servants and ex-Ministers undertaken for the Commission for Local Democracy: 'the general view of local government in Whitehall and Westminister is that it is a service provider, unlike elsewhere in Europe where the emphasis is on expressing local community feeling' (Jones and Travers, 1994, p. 12). The drive towards local government as an enabling mechanism for service delivery rather than a forum for political debate illustrates this economistic propensity (Hill, 1994, ch. 5).

Politically, the motive for considering normative values as being germane to designing local government is unproblematic. The establishment of new forms of political administration alongside traditional local authorities, the transfer of decision-making powers for some policies from elected authorities to unelected agencies, the fostering of 'opted-out' schools and hospitals, and the growth of interest in new issues, such as 'environmental' ones, among local communities all suggest a context that is stimulating enquiry about first-order political values. Of course, the relationship between political institutions and normative values is not one of identity and it would be foolish to attempt to 'read off' the former from the latter. The consideration of normative values should be undertaken with some reference to existing local democratic institutions but not with the assumption that they correlate directly.

The new context of local government

The shape of modern local government has changed significantly since the early 1980s, in part driven by the public choice logic explicated by Keith Dowding in Chapter 3 of this book. The number of elected and accountable bodies has declined, while those agencies with only limited or nil accountability (measured by elections) among electors has increased. The Conservatives' post-1979 legislation has created a new system of *informal local government* composed of centrally controlled agencies whose work parallels that of elected local authorities. The environment of local governance has evolved. Part of the Conservative Administration's strategy for local government is to centralise in the short-term as the basis for decentralising, on its own terms, over the long-term. Agencies constituting the informal local government system effect this strategy. They are complemented by government programmes to increase public–private partnerships in urban policy, such as those associated with City Challenge, City Technology Colleges and enterprise agency schemes. The system is informal in that a range of agencies and organisations enjoying policy-making powers and financial resources operate independently of formal local government to which members are elected and held accountable by voters.

Informal local government agencies are not directly accountable to local voters (and are indirectly accountable in only a few cases), but they chart many of the policies – such as education, health, and training urban regeneration – which affect some local voters. In terms of decentralisation, however, many of these touted changes may prove to be little more than rhetorical.

Within this new institutional context, one of the most important developments is the increased used of non-elected quangos with which to administer government policy and to formulate local practices. This institutional development marks a qualitative modification to British local democracy. According to some writers, Britain now deserves the sobriquet 'quango state', such is the prevalence of non-elected authorities with administrative responsibilities (see Stewart *et al.*, 1995; and Stoker, 1994). Commonly cited examples include Training and Enterprise Councils (TECs), hospital trusts, grant maintained schools, housing associations, housing action trusts, urban development corporations, and district health authorities. The trend is set to continue; G. Jones and T. Travers report support among central government policy-makers for it: 'the growth of appointed bodies is viewed with suspicion, though only a minority of ministers and ex-ministers would transfer services back to elected local government. Further shifts between local and central government are seen as inevitable' (Jones and Travers, 1994, p. 12).

The growth of quangos has several consequences for local government and local democracy. First, it narrows the responsibilities exercised by formally-elected local authorities, modifying the relationship between voters and the government. Second, the channel of accountability between voter and government is no longer a comprehensive mechanism for assessing local administration. By shifting service delivery responsibilities to unelected authorities and agencies, the government requires either that locally elected authorities achieve representation by right on the former, or that central government demonstrates publicly its role in monitoring the institutions of informal local governance. Either way, the lines of accountability between voters and quangos are murky.

An additional dimension of contemporary local government concerns the importance of national budget allocation for local government finances. Even where voters express strong views about local issues, the discretion enjoyed by local authorities actively to raise additional revenues or to shape spending priorities is slight.

Since the shift of business tax revenues to the centre, less than a quarter of local authorities' spending is financed by their own revenues, the council tax. Miscreants are subject to capping which set maximum expenditure allowances and to penalties if these levels are transgressed. One recent commentator concludes, regarding recent trends in local government finance, that, 'the whole rationale for the state has been questioned and local government has been subject to a welter of legislation which has eroded its role in the direct provision of services and its discretion over the level of local spending' (Sanderson, 1995, p. 5).

It is this new context which, unsurprisingly, has stimulated interest among students of local government as to the political values from which local democracy should derive. The decline of local government powers and autonomy has not been mirrored by a decline in academic interest.

Designing local government: new frameworks and old problems

The post-war expansion of the welfare state through nationally formulated and administered programmes was premised on a particular assumption about how best to remedy inequality. It was assumed that to promote equality of opportunity and of conditions across a polity required the maintenance of more-or-less uniform standards throughout the political system. For instance, in order that citizens living in different parts of the country received access to comparable public education and medical facilities, it was necessary that standards of delivery were set nationally and that interregional inequalities were – in theory at least – eradicated. This logic informed David Harvey's principles of 'territorial distributive justice', themselves borrowed from the work of John Rawls on liberal justice (Harvey, 1973; Rawls, 1971; see also Elster, 1992; Judge, 1978; and Smith, 1985). In Britain, this philosophy reflected the arguments influentially articulated by T. H. Marshall in his thesis about the social rights of citizenship (Marshall and Bottomore, 1992). The twin concerns with universalism – though not uniformity – and equality of opportunity driving this social rights framework implied an administrative role for local government to complement the policy-making work of national governments. Local autonomy constituted a danger to equality and the social rights of citizenship by providing the potential for malevolent variations between the services received by citizens according to where they lived.

The contributors to the present collection who are engaged in reflecting upon the normative values to be promoted in political institutions, including local ones, have implicitly or explicitly side-stepped this issue. For them, it is more important to advance political aims than to be unduly trammelled by distributive justice. For several of the contributors, local democracy and local autonomy are attractive mechanisms for maximising the value to which they are especially committed. Green theorists, as Hugh Ward explains in Chapter 7 in this volume, believe in 'small is good' and 'local is preferable' arguments, while, as Anne Phillips adumbrates in Chapter 6 of this book, feminists also advocate local institutions as a means of enhancing equality (see Young, 1990; Garber, 1995; and Staeheli and Clarke, 1995). Such an endorsement of local democracy implies the assurance of greater local autonomy and discretion – and both Ward and Phillips deal admirably with the implications of the normative claims they review. Ward focuses judiciously upon the pragmatic grounds for embracing Green localist claims, placing less value on intrinsic normative arguments. Phillips is fully cognisant of the dangers of local control for a feminist agenda, stressing the potential for innovation to redefine political priorities eventually at the national level, within strict constraints offered by local institutions. Thus local democracy is important, for these arguments, in its ability to generate debates that feed into national politics. These positive claims, however, despite their cautious character, still seem to me to address insufficiently the historical evidence about local government and democracy (though, of course, unfettered centralisation is not without its pellucidly deleterious effects). The twentieth century expansion of citizenship rights has rested upon the curtailing of local discretion and the realization of democratic values through national policy. The aim has been the limiting of variation within a polity once agreement upon certain national objectives has been reached. This is a problem about which I have written before and, in part because of its intrinsic difficulty, this fundamental problem continues to exercise scholars' concerns (see King, 1995; also Sancton, 1976).

The problem derives from the classic Millian liberal conception of local government, according to which local authorities are most appropriate for promoting efficiency of resource allocation within a local area, facilitiating political participation and thereby education, and finally offering a nebulous form of power for local residents by constituting a bulwark between them and the central state (see Mill, 1972; Sharpe, 1970; Hill, 1976; Seyd, 1966; Peterson, 1981; and Elkin, 1987). An obvious and non-trivial stumbling block to these principles is the reconciliation of local traditions with national rights. A glaring example is posed by the memory of the American South in the period of segregation, sanctified by the Supreme Court in 1896, until the passage of the Civil Rights Act of 1964 (for an admirable and compelling discussion of how this pernicious system operated in one southern state, see Fairclough, 1995). While substantial local discretion may not result in the erosion of a whole group's political rights, as occurred in the American South, it is possible to imagine targeted groups suffering discrimination, or at least dilatory treatment, in the allocation of local services. That this is not a purely academic anxiety is demonstrated by recent events in the London Borough of Tower Hamlets. Its experience in housing policy reminds us what a potent coagulation local prejudices and local decisions about services can become (for a fuller account see King *et al.*, 1995).

Tower Hamlets attained national notoriety in 1993 when a member of the fascist British National Party was elected in a local by-election from a Ward in the Isle of Dogs. Subsequently rejected by the electorate in May 1994, the election of a BNP councillor reflected the palpable racial tension – described by one Asian councillor as the 'smell of fear in the streets'[1] – and the effects of racism by divisive housing policies in the borough. As in other London boroughs, public service delivery – particularly housing though also education and social services – was pivotal to the character of local politics. However, unlike other boroughs, public service delivery in Tower Hamlets became entangled with racial divisions during the period of Liberal Democrat control (1986–94).

The Liberal Democrats were committed to decentralisation of power, policy formation and service delivery in Tower Hamlets. This programme was partly a reaction to the previous Labour party tradition, which was statist and highly bureaucratic, though it also rested upon a peculiar Liberal concern with decentralisation and community. Consequently, on winning borough-wide power in 1986, the party initiated a decentralisation programme, dividing the borough into seven neighbourhood areas (Isle of Dogs, Globe, Bow, Poplar, Stepney, Wapping and Bethnal Green). The neighbourhood system involved both service decentralisation and political decentralisation, the latter arrangement implying a high degree of consultation between neighbourhood committees and officers. In party political terms, some of the neighbourhoods were Liberal or Labour, and the borough as a whole was dominated by the Liberal group.

The principal case advanced in favour of decentralisation was that there would be benefits for service delivery and community accountability: 'service delivery was primary because accountability to the electorate was very direct'. Even critics of the system accepted that the 'good side was service delivery'. However, this close consultation also constituted a vulnerability. Because the neighbourhoods were based on a geographical area, rigidly demarcated, consultation processes were quickly exploited by groups unrepresentative of the local community at the expense of other groups. The neighbourhood system – with its excessive autonomy and generous decision-making powers – provided an organisational focus for groups determined to shift policy toward there own interests (it also bloated the borough's bureaucracy, reproducing several offices where one central one with appropriate staff would have sufficed).

The autonomy granted to neighbourhood areas limited the ability of the council as a whole to monitor and oversee local service delivery. In one officer's view, autonomy

> did help [areas] focus on service delivery and shape neighbourhoods' performance but it made neighbourhoods very inward focused (and competing against six other neighbourhoods) . . . [there was] intense rivalry between the neighbourhoods . . .

Attempts to assess neighbourhood standards by a Performance Review Committee faltered, and the decentralised system precluded comparisons with other boroughs' performances. The neighbourhood system was divisive.

The weakness of this extravagant neighbourhood autonomy became most pronounced in housing policy. In 1988, the Commission for Racial Equality (CRE) accused the borough of discrimination, issuing a non-discrimination notice after taking Tower

Hamlets to court (an out-of-court settlement was reached). According to one former housing officer, this discrimination reflected in part 'differing priorities in different neighbourhoods', a discreet way of expressing this baneful practice. According to one of the new councillors, the 1986–94 Liberal period constituted a 'regime of racial hatred'. Housing allocation resulted in some members of ethnic minorities receiving poorer housing. Housing was allegedly allocated by race, restricting Asian families to accommodation in housing blocks rather than in houses; the neighbourhood system also placed limits on moving between the seven neighbourhood areas. Strikingly, there was no council-level committee for housing which might have exercised supervision of the neighbourhoods' practices.

In sum, instead of fostering local identity and creating a direct relationship between voters and local government, neighbourhood areas, as they operated in Tower Hamlets, were at best divisive and at worst instruments of discimination. Local control can be pusillanimous. Regrettably, it may not necessarily be the *beau monde* anticipated by its supporters.

One response to this concern is the influential communitarian thesis advanced by G. Jones and J. Stewart. They stress how implementation defines policy:

> national minimum standards, in statutes or statutory instruments, are in fact rare. Most mandatory obligations laid on local authorities are general, empowering local authorities to perform certain functions, giving them duties and laying down procedures, while leaving local authorities discretion about the level and extent of the service provided, its frequency and intensity. The standards which emerged are not nationally determined. Such standards are in effect standards achieved through local choice. (Jones and Stewart, 1985, pp. 81–2)

Although this is presented as an argument for greater local autonomy, it could be seen as having the obverse implication: national statements of policy should be more detailed about administration than they are at present. Taking the statement on Jones and Stewart's own intended terms, the argument still gives grounds for enhancing local autonomy on major decisions, such as eligibility for housing benefits or access to schools. It is these latter sort of decisions which derive from rights of citizenship articulated and entrenched nationally. Defenders of local autonomy need to offer a resolution of the familiar problem of determining which decisions are best reached locally and which nationally. Polemics for expanded local politics – a wholly reasonable ambition – do not dissipate this problem (see Stoker, 1994). Such pleas might more usefully be directed towards constitutional reform and perhaps a Bill of Rights.

A problem also attaches to the communitarian defence of local democracy. Leaving aside the dense definitional confusion necessarily associated with conceptualising 'community' (see Elizabeth Frazer's valuable chapter in this volume (Chapter 5); and Hill, 1994, ch. 3), this new enthusiasm carries some troublesome implications (and some positive ones). The central issue is straightforward: whose conception of community – and relatedly, community traditions – is going to prevail? How do we determine which aspects of a community's values and traditions are apposite to contemporary institutional design and policy choices? To some extent, it is this very issue that tantalises communitarians and stimulates their endorsement of the approach. Communitarianism implies deliberation and decision-making on the basis of appealing to agreed upon traditional values and proceeding through compromise. However, even a cursory knowledge of history suggests that this strategy may, regrettably, constitute a mechanism for empowering those more able to articulate and mobilise their preferred values at the cost of marginalising the already marginal (for one discussion that points towards such consequences see Geddes, 1995, though the problems addressed by Geddes have somewhat similar implications for national politics as those drawn regarding local political participation). Such an outcome is not inevitable. It is, however, far from unimaginable as the Tower Hamlets *cause celebre* all too powerfully testifies.

In sum, advocates of decentralisation must be prepared to tolerate the often egregious consequences of empowering local communities (and their associated prejudices). From a Tieboutian perspective, such local effects are adjured, both on the grounds that citizens may move around if they dislike local conditions, and on the efficiency market analogy. If current discussions about decentralising the administration of social security benefits and the setting of levels meeting local circumstances are acted upon, then such inter-area variations will arise ineluctably. Those critics of recent local government restructuring – charging its emasculation – need to be mindful of the unsalubrious effects of local authorities intoxicated by local views (a point Keith Dowding makes in his discussion of left-wing appraisals of the Tieboutian framework).

The debates among political theorists collected in this volume are attempts to enrich discussion of local government and local democracy in Britain. If local democracy is a value accepted as part of the political culture and aligned with a commitment to some set of local democratic institutions, then thinking about normative values is elemental. It is particularly useful to reflect upon them during a period of great institutional turbulence and change of the sort experienced since 1979. However, new frameworks do not erode historic problems. Of these latter, that of balancing principles of social justice and equality of treatment with meaningful local autonomy, which has dogged encomiasts of local democracy for well over a century, persists and, as the contributors to this volume demonstrate, it cannot be ignored.

Note

1. All the quotations included in this section come from interviews conducted by the author with councillors and officers in Tower Hamlets under the condition of anonymity. For further details, see King *et al.*, 1995.

Bibliography

Abbot, P. (1991) *Political Thought in America* (Itasca, Ill.: F. E. Peacock).

Adam Smith Institute (1989a) *Wiser Councils (England and Wales)* (London: Adam Smith Institute).

Adam Smith Institute (1989b) *Shedding a Tier (Scotland)* (London: Adam Smith Institute).

Advisory Commission on Intergovernmental Relations (1987) *The Organisation of Local Political Economies* (Washington, DC: Advisory Commission on Intergovernmental Relations).

Alexander, A. (1991) 'Managing Fragmentation – Democracy, Accountability and the Future of Local Government', *Local Government Studies*, vol. 17, no. 6, pp. 63–76.

Alfonso, L. P. (1991): 'Local Government in Spain: Implementing the Basic Law', in J. Hesse and L. J. Sharpe, *Local Government*, pp. 497–516.

Alladina, S. and V. Edwards (1991) *Multilingualism in the British Isles* (London: Longman).

Allum, P. (1973) *Politics and Society in Postwar Naples* (London: CUP).

Anderson, B. (1991) *Imagined Communities*, 2nd edn (London: Verso).

Arrow, K. (1951) *Social Choice and Individual Values* (New York: John Wiley).

Ascher, K. (1987) *The Politics of Privatization* (London: Macmillan).

Ashford, D. E. (ed.) (1980) *Financing Urban Government in the Welfare State* (London: Croom Helm).

Ashford, D. E. (1982) *French Pragmatism and British Dogmatism* (London: Allen & Unwin).

Audit Commission (1993) *Passing the Bucks: The Impact of Standard Spending Assessments on Efficiency, Economy and Effectiveness* (London: HMSO).

Avinera, S. and De-Shalit, A. (eds) (1992) *Individualism and Communitarianism* (Oxford University Press).

Bachrach, P. and M. Baratz (1962) 'Two Faces of Power', *American Political Science Review*, vol. 56, no. 4, pp. 947–52.

Bahrenberg, G. (1989) 'West Germany: From Decentralisation in Theory to Centralisation in Practice', in R. Bennett (ed.), *Territory and Administration in Europe* (London: Pinter).

Banfield, E. and J. Q. Wilson (1963) *City Politics* (New York: Vintage Books).

Barber, B. R. (1984) *Strong Democracy* (Berkeley, Calif.: University of California Press).

Barry, B. (1989) *'Does Society Exist? The Case for Socialism'*, Fabian Tract 536.

Barry, B. (1991) *Political Argument: A Resissue with a New Introduction* (Hemel Hempstead: Harvester Wheatsheaf).

Bauer, H. (1991) 'Reviving Local Government in Austria', in J. Hesse and L. J. Sharpe, *Local Government*, pp. 387–409.

Beckett, A. (1994) 'How Clean was my Valley?', *The Independent on Sunday Supplement*, 28 August, pp. 4–8.

Beetham, D. (1994) 'Key Principles and Indices for a Democratic Audit', in D. Beetham (ed.), *Defining and Measuring Democracy* (London: Sage) pp. 25–43.

Beetham, D. and K. Boyle (1995) *Introducing Democracy: 80 Questions and Answers* (Cambridge: UNESCO and Polity Press).

Bell, C. and H. Newby (1971) *Community Studies: An Introduction to the Sociology of the Local Community* (London: George Allen & Unwin).

Bendor, J. (1985) *Parallel Systems: Redundancy in Government* (Berkeley and Los Angeles: University of California Press).

Bendor, J. and D. Mookherjee (1987) 'Institutional Structure and the Logic of Ongoing Collective Action', *American Political Science Review*, vol. 81, pp. 129–54.

Benhabib, S. (1992) *Situating the Self: Gender, Community and Postmodernism in Contemporary Ethics* (Oxford: Polity Press).

Benhabib, S. (1994) 'Democracy and Difference: Reflections on the Metapolitics of Lyotard and Derrida', *Journal of Political Philosophy*, vol. 2, pp. 1–23.

Benington, J. (1994) *Local Democracy and the European Union: The Impact of Europeanisation on Local Governance*, Research Report No. 6 (London: Commission for Local Democracy).

Bennett, R. J. (1980) *The Geography of Public Finance: Welfare Under Fiscal Federalism and Local Government Finance* (London: Methuen).

Bennett, R. J. (1989) 'Assessment of Competence and Resources', in R. J. Bennett (ed.), *Territory and Administration in Europe* (London: Pinter).

Bennett, R. J., M. Barrow and P. Smith (1991) 'Representation without Taxation: An Empirical Assessment of the Validity of the Accountability Argument Underlying the Reform of Local Government in England', *Fiscal Studies*, vol. 12, pp. 30–46.

Bennie, L., M. Franklin and W. Rudig (1993) 'Green Dimensions: The Ideology of the British Greens', Paper presented at the UK Political Studies Association Annual Conference, University of Leicester, April 20–22.

Biggs, S. and Dunleavy, P. (1995) 'Local Government Structures Transformed: A Bureau Shaping Analysis of Four London Boroughs', *Contemporary Political Studies*, vol. 2 (Belfast: Political Studies Association).

Bish, R. L. (1987) 'Federalism – A Market Economics Perspective', *CATO Journal*, vol. 7, pp. 377–96.

Bish, R. L. and V. Ostrom (1973) *Understanding Urban Government* (Washington, DC: American Enterprise Institute).

Blunkett, D. and G. Green (1983) *Building from the Bottom. The Sheffield Experience*, Fabian Tract 491 (London: The Fabian Society).

Boadway, R. W. and N. Bruce (1984) *Welfare Economics* (Oxford: Basil Blackwell).

Bock, G. and S. James (1993) *Beyond Equality and Difference* (London: Routledge).

Boddy, M. and C. Fudge (eds) (1984) *Local Socialism? Labour Councils and New Left Alternative* (London: Macmillan).

Bogason, P. (1987) 'Denmark', in E. Page and M. Goldsmith, *Central and Local Government Relations*, pp. 46–67.

Bogason, P. (1991) 'Danish Local Government: Towards an Effective and Efficient Welfare State', in L. Hesse and L. J. Sharpe, *Local Government and Urban Affairs in International Perspective*, pp. 261–90.

Bookchin, M. (1989) *Remaking Society* (Montreal: Black Rose Books).

Borraz, O. (1994) 'Mayoral leadership in France', in O. Borraz, R. Hambleton, N. Rao, U. Bullmon, E. Page, K. Young, *Local Leadership and Decision Making* (London: Joseph Rowntree Foundation) pp. 11–32.

Brennan, G. and J. Buchanan (1980) *The Power to Tax: Analytical Foundations of a Fiscal Constitution* (Cambridge University Press).

British Youth Council (1986) *The Voices of Young People* (London: British Youth Council).

Bromley, D. W. (1989) *Economic Interests and Institutions* (Oxford: Basil Blackwell).

Buchanan, J. M. (1971) 'Principles of Urban Fiscal Strategy', *Public Choice*, vol. 11, pp. 1–16.

Buchanan, J. M. (1975) *The Limits of Liberty: Between Anarchy and Leviathan* (Chicago: University of Chicago Press).

Buchanan, J. M. (1991) *Constitutional Economics* (Oxford: Basil Blackwell).

Buchanan, J. M. and G. Tullock (1962) *The Calculus of Consent* (Ann Arbor, Mich.: University of Michigan Press).

Buchanan, J. M., R. Tollison and G. Tullock (eds) (1980) *Towards a Theory of the Rent-Seeking Society* (College Station, Texas: Texas A&M University Press).

Bulmann, U. and E. Page (1994) 'Executive Leadership in German local government', in D. Borraz, R. Hambleton, N. Raw, U. Bullman, E. Page, K. Young, *Local Leadership and Decision Making* (London: Joseph Rowntree Foundation), pp. 33–54.

Bulmer, M. (1986) *Neighbours: The Work of Phillip Abrams* (Cambridge University Press).

Bulpitt, J. (1983) *Territory and Power in the United Kingdom* (Manchester: Manchester University Press).

Burnheim, J. (1985) *Is Democracy Possible? The Alternative to Democratic Politics* (Cambridge: Polity Press).

Burns, D., R. Hambleton and P. Hoggett (1994) *The Politics of Decentralisation. Revitalising Local Democracy* (London: Macmillan).

Butler, D., A. Adonis and T. Travers (1994) *Failure in British Government: the Politics of the Poll Tax* (Oxford University Press).

Byrne, D. (1995) 'Deindustrialisation and Dispossession: An Examination of Social Division in the Industrial City', *Sociology*, vol. 29, pp. 95–115.

Byrne, T. (1992) *Local Government in Britain. Everyone's Guide to How it All Works* (Harmondsworth: Penguin).

Campbell, B. (1993) *Goliath: Britain's Dangerous Places* (London: Methuen).

Carter, A. (1993) 'Towards a Green Political Theory', in A. Dobson and P. Lucardie (eds) *The Politics of Nature: Explorations in Green Political Theory* (London: Routledge).

Carter, N., R. Klein and P. Day (1992) *How Organisations Measure Success: The Use of Performance Indicators in Government* (London: Routledge).

Chandler, J. (1989) 'The Liberal Justification for Local Government: Values and Administrative Expediency', *Political Studies*, vol. 37, pp. 604–11.

Charlesworth, J., J. Clarke and A. Cochrane (1995) 'Managing Local Mixed Economies of Care', *Environment and Planning A*, vol. 27, No. 9, pp. 1419–35.

Clarke, J., A. Cochrane and E. McLaughlin (eds) (1994) *Managing Social Policy* (London: Sage).

Clarke, M. and J. Stewart (1988) *The Enabling Council* (Luton: Local Government Training Board).

Clarke, M. and J. Stewart (1991) *Choices for Local Government for the 1990's and Beyond* (London: Longman).

Clarke, M. and J. D. Stewart (1992) 'Empowerment: A Theme for the 1990s', *Local Government Studies*, vol. 18, no. 2, pp. 18–26.

Clavel, P. and N. Kleniewski (1990) 'Space for Progressive Local policy: Examples from the United States and United Kingdom', in J. R. Logan and T. Swanstrom (eds), *Beyond the City Limits* (Philadelphia, Pa.: Temple University Press).

Clegg, S. R. (1993) *Modern Organisations: Organisation Studies in the Postmodern World* (London: Sage).

Clegg, S. R. and D. Dunkerley (1980) *Organisation, Class and Control* (London: Routledge & Kegan Paul).

Clegg, T. (1987) 'Spain', in E. Page and M. Goldsmith (eds), *Central and Local Government Relations*, pp. 130–156.

Cochrane, A. (1986) 'Community Politics and Democracy', in D. Held and C. Pollitt (eds), *New Forms of Democracy* (London: Sage).

Cochrane, A. (1993) *Whatever Happened to Local Government?* (Buckingham: Open University Press).

Cochrane, A. (1994) 'Managing Change in Local Government', in J. Clarke *et al.* (eds), *Managing Social Policy*.

Cohen, J. (1989) 'Deliberation and Democratic Legitimacy', in A. Hamlin and P. Petitt (eds), *The Good Polity: Normative Analysis of the State* (Oxford: Basil Blackwell).

Cooke, P. (ed.), (1989) *Localities. The Changing Face of Urban Britain* (London: Unwin Hyman).

Cooke, P. (1990) *Back to the Future: Modernity, Postmodernity and Locality* (London: Unwin Hyman).

Coote, A. and P. Patullo (1990) *Power and Prejudice: Women and Politics* (London: Weidenfeld and Nicolson).

Cope, S. (1994) 'Making Spending Cuts in Local Government: Budget Maximizing or Bureau Shaping', in P. Dunleavy and J. Stanyer (eds),

Contemporary Political Studies 1994, vol. 2 (Belfast: Political Studies Association of UK).

Dahl, R. (1961) *Who Governs?* (New Haven, Conn.: Yale University Press).

Dahlgren, P. and Sparks, C. (eds) (1991) *Communication and Citizenship: Journalism and the Public Sphere in the New Media Age* (London: Routledge).

Dalton, R. J. (1988) *Citizen Politics in Western Democracies: Public Opinion and Political Parties in the United States, Great Britain, West Germany and France* (Chatham, NJ: Chatham House).

Daly, H. (1993) 'The Perils of Free Trade', *Scientific American*, November, pp. 24–9.

Dauncey, G. (1986) 'A New Local Economic Order', in P. Ekins (ed.), *The Living Economy* (Routledge: London).

Davis, H. and J. D. Stewart (1993) *The Growth of Government by Appointment: Implications for Local Democracy* (Luton: Local Government Management Board).

De Tocqueville, A. (1954) *Democracy in America*, vol. 1 (New York: Vintage Books).

Dente, B. (1987) 'Local Government Reform and Legitimcy', in F. Kjellberg and B. Dente (eds), *The Dynamics of Institutional Change* (London: Sage) pp. 171–86.

Dente, B. (1991) 'The Fragmented Reality of Italian Local Government', in L. Hesse and L. J. Sharpe, *Local Government and Urban Affairs in International Perspective*, pp. 517–50.

Department of the Environment (1991) *Local Government Review Consultation Paper: The Internal Management of Local Authorities* (London: HMSO).

Devall, B. (1988) *Simple in Means, Rich in Ends: Practising Deep Ecology* (London: Greenprint).

Die Gruenen (1983) *Programme of the German Greens* (London: Heretic Books).

Dobson, A. (1990) *Green Political Thought* (London: Unwin Hyman).

Domberger, S., S. Meadowcroft and D. Thompson (1986) 'Competitive Tendering and Efficiency: The Case of Refuse Collection', *Fiscal Studies*, vol. 7, no. 4, pp. 69–87.

Donnison, D. (1994) *Act Local: Social Justice from the Bottom Up* (London: Institute for Public Policy Research).

Dowding, K. (1991) *Rational Choice and Political Power* (Aldershot: Edward Elgar).

Dowding, K. (1992) 'Choice: Its Increase and Its Value', *British Journal of Political Science*, vol. 22, no. 3, pp. 301–14.

Dowding, K. (1995) *The Civil Service* (London: Routledge).

Dowding, K., P. John and S. Biggs (1994a) 'Population Movements in Response to Taxes and Service: Results from Four London Boroughs', LSE Public Policy Paper, vol. 8 (London: London School of Economics).

Dowding, K., P. John and S. Biggs (1994b) 'Tiebout: A Survey of the Empirical Literature', *Urban Studies*, vol. 31, pp. 767–97.

Dowding, K. and P. Dunleavy (1994) 'Production, Disbursement and Consumption: The Modes and Modalities of Goods and Services', ESRC Seminars – Conceptualizing Consumption Issues – The Marketization of Consumption: Public and Private, Salford University, 8 July.

Dowding, K. and D. King (1995) 'Introduction', in K. Dowding and D. King (eds), *Preferences, Institutions and Rational Choice* (Oxford: Oxford University Press).

Downs, A. (1957) *An Economic Theory of Democracy* (New York: Harper Row).

Dryzek, J. (1990) *Discursive Democracy: Politics, Policy and Political Science* (Cambridge: Cambridge University Press).

Duncan, S. and M. Goodwin (1988) *The Local State and Uneven Development* (Cambridge: Polity).

Dunleavy, P. (1980) *Urban Political Analysis* (London: Macmillan).

Dunleavy, P. (1991) *Democracy, Bureaucracy and Public Choice* (Hemel Hempstead: Harvester Wheatsheaf).

Dunleavy, P. (1993) 'Micro Agencies, Tiebout and the Theory of Clubs', Paper presented to PSA Rational Choice Group, London, 12 May.

Dworkin, R. (1986) *Law's Empire* (London: Fontana).

Dye, T. (1990) *American Federalism: Competition Amongst Governments* (Lexington Mass.: Lexington Books).

Eckersley, R. (1992) *Environmentalism and Political Theory: Towards an Ecocentric Approach* (London: UCL Press).

Editors of the *Ecologist* (1972) *Blueprint for Survival* (Boston, Mass.: Houghton Mifflin).

Edwards, J. (1988/9) 'Local Government Women's Committees', *Critical Social Policy*.

Eggertsson, T. (1990) *Economic Behaviour and Institutions* (Cambridge: Cambridge University Press).

Ekins, P. (1986) 'Co-operation: Where the Social Meets the Economic', in P. Ekins (ed.), *The Living Economy* (London: Routledge).

Elkin, S. (1987) *City and Regime in the American Republic: Chicago and London* (Chicago: University of Chicago Press).

Elshtain, J. B. (1981) *Public Man, Private Woman: Women in Social and Political Thought* (Princeton, NJ: Princeton University Press).

Elster, J. (1992) *Local Justice* (Cambridge University Press).

Etzioni, A. (1988) *The Moral Dimension: Towards a New Economics* (New York: Free Press).

Fairclough, A. (1995) *Race and Democracy: The Civil Rights Struggle in Louisiana, 1915–1972* (Athens, Georgia: University of Georgia Press).

Fergusson, R. (1994) *Managerialism in Education*, in Clarke *et al.* (eds), *Managing Social Policy*.

Fishkin, J. S. (1991) *Democracy and Deliberation. New Directions for Democratic Reform* (New Haven, Conn.: Yale University Press).

Frazer, E. and N. Lacey (1993) *The Politics of Community: A Feminist Critique of the Liberal Communitarian Debate* (Hemel Hempstead: Harvester Wheatsheaf).

Frey, B. (1992) 'Efficiency and Democratic Political Organisation: the Case for the Referendum', *Journal of Public Policy*, vol. 12, pp. 209–22.

Friedman, M. (1990) 'Feminism and Modern Friendship: Dislocating the Community', in C. Sunstein (ed.), *Feminism and Political Theory* (Chicago: University of Chicago Press).

Game, C. (1991) 'Local Elections', in J. Stewart and C. Game, *Local Democracy: Representation and Elections* (Luton: Local Government Management Board).

Garber, J. A (1995) 'Defining Feminist Community: Place, Choice and the Urban Politics of Difference', in Garber and Turner, *Gender in Urban Research*.

Garber, J. A. and R. S. Turner (eds) (1995) *Gender in Urban Research* (London: Sage).

Geddes, M. (1995) *Poverty, Excluded Communities and Local Democracy*, Research Report No.9 (London: Commission for Local Democracy).

Gerlach, M. (1988) 'Business Alliances and the Strategy of the Japanese Firm', *California Management Review*, vol. 30, pp. 126–42.

Glaser, D. (1995) 'Normative Theory', in D. Marsh and G. Stoker, *Theory and Methods in Political Science* (London: Macmillan).

Glennerster, H., A. Power and T. Travers (1991) 'A New Era for Social Policy: a New Enlightenment or a New Leviathan?', *Journal of Social Policy*, vol. 20, no. 3, pp. 389–414.

Goodin, R. (1992) *Green Political Theory* (Cambridge: Polity).

Gordon, J. (1993) 'Letting the Genie Out: Local Government and the UNCED', *Environmental Politics*, vol. 2, pp. 137–55.

Gorz, A. (1980) *Ecology as Politics* (Boston, Mass.: South End Press).

Goss, S. (1984) 'Women's Initiatives in Local Government', in M. Boddy and C. Fudge (eds), *Local Socialism? Labour Councils and New Left Alternative* (London: Macmillan).

Grandy, R. (1973) 'Reference, Meaning and Belief', *Journal of Philosophy*, vol. LXX, pp. 439–52.

Gray, J. (1989) *Liberalisms: Essays in Political Philosophy* (London: Routledge).

Green Party, The (1992a) *New Directions: The Path to a Green Britain Now* (London: The Green Party).

Green Party, The (1992b) *New Directions: Policies for a Green Britain Now* (London: The Green Party).

Greer, A. and P. Hoggett (1995) 'Non-elected Bodies and Local Governance', in J. Stewart, A. Greer and P. Hoggett, *The Quango State: An Alternative Approach*, Research Report No. 10 (London: Commission for Local Democracy).

Guinier, L. (1993) *The Tyranny of the Majority Fundamental Fairness in Representative Democracy* (New York: Free Press).

Gunlicks, A. B. (ed.) (1981) *Local Government Reform and Reorganisation* (New York: Kennikat Press).

Gunlicks, A. B (1986) *Local Government in the Federal German System* (Durham, NC: Duke University Press).

Gurr, T. R and D. S. King (1987) *The State and the City* (Chicago: University of Chicago Press).

Gustafsson, A. (1983) *Local Government in Sweden* (Stockholm: The Swedish Institute).

Gustafsson, G. (1980) *Local Government Reform in Sweden* (Lund: CWK Gleerup).

Gustafsson, G. (1981) 'Local Government Reform in Sweden', in A. B. Gunlicks (ed.) *Local Government Reform and Reorganisation* (Perk Washington: Kennikat Press), pp. 76–92.

Gustafsson, G. (1991) 'Swedish Local Government: Reconsidering Rationality and Consensus', in J. Hesse and L. J. Sharpe (eds), *Local Government and Urban Affairs in International Paerspective*, pp. 241–60.

Gutch, R. (1992) *Contracting Lessons from the US* (London: National Council for Voluntary Organisations).

Gutch, R. and K. Young (1988) *Partners or Rivals? A Discussion Paper on the Relationship between Local Government and the Voluntary Sector* (Luton: Local Government Training Board).

Gyford, J. (1985) *The Politics of Local Socialism* (London: Allen & Unwin).

Gyford, J. (1986) 'Diversity, Sectionalism and Local Democracy', *Research vol. IV* of *Widdicombe Report on The Conduct of Local Authority Business. Committee of Inquiry into the Conduct of Local Authority Business*, Cmnd 9797–9801 (London: HMSO).

Gyford, J. (1991a) *Citizens, Consumers and Councils: Local Government and the Public* (Basingstoke: Macmillan).

Gyford, J. (1991b) *Does Place Matter? Locality and Local Democracy* (London: Local Government Management Board).

Hansen, T. (1991) 'Norwegian Local Government: Stability through Change', in J. Hesse and L. J. Sharpe, *Local Government*, pp. 211–41.

Hardin, G. (1968) 'The Tragedy of the Commons', *Science*, vol. 162, pp. 1243–8.

Harding, A. (1995) 'Elitism', in D. Judge, G. Stoker and H. Wolman, *Theories of Urban Politics* (London: Sage).

Harvey, D. (1973) *Social Justice and the City* (Baltimore, MD: Johns Hopkins University Press).

Harvey, D. (1989) *The Condition of Postmodernity* (Oxford: Basil Blackwell).

Hayek, F. A. (1982) *Law, Legislation and Liberty* (London: Routledge & Kegan Paul).

Held, V. (1990) 'Mothering Versus Contract', in J. J. Mansbridge (ed.), *Beyond Self-Interest* (Chicago and London: University of Chicago Press).

Held, D. (1992) 'Democracy: From City States to a Cosmopolitan Order?', *Political Studies*, vol. XL Special Issue, pp. 10–39.

Herbert Report (1960) *Royal Commission on Local Government in Greater London*, Cmnd 1164 (London: HMSO).

Hesse, J. (1987) 'The Federal Republic of Germany: From Co-operative Federalism to Joint Policy Making', in R. A. W. Rhodes and V. Wright (eds), *Territorial Politics in Western Europe*, pp. 71–87).

Hesse, J. (1991) 'Local Government in a Federal State: The Case of West Germany' in J. Hesse and L. J. Sharpe (eds), *Local Government and Urban Affairs in International Perspective* (Baden-Baden: Nomos Verlagsgesellschaft).

Hesse, J. and L. J. Sharpe (1991) 'Local Government in International Perspective – some comparative observations', in J. Hesse and L. J. Sharpe (eds), *Local Government*, pp. 603–621.

Hesse J. and Sharpe L. J. (1991) *Local Government and Urban Affairs in International Perspective* (Baden-Baden, Nomos Verlagsgesellschaft).

Hill, D. M. (1974) *Democratic Theory and Local Government* (London: Allen & Unwin).

Hindmoor, A. and K. Dowding (1994) *'Can Rational Choice Writers Choose their Politics?'*, MS.

Hirschman, A. O. (1982) *Shifting Involvements. Private Interest and Public Action* (Oxford: Martin Robertson).

Hirst, P. (1994) *Associative Democracy. New Forms of Economic and Social Governance* (Cambridge: Polity Press).

Hoggett, P. (1991) 'A New Management in the Public Sector?', *Policy and Politics*, vol. 19, no. 4, pp. 243–56.

Hoggett, P. and Hambleton, R. (eds) (1987) *Decentralisation and Democracy* (University of Bristol: School for Advanced Urban Studies).

Hollis, P. (1987) *Ladies Elect: Women in English Local Government 1865–1914* (Oxford: Clarendon Press).

Hoyt, W. H. (1993) 'Tax Competition, Nash Equilibrium and Residential Mobility', *Journal of Urban Economics*, vol. 34, pp. 358–79.

Hulmes, S. (1991) *Local Governance and National Power* (London: Harvester Wheatsheaf).

Humphrey, C. and K. Pease (1991) 'After the Rainbow', *Local Government Studies*, vol. 17, no. 4, pp. 1–5.

Hunter, F. (1953) *Community Power Structure* (Chapel Hill, NC: University of North Carolina Press).

Illich, I. (1973) *Tools for Conviviality* (London: Fontana).

Ingham, G. K. (1970) *Size of Industrial Organisation and Worker Behaviour* (Cambridge: Cambridge University Press).

Jackson, P. M. (1982) *The Political Economy of Bureaucracy* (Oxford: Philip Allan).

Jacobs, B. D. (1992) *Fractured Cities. Capitalism, Community and Empowerment in Britain and America* (London: Routledge).

John, P., K. Dowding and S. Biggs (1994) 'Residential Mobility in London: A Micro Level Test of the Behavioural Assumptions of the Tiebout Model', MS.

Jonasdottir, A. (1988) 'On the Concept of Interests, Women's Interests, and the Limitations of Interest Theory', in K. B Jones and A. G. Jonasdottir (eds), *The Political Interests of Gender* (London: Sage).

Jones, B. and L. Bachelor (1986) *The Sustaining Hand* (Lawrence, Kan.: University of Kansas Press).

Jones, G. (1988) 'The Crisis in British Central–Local Government', *Governance*, vol. 1, no. 2, pp. 163–83.

Jones, G. W. (1992) 'The Search for Local Accountability', in S. Leach (ed.), *Strengthening Local Government in the 1990s* (London: Longman) pp. 49–78.

Jones, G. and S. Ranson (1989) 'Is There A Need for Participatory Democracy? An Exchange', *Local Government Studies*, vol. 15, no. 3, pp. 1–10.

Jones, G. and J. Stewart (1985) *The Case for Local Government* (2nd edn) (London: Allen & Unwin).

Jones, G. W. and J. D. Stewart (1983) *The Case for Local Government* (London: Allen & Unwin).

Jones, G. and J. Stewart (1992) 'Selected Not Elected', *Local Government Chronicle*, vol. 13 November.

Jones, G. and T. Travers (1994) *Attitudes to Local Government in Westminster and Whitehall*, Research Report No. 5 (London: Commission for Local Democracy).

Judge, D. (1995) 'Pluralism', in D. Judge, G. Stoker and H. Wolman (eds), *Theories of Urban Politics* (London: Sage).

Judge, K. (1978) *Rationing Social Services* (London: Heinemann).

Kaplan, G. (1992) *Contemporary Western European Feminism* (London: UCL Press).

Keating, M. and A. Midwinter (1994) 'The Politics of Central–Local Grants in France', *Government and Policy*, vol. 12, pp. 177–94.

Kesselman, M. (1967) *The Ambiguous Consensus* (New York: Knopf).

King, D. (1984) *Fiscal Tiers: The Economics of Multi-Level Government* (London: Allen & Unwin).

King, D. S. (1987) *The New Right* (London: Macmillan).

King, D. S. (1990) 'Economic Activity and the Challenge to Local Government', in D. S. King and J. Pierre (eds), *Challenges to Local Government* (London: Sage).

King, D. S. (1989) 'The New Right, the New Left, and Local Government', in J. Stewart and G. Stoker (eds), *The Future of Local Government* (Basingstoke: Macmillan).

King, D. S. (1993) 'Government beyond Whitehall', in P. Dunleavy, A. Gamble, I. Holliday and G. Peele (eds), *Developments in British Politics 4* (London: Macmillan) pp. 194–220.

King, D. S. (1995) 'From the Urban Left to the New Right: Normative Theory and Local Government', in J. Stewart and G. Stoker (eds), *Local Government in the 1990s* (London: Macmillan).

King, D. S, K. Dowding, P. Dunleavy and H. Margetts (1995) 'Regime Politics – London Style', Paper presented at the annual meeting of the American Political Science Association, Chicago, August.

Kiser, L. L. and E. Ostrom (1982) 'The Three Worlds of Action: A Metatheoretical Synthesis of Institutional Approaches', in E. Ostrom (ed.), *Strategies of Political Inquiry* (Beverly Hills: Sage).

Kiviniemi, M. (1987) 'Local Government Reorganisation and Structural Changes in Public Administration: The Finnish Case', in F. Kjellberg and B. Dente, *The Dynamics of Institutional Change*, pp. 70–88.

Kjellberg, F. (1987) 'Local Government and the Welfare State: Reorganisation in Scandinavia', in F. Kjellberg and B. Dente (eds), *The Dynamics of Institutional Change* (London: Sage) pp. 39–69.

Kjellberg, F. and B. Dente (eds) (1987) *The Dynamics of Institutional Change* (London: Sage).

Kymlicka, W. (1989) *Liberalism, Community and Culture* (Oxford: Clarendon Press).

Lacey, N. (1995) 'Community in Legal Theory: Idea, Ideal or Ideology', *Studies in Law, Politics and Society*, vol. 15, forthcoming.

Lane, J. and T. Magnusson (1987) 'Sweden', in E. Page and M. Goldsmith, *Central and Local Government Relations*, pp. 12–28.

Langan, M. and J. Clarke (1994) 'Managing in the mixed economy of care, in Clarke *et al.* (eds), *Managing Social Policy*.

Langrod, G. (1953) 'Local Government and Democracy', *Public Administration*, vol. 31, pp. 26–31.

Layfield Report (1976) *Report of the Committee of Inquiry into Local Government Finance*, Cmnd 6453 (London: HMSO).

Le Grand, J. (1990) *Quasi-markets and Social Policy. Studies in Decentralisation and Quasi-markets* (Bristol: School for Advanced Urban Studies).

Le Grand, J. (1991) *Equity and Choice. An Essay in Economics and Applied Philosophy* (London: HarperCollins).

Leach, S. (1995) 'The Strange Case of the Local Government Review', in J. Stewart and G. Stoker (eds), *Local Government in the 1990s* (London: Macmillan).

Leibenstein, H. (1966) 'Allocative Efficiency vs X-Efficiency', *American Economic Review*, vol. 56, pp. 392–415.

Lindblom, C. (1977) *Politics and Markets* (New York: Basic Books).

Linder, W. (1991) 'Local Government in Switzerland: Adaptation as Self-Help', in J. Hesse and L.J. Sharpe (eds), *Local Government and Urban Affairs in International Perpective* (Baden-Baden: Nomos Verlagsgesellschaft) pp. 409–29.

Lipset, S. M. and S. Rokken (1967) 'Cleavage Structures, Party Systems and Voter Alignment: An Introduction', in S.M. Lipset and S. Rokken (eds), *Party Systems and Voter Alignment* (New York: Free Press) pp. 1–66.

Lloyd, G. (1984) *The Man of Reason: Male and Female in Western Philosophy* (London: Methuen).

Lovenduski, J. and V. Randall (1993) *Contemporary Feminist Politics: Women and Power in Britain* (Oxford: Oxford University Press).

Lukes, S. (1974) *Power: A Radical View* (London: Macmillan).

Mabileau, A., G. Moyser, G. Parry and P. Quantin (1989) *Local Politics and Participation in Britain and France* (Cambridge: Cambridge University Press).

MacIntyre, A. (1981) *After Virtue* (London: Duckworth).

Mackenzie, W. (1961) *Theories of Local Government*, Greater London Papers No. 2 (London: London School of Economics and Political Science).

Magnusson, W. (1986) 'Bourgeois Theories of Local Government', *Political Studies*, vol. 34, pp. 1–18.

Mansbridge, J. (1992) 'A Deliberative Theory of Interest Representation', in M. P. Pettraca (ed.), *The Politics of Interest* (Boulder, Col./San Francisco/Oxford: Westview Press).

Marin, B. (ed.) (1990) *Generalized Political Exchange: Antagonistic Cooperation and Integrated Policy Circuits* (Boulder, Col.: Westview Press).

Marshall, T. H. (1950) *Citizenship and Social Class and Other Essays* (Cambridge: Cambridge University Press).

Marshall, T. H. and T. Bottomore (1992) *Citizenship and Social Class* (London: Pluto Press).

Mather, G. (1989) 'Thatcherism and Local Government Finance', in J. Stewart and G. Stoker (eds), *The Future of Local Government* (London: Macmillan).

Mayo, M. (1994) *Communities and Caring: The Mixed Economy of Welfare* (London: Macmillan).

Meadows, D. H., D. L. Meadows and J. Randers (1992) *Beyond the Limits: Global Collapse or a Sustainable Future?* (London: Earthscan).

Mény, Y. (1980): 'Financial Transfers and Local Government in France', in D. E. Ashford, *Financial Urban Government*, pp. 142–57.

Mény, Y. (1987): 'France: The Construction and Reconstruction of the Centre, 1945–1986', in R. A. W. Rhodes and V. Wright (eds), *Territorial Politics in Western Europe* (London: Frank Cass).

Mény, Y. (1992) *La Corruption de la Rèpublique* (Paris: Fayard).

Mény, Y. and Wright, V. (eds) (1985) *Centre–Periphery Relations in Western Europe* (London: Allen & Unwin).

Milgrom, P. and J. Roberts (1990) 'Bargaining Costs, Influence Costs and the Organisation of Economic Activity', in J. E. Alt and K. A. Shepsle (eds), *Perspectives on Positive Political Economy* (Cambridge: Cambridge University Press).

Milgrom, P. and J. Roberts (1992) *Economics, Organization and Management* (Englewood Cliffs, NJ: Prentice-Hall).

Mill, J. S. (1861) *Considerations on Representative Government in Utilitarianism, Liberty, Representative Government* (London: J. M. Dent).

Mill, J. S (1911) *Utilitarianism, Liberty and Representative Government* (London: Dent).

Mill, J. S (1962) *Considerations on Representative Government* (Chicago: Henry Regency Co).

Mill, J. S. (1972) *Considerations on Representative Government* (London: Dent).

Miller, W. L. (1986) 'Local Electoral Behaviour', in Widdicombe Report, (1986) Research vol. 3, pp. 105–72.

Miller, W. L. (1988) *Irrelevant Elections? The Quality of Local Democracy in Britain* (Oxford: Clarendon Press).

Mills, L. (1994) 'Economic Development, the Environment and Europe: Areas of Innovation in UK Local Government', *Local Government Policy Making*, vol. 20, pp. 3–10.

Moore, J. (1992) 'The Firm as a Collection of Assets', *European Economic Review*, vol. 36, pp. 493–507.

Moran, R. L. (1981) 'Territorial Reorganisation and Administrative Reform in Denmark', in A. B. Talicki (ed.) *Local Government Reform and Reorganisation* (Park Washington: Kennikat Press).

Mouffe, C. (1992a) 'Democratic Citizenship and the Political Community', in C. Mouffe, (ed.), *Dimensions of Radical Democracy* (London: Verso).

Mouffe, C. (1992b) *Dimensions of Radical Democracy. Pluralism and Citizenship* (London: Verso).

Mulgan, G. (1994a) *Politics in an Antipolitical Age* (Cambridge: Polity Press).

Mulgan, G. (ed.) (1994b) 'Lean Democracy', *Demos Quarterly*, no. 3.

Musgrove, R. A. (1989) *Theory of Public Finance* (New York: McGraw-Hill).

Naess, A. (1989) *Ecology, Community and Life Style* (Cambridge: Cambridge University Press).

Nassmacher K.-H. (1990) 'The Changing Functions of Local Government', in K.-H. Nassmacher and A. Norton (eds), *Local Government in Britain and Germany* (Birmingham: INLOGOV) pp. 35–48.

Nassmacher K.-H. and A. Norton (eds) (1990a) *Local Government in Britain and Germany* (Birmingham, INLOGOV).

Nassmacher K.-H. and A. Norton (1990b) 'Background to Local Government in Western Germany', in K.-H. Nassmacher and A. Norton, *Local Government in Britain and Germany*, pp. 105–15.

National Municipal League (1939) *Forms of Government: How Have They Worked?* (New York: National Municipal League).

Nevers, J. (1983) 'Du clientélisme à la technocratie: cent ans de démocratie dans une grande ville, Toulouse', *Révue française de Science Politique*, vol. 33, pp. 428–54.

Newton, K. (1976) *Second City Politics* (Oxford: Oxford University Press).

Niskanen, W. A. (1971) *Bureaucracy and Representative Government* (Chicago: Aldine-Atherton).

Niskanen, W. A. (1973) *Bureaucracy: Servant or Master?* (London: Institute of Economic Affairs).

Noddings, N. (1984) *Caring: A Feminine Approach to Ethics and Moral Education* (Berkeley, Calif.: University of California Press).

North, D. C. (1990) *Institutions, Institutional Change and Economic Performance* (Cambridge: Cambridge University Press).

Norton, A. (1985) 'German and British Government and Administration: Some Comparisons', in A. Norton (ed.), *Local Government in Britain and Germany* (Birmingham: INLOGOV).

Norton, A. (1994) *International Handbook of Local and Regional Government* (London: Edward Elgar).

Nove, A. (1983) *The Economics of Feasible Socialism* (London: George Allen & Unwin).

Nurmi, H. (ed.) (n.d.) 'Referenda in Representative Democracies', MS.

Oates, W. E. (1972) *Fiscal Federalism* (New Haven, Conn.: Yale University Press).

Oates, W. E. (1977) *The Political Economy of Fiscal Federalism* (Lexington, Mass.: Lexington Books).

Offe, C. (1989) 'New Social Movements: Challenging the Boundaries of Institutional Politics', *Social Research*, vol. 52, no. 4, pp. 817–65.

Okun, A. (1975) *Equality and Efficiency: The Big Trade Off* (Washington DC: Brooking Institution).

Olson, M. (1965) *The Logic of Collective Action* (Cambridge, Mass.: Harvard University Press).

Olson, M. (1984) *The Rise and Decline of Nations* (New Haven, Conn.: Yale University Press).

Ophuls, W. and A. Boyan Jr. (1992) *Ecology and the Politics of Scarcity Revisited: The Unravelling of the American Dream* (New York: Freeman).

Osborne, D. and T. Gaebler (1992) *Reinventing Government. How the Entrepreneurial Spirit is Transforming the Public Sector* (Reading, Mass.: Addison Wesley).

Ostrom, E. (1990) *Governing the Commons: The Evolution of Institutions for Collective Action* (Cambridge: Cambridge University Press).

Ostrom, E. (1991) 'Rational Choice Theory and Institutional Analysis: Towards Complementarity', *American Political Science Review*, vol. 85, pp. 237–43.

Ostrom, V. (1987) *The Political Theory of a Compound Republic* (Lincoln, Neb.: University of Nebraska Press).

Ostrom, V., C. Tiebout and R. Warren (1961) 'The Organization of Government in Metropolitan Areas – A Theoretical Inquiry', *American Political Science Review*, vol. 55, pp. 831–42.

Paehlke, R. (1989) *Environmentalism and the Future of Progressive Politics* (New Haven, Conn.: Yale University Press).

Page, E. (1982) 'The Value of Local Autonomy', *Local Government Studies*, vol. 8, no. 1, pp. 21–42.

Page E. C. (1990) 'The Political Origins of Bureaucracy and Self-Government: Otto Hintze's conceptual Map of Europe', *Political Studies*, vol. 31, no. 1, pp. 39–55.

Page E. C. (1991) *Localism and Centralism in Europe* (Oxford: Oxford University Press).

Page E. C. and M. Goldsmith (eds) (1987) *Central and Local Government Relations* (London: Sage).

Paley, J., J. Thomas and J. Norman (1986) *Rethinking Youth Social Work* (Leicester: National Youth Bureau).

Panter-Brick, K. (1954) 'Local Government and Democracy: A Rejoinder', *Public Administration*, vol. 31, pp. 344–7, and vol. 32, pp. 438–40.

Pareto, V. (1906) *Manual of Political Economy*, trans. 1971 by Ann S. Schwier, ed. A. S. Schwier and A. N. Page (London: Macmillan).

Parry, G., G. Moyser and N. Day (1992) *Political Participation and Democracy in Britain* (Cambridge: Cambridge University Press).

Paterson, M. (1994) 'Green Political Strategy and the State', Paper given at the Third IRNES Conference, September 1994.

Percy-Smith, J. (1995) *Digital Democracy: Information and Communication Technologies in Local Politics*, Research Report No. 14 (London: Commission for Local Democracy).

Peterson, P. (1981) *City Limits* (Chicago and London: University of Chicago Press).

Pettigrew, A. and R. Whipp (1991) *Managing for Competitive Success* (Oxford: Basil Blackwell).

Phillips, A. (1991) *Engendering Democracy* (Cambridge: Polity Press).

Phillips, A. (1994) *Local Democracy: The Terms of the Debate*, Research Report No. 2 (London: Commission for Local Democracy).

Phillips, M. (1986) 'What Small Business Experience Teaches About Economic Theory', in P. Elkins (ed.), *The Living Economy* (London: Routledge).

Philp, M. (1994) 'On Politics and Its Corruption', *Political Theory Newsletter*, vol. 6, pp. 1–18.

Porrit, J. (1984) *Seeing Green* (Oxford: Basil Blackwell).

Prest, J. (1990) *Liberty and Locality: Parliament, Permissive Legislation, and Ratepayers', Democracies in the Mid-Nineteenth Century* (Oxford: Clarendon Press).

Pringle, R. and S. Watson (1992) '"Women's Interests" and the Post-Structuralist State', in M. Barrett and A. Phillips (eds), *Destabilizing Theory: Contemporary Feminist Debates* (Cambridge: Polity Press).

Putnam R. D. (1993) *Making Democracy Work* (Princeton, NJ: Princeton University Press).

Rallings, C., M. Temple and M. Thrasher (1994) *Community Identity and Participation in Local Democracy*, Research Report No. 1 (London: Commission for Local Democracy).

Randall, V. (1987) *Women and Politics* (London: Macmillan).

Rawls, J. (1971) *A Theory of Justice* (Oxford: Oxford University Press).

Rawls, J. (1993) *Political Liberalism* (New York: Columbia University Press).

Reed, A. (1988) 'The Black Urban Regime: Structural Origins and Constraints', *Comparative Urban and Community Research*, vol. 1.

Reissert, B. (1980) 'Federal and State Transfers to Local Governments in the Federal Republic of Germany', in D. E. Ashford, *Financial Urban Government*, pp. 158–79.

Reissert, B. and G. F. Schaefer (1985) 'Centre-Periphery Relations in the Federal Republic of Germany', in Y. Mèny and V. Wright (eds), *Centre-Periphery Relations in Western Europe* (London: Allen & Unwin) pp. 104–24.

Rhodes, R. A. W. and V. Wright (1987) *Territorial Politics in Western Europe* (London: Frank Cass).

Ridley, N. (1988) *The Local Right: Enabling Not Providing* (London: Centre for Policy Studies).

Riker, W. H. (1982) *Liberalism Against Populism* (New York: Freeman).

Riker, W. H. and S. J. Brams (1973) 'The Paradox of Vote Trading', *American Political Science Review*, vol. 67: pp. 1235–47.

Roche, M. (1987) 'Citizenship, Social Theory and Change', *Theory and Society*, vol. 16, pp. 363–99.

Roddick, J. and F. Dodds (1993) 'Agenda 21's Political Strategy', *Environmental Politics*, vol. 2, pp. 242–8.

Rokkan, S. (1970) *Citizens, Electors, Parties* (Oslo: Universitatsferlayet).

Rokkan, S. and D. Unwin (eds) *Economy, Territory, Identity* (London: Sage).

Rose, L. (1990) 'Nordic Free Commune Experiments: Increased Local Autonomy or Continued Central Control', in D. King and J. Pierre (eds), *Challenges to Local Government* (London: Sage) pp. 212–41.

Rowley, C. K., R. Tollison and G. Tullock (eds) (1988) *The Political Economy of Rent-Seeking* (Boston: Kluwer Academic).

Ruddick, S. (1984) *Maternal Thinking: Towards a Politics of Peace* (London: Women's Press).

Sachs, W. (1986) 'Delinking from the World Market', in P. Elkins (ed.), *The Living Economy* (Routledge: London).

Sale. K. (1985) *Dwellers in the Land* (San Francisco: Sierra Club Books).

Salecl, R. (1994) *The Spoils of Freedom: Psychoanalysis and Feminism after the Fall of Socialism* (London: Routledge).

Samuelson, P. A. (1954) 'The Pure Theory of Public Expenditure', *Review of Economics and Statistics*, vol. 36, pp. 387–9.

Samuelson, P. A. (1955) 'Diagrammatic Exposition of a Theory of Public Expenditure', *Review of Economics and Statistics*, vol. 37, pp. 350–6.

Samuelson, P. A. (1958) 'Aspects of Public Expenditures Theories', *Review of Economics and Statistics*, vol. 40, pp. 332–7.

Sanantonio, E. (1987) 'Italy', in E. C. Page and M. Goldsmith, *Central and Local Government Relations*, pp. 107–29.

Sancton, A. (1976) 'British Socialist Theories in the Division of Power by Area', *Political Studies*, vol. 24, pp. 158–70.

Sandel, M. (1982) *Liberalism and the Limits of Justice* (Cambridge: Cambridge University Press).

Sandel, M. (1984) 'The Procedural Republic and the Unencumbered Self', *Political Theory*, vol. 12, pp. 81–96.

Sanderson, I. (1995) *'Current Issues in Local Government Finance'*, Research Report No. 12 (London: Commission for Local Democracy).

Santerre, R. E. (1986) 'Representative versus Direct Democracy. A Tiebout Test of Relative Importance', *Public Choice*, vol. 48, pp. 55–63.

Sapiro, V. (1981) 'When are interests interesting? The problem of political representation of women', *American Political Science Review*, vol. 75, no. 3.

Saunders, P. (1984) 'Rethinking Local Politics', in M. Boddy and C. Fudge (eds), *Local Socialism? Labour Councils and New Left Alternatives* (London: Macmillan).

Savas, E. S. (1987) *Privatization: The Key to Better Government* (Chatham House, NJ: Chatham House).

Schumpeter, J. A. (1952) *Capitalism, Socialism and Democracy*, 5th edn. (London: Allen & Unwin).

Schwartz, T. (1975) 'Vote Trading and Pareto Efficiency', *Public Choice*, vol. 24, pp. 101–9.

Seldon, A. (1990) *Capitalism* (Oxford: Basil Blackwell).

Self, P. (1962) 'The Herbert Report and the Values of Local Government', *Political Studies*, vol. 10, pp. 146–62.

Selznick, P. (1987) 'The Idea of a Communitarian Morality', *California Law Review*, vol. 77, pp. 445–63.

Seyd, A. (1966) *The Political Theory of American Local Government* (New York: Random House).

Shackle, G. L. S. (1979) *Imagination and the Nature of Choice* (Edinburgh: Edinburgh University Press).

Sharpe, L. J. (1970) 'Theories and Values of Local Government', *Political Studies*, vol. 18, pp. 153–74.

Sharpe, L. J. (1973) 'American Democracy Reconsidered Parts I and II', *British Journal of Political Science*, vol. 1, no. 1–2, pp. 129–67.

Sharpe, L. J. (1988) 'Local Government Reorganisation: General Theory and UK Practice' in B. Dente and F. Kjellberg (eds), *The Dynamics of Institutional Change* (London: Sage), pp. 89–129.

Sharpe, L. J. (1993) 'The European Meso: An Appraisal', in L. J. Sharpe (ed.), *The Rise of Meso Government in Europe* (London: Sage) pp. 1–34.

Sharpe, L. J. and K. Newton (1984) *Does Politics Matter? The Determinants of Public Policy* (Oxford: Clarendon Press).

Skjeie, H. (1991) 'The Rhetoric of Difference: On Women's Inclusion into Political Elites', *Politics and Society*, vol. 19, no. 2.

Smith, B. C. (1985) *Decentralisation: The Territorial Dimension of the State* (London: Allen & Unwin).

Smith, S. R. and M. Lipsky (1993) *Non-Profits for Hire: The Welfare State in the Age of Contracting* (Cambridge Mass.: Harvard University Press).

Stacey, M. (1969) 'The Myth of Community Studies', *British Journal of Sociology*, vol. 20, no. 2, pp. 134–47.

Staeheli, L. A. and S. E. Clarke (1995) 'Gender, Place and Citizenship', in J. A. Garber and R. S. Turner (eds), *Gender in Urban Research* (London: Sage).

Stanyer, J. (1994) 'The Protection of Wildlife as an Organisational Problem for Local Authorities', Paper given at the Political Studies Association Urban Politics Group Conference, Manchester University, 1 July.

Stewart, J. (1989) 'The Changing Organisation and Management of Local Authorities', in J. Stewart and G. Stoker (eds), *The Future of Local Government* (London: Macmillan).

Stewart, J. (1989) 'A Future for Local Authorities as Community Government', in J. D. Stewart and G. Stoker (eds), *The Future of Local Government* (London: Macmillan) pp. 236–54.

Stewart, J. (1991) *An Experiment in Freedom* (London: IPPR).

Stewart, J. (1992) *Accountability to the Public* (London: European Policy Forum).

Stewart, J. and G. Stoker (1988) *From Local Administration to Community Government*, Fabian Research Series No. 351 (London: Fabian Society).

Stewart, J. and G. Stoker (eds) (1989) *The Future of Local Government* (London: Macmillan).

Stewart, J. and G. Stoker (eds) (1995) *Local Government in the 1990s* (London: Macmillan).

Stewart, J. and T. Hams (1992) *Local Government for Sustainable Growth: The UK Local Government Agenda for the Earth Summit* (Luton: Local Government Management Board).

Stewart, J. and K. Walsh (1994) 'Performance Measurement When Performance Can Never Be Finally Defined', *Public Money and Management*, vol. 14, no. 2, pp. 45–9.

Stewart, J., E. Kendall and A. Coote (1994) *Citizens' Juries* (London: IPPR).

Stewart, J., A. Greer and P. Hoggett (1995) *The Quango State: An Alternative Approach*, Research Report No. 10 (London: Commission for Local Democracy).

Stigler, G. (1976) 'The Existence of X-efficiency', *American Economic Review*, vol. 66, pp. 213–16.

Stillman, R.J. (1974) *The Rise of the City Manager* (Albuquerque, NM: University of New Mexico Press).

Stoker, G. (1991) *The Politics of Local Government*, 2nd edn., (London: Macmillan).

Stoker, G. (1994) *The Role and Purpose of Local Government* (London: Commission for Local Democracy).

Stoker, G. (1995) 'Regime Theory', in D. Judge, G. Stoker and H. Wolman (eds), *Theories of Urban Politics* (London: Sage).

Stone, C. (1980) 'Systematic Power in Community Decision-making: A Restatement of Classification Theory', *American Political Science Review*, vol. 74, no. 4, pp. 978–90.

Stone, C. (1989) *Regime Politics: Governing Atlanta* (Lawrence, Ks: University of Kansas Press).

Stromberg, L. and J. Westerstall (1984) *The New Swedish Commune* (Stockholm: Liber Books).

Sugden, R. (1986) *The Economics of Rights, Co-operation and Welfare* (Oxford: Basil Blackwell).

Sunstein, C. (1991) 'Preferences and Politics', *Philosophy and Public Affairs*, vol. 20, no. 1.

Surrey County Council (1992) *Options for Local Government in Surrey* (Kingston-upon-Thames: Surrey County Council).

Syed, A. (1966) *The Political Theory of American Local Government* (New York: Random House).

Tarrow, S. (1977) *Between Centre and Periphery* (New Haven, Conn.: Yale University Press).

Taylor, C. (1985a) 'Interpretation and the Sciences of Man', in *Philosophy and the Human Sciences* (Cambridge: Cambridge University Press).

Taylor, C. (1985b) 'Self-Interpeting Animals', in *Human Agency and Language* (Cambridge University Press).

Taylor, C. (1985c) 'What is Human Agency?', *Human Agency and Language* (Cambridge University Press).

Taylor, C. (1989) *Sources of the Self: the Making of the Modern Identity* (Cambridge: Cambridge University Press).

Taylor, M. (1982) *Community, Anarchy and Liberty* (Cambridge: Cambridge University Press.

Taylor, M. (1987) *The Possibility of Cooperation* (Cambridge: Cambridge University Press).

Thorbecke, J. R. (1841; 1843) *Aanteekening op de gradwet*, vols 1 and 2 (Amsterdam: Muller), quoted in Toonen (1991).

Tiebout, C. M. (1956) 'A Pure Theory of Local Expenditure', *Journal of Political Economy*, vol. 64, pp. 416–24.

Tiebout, C. (1957) 'A Regional Framework for Government Expenditures', in Joint Economic Committee (eds), *Federal Expenditure Policy for Economic Growth and Stability* (Washington, DC: Government Printing Office).

Tiebout, C. (1961) 'Economic Theory of Fiscal Decentralization', in *Public Finance: Needs, Sources and Utilization* (no listed ed.) (Princeton, NJ: National Bureau of Economic Research).

Toonen T. (1987) 'The Netherlands: a decentralised state in a welfare society', in R. A. W. Rhodes and L. V. Wright (eds), *Territorial Politics in Western Europe* (London: Frank Cass), pp. 108–29.

Toonen, T. (1991) 'Change in Continuity: Local Government and Urban Affairs in the Netherlands', in J. Hesse and L. J. Sharpe, *Local Government and Urban Affairs in International Perspective*, pp. 291–332.

Toonen, T. (1993) 'Dutch Provinces and the Struggle for the Meso', in L. J. Sharpe (ed.), *The Rise of Meso Government in Western Europe* (London: Sage).

Trainer, T. (1989) *Developed to Death* (London, Green Print).

Travers, T., G. Jones and J. Burnham (1993) *The Impact of Population Size on Local Authority Costs and Effectiveness* (York: Joseph Rowntree Foundation).

Tullock, G. (1965) *The Politics of Bureaucracy* (Washington, DC: Public Affairs Press).

Tullock, G. (1969) 'Federalism: Problems of Scale', *Public Choice*, vol. 6, pp. 19–30.

Tullock, G. (1990) 'The Costs of Special Privilege', in J. E. Alt and K. A. Shepsle (eds), *Perspectives on Positive Political Economy* (Cambridge: Cambridge University Press).

Tullock, G. (1992) 'Is There a Paradox of Voting?', *Journal of Theoretical Politics*, vol. 4, pp. 225–30.

Tullock, G. (1994) 'Is Public Choice Inherently Anti-Socialist', Public debate, London School of Economics, 10 May.

Vining, A. R. and D. L. Weimer (1990) 'Government Supply and Government Production Failures: A Framework Based on Contestability', *Journal of Public Policy*, vol. 10, no. 1, pp. 166–86.

Wainwright, H. (1994) *Arguments for a New Left: Answering the Free Market Right* (Oxford: Basil Blackwell).

Waldegrave, W. (1993) *The Reality of Reform and Accountability in Today's Public Service* (London: Public Finance Foundation, BDP Consulting, Chartered Institute of Public Finance and Accountability).

Walker, K. (1988). 'The Environmental Crisis: A Critique of Neo-Hobbesian Responses', *Polity*, vol. 21, pp. 67–81.

Wall, D. (1990) *Getting There: Steps to a Green Society* (London: Green Print).

Waller, P. J. (1983) *Town, City and Nation. England 1850–1914* (Oxford: Oxford University Press).

Walsh, K. (1991) 'Quality and Public Services', *Public Administration*, vol. 69, pp. 503–14.

Walsh, K. and H. Davis, (1993) *Competition and Service: The Impact of the Local Government Act, 1988* (London: HMSO).

Walzer, M. (1983) *Spheres of Justice* (New York: Basic Books).

Walzer, M. (1990) 'The Communitarian Critique of Liberalism', *Political Theory*, vol. 18, pp. 6–23.

Ward, H. and D. Samways (1992) 'Environmental Policy', in D. Marsh and R. Rhodes (eds), *Implementing Thatcherite Policies: Audit of an Era* (Milton Keynes: Open University Press).

Ward, S. (1993) *Thinking Global, Acting Local? Local Authorities and their Environmental Plans*, University of the West of England Papers in Politics, No. 2.

Watson, S. (ed.) (1989) *Playing the State* (London: Verso).

Weir, S. and W. Hall (ed.) (1994) *EGO Trip: Extra-governmental Organizations in the United Kingdom and their Accountability* (London: Charter 88 Trust).

Whitty, G. (1990) 'The Politics of the 1988 Education Reform Act', in P. Dunleavy, A. Gamble and G. Peele, *Developments in British Politics 3* (London: Macmillan).

Widdicombe Report (1986) *Report of the Committee of Inquiry into the Conduct of Local Authority Business: The Conduct of Local Authority Business* (Chairman Mr David Widdicombe QC) Cmnd 9798 (London: HMSO).

Williams O. P. and G. J. Clijn (1980) 'Territorial Politics and Resource Transfers in the Netherlands', in D. E. Ashford, *Financial Urban Government*.

Williamson, O. (1986) *The Economic Institutions of Capitalism* (New York: Free Press).

Willig, R. (1979) 'Multiproduct Technology and Market Structure', *American Economic Review*, vol. 69, pp. 346–51.

Wilson, D. and C. Game (1994) *Local Government in the United Kingdom* (with S. Leach and G. Stoker) (London: Macmillan).

Wistow, G., M. Knapp, B. Hardy and C. Allen (1994) *Social Care in a Mixed Economy* (Buckingham, Open University Press).

Wolf, M. (1988) *Markets or Government: Choosing between Imperfect Alternatives* (Cambridge Mass.: MIT Press).

Wolman, H. and M. Goldsmith (1992) *Urban Politics and Policy: A Comparative Approach* (Oxford: Basil Blackwell).

Wolman, H. (1993) 'Between Rupture and Legacies: Local Government Transformation in Eastern Germany', paper presented to conference on economic transformation in Central and Eastern Europe WZB Berlin, 24–25 September.

Yates, D. (1977) *The Ungovernable City* (Cambridge Mass; MIT Press).

Young, I. M. (1990) *Justice and the Politics of Difference* (Princeton, NJ: Princeton University Press).

Young, I. M. (1993) 'Justice and Communicative Democracy', in R. Gottlieb (ed.), *Radical Philosophy: Tradition, Counter-tradition, Politics* (Philadelphia, Pa.: Temple University Press).

Young, K. (1986a) 'The Local Government Elector: Attitudes to Local Government', in Widdicombe Report (1986) Research vol. 3, pp. 105–72.

Young, K. (1986b) 'The Justification of Local Government', in M. Goldsmith (eds), *Essays on the Future of Local Government* (Birmingham: INLOGOV).

Young, K. and Rao, N. (1994) *Coming to Terms with Change? The Local Government Councillor in 1993* (London: Joseph Rowntree Foundation/ Local Government Chronicle Communication).

Young, O. (1989) *International Cooperation: Building Regimes for Natural Resources and the Environment* (Ithaca, NY: Cornell University Press).

Young, S. (1993) 'Sustainable Development at the City Level', in G. Stoker and S. Young, *Cities in the 90s* (London: Longman).

Zucker, L. (1988) 'Normal Change or Risky Business? Institutional Effects of the "Hazard" of Change in Hospital Organizations, 1959–1979', *Journal of Management Studies*.

Index